RACE, POVERTY, AND SOCIAL JUSTICE

About the Cover

The mural on the cover, titled "Building Community," was painted by artist Paul Botello, students, and immigrant workers from the Pomona Day Labor Center. Botello gathered dozens of sketches and proposals from the day laborers before presenting a drawing that they all agreed to. In addition to the image of Cesar Chavez, the final mural includes the many faces of day laborers, students, faculty, and supporters who comprise the center's "community."

Service Learning for Civic Engagement Series
Series Editor: Gerald Eisman

Available:

Race, Poverty, and Social Justice
Multidisciplinary Perspectives Through Service Learning
Edited by José Z. Calderón

Gender Identity, Equity, and Violence
Multidisciplinary Perspectives Through Service Learning
Edited by Geraldine B. Stahly

Forthcoming Topics:

**Promoting Health and Wellness in Underserved
    Communities**
Multidisciplinary Perspectives Through Service Learning
Edited by Anabel Pelham and Elizabeth Sills

Research, Advocacy, and Political Engagement
Multidisciplinary Perspectives Through Service Learning
Edited by Sally Tannenbaum

RACE, POVERTY, AND

SOCIAL JUSTICE

Multidisciplinary Perspectives
Through Service Learning

Edited by
José Z. Calderón

Foreword by Robert A. Corrigan

STERLING, VIRGINIA

Sty/us

COPYRIGHT © 2007 BY
STYLUS PUBLISHING, LLC

Published by Stylus Publishing, LLC
22883 Quicksilver Drive
Sterling, Virginia 20166-2102

Library of Congress Cataloging-in-Publication-Data
Race, poverty, and social justice : multidisciplinary
perspectives through service learning / edited by José Z.
Calderón.
    p.   cm.
    Includes bibliographical references and index.
    ISBN 1-57922-219-6 (cloth : alk. paper)—
    ISBN 1-57922-220-X (pbk. : alk. paper)
    1. Student service—United States.   2. Social justice—
Study and teaching—United States.   3. Multicultural
education—United States.   I. Calderón, José Z. (José
Zapata), 1946-
LC220.5.R33   2007
361.3'7—dc22   2006033684

ISBN: 978-1-57922-219-2 (cloth)
ISBN: 978-1-57922-220-8 (paper)

Printed in the United States of America

All first editions printed on acid-free paper
that meets the American National Standards Institute
Z39-48 Standard.

Bulk Purchases

Quantity discounts are available for use in workshops
and for staff development. Call 1-800-232-0223

First Edition, 2007

10 9 8 7 6 5 4 3 2 1

CONTENTS

ACKNOWLEDGMENTS

We would like to give special thanks to colleagues both within and external to the California State University who serve on the Advisory Board for the monograph series. Debra David, Barbara Holland, Kathy O'Byrne, Seth Pollack, and Maureen Rubin continue to provide invaluable advice on the development of the current volumes and the dimensions the series will explore in the future.

We also wish to give a special acknowledgement to Dr. Gilda Ochoa, Professor in Sociology and Chicano Studies at Pomona College, for her extensive contributions to conceptualizing and editing this volume.

This material is based upon work supported by the Corporation for National and Community Service under Learn and Serve America Grant No. 03LHHCA003. Opinions or points of view expressed in this document are those of the authors and do not necessarily reflect the official position of the Corporation or the Learn and Serve America Program.

FOREWORD

Perhaps once in a generation a movement comes along to redefine—even transform—higher education. I can point to the GI Bill of 1944, which opened the gates to a much broader population than had ever before enjoyed the opportunity to receive higher education. The civil rights struggle and the later antiwar movement galvanized students and faculty across the nation. Many of us participated directly in these movements; many more worked then, and in the years that followed, to overhaul what we perceived as an outmoded university curriculum as we struggled to open up the university to new ideas, new teaching strategies, and most of all, to underrepresented populations.

To this list, I would now add community service learning. I consider this movement in higher education as exciting as anything I have experienced as an educator. Service learning, and its central role in our goals of campuswide civic engagement and ethical education, may be the most significant development on our campuses since the curricular reforms of the 1960s. In fact, I believe that it will prove to be *the* higher education legacy of the early 21st century, and that it will have a lifelong impact on our students.

Since service learning began to take formal hold throughout the nation in the early 1990s, it has come to be seen as much more than community volunteerism linked with academic study. It is a vehicle for character and citizenship development—in short, for all that we most value in a liberal education. Through thoughtfully structured service-learning experiences, students can test and apply the values of a healthy democracy to some of the most complex and challenging issues of our time.

In recent years, higher education has begun more deliberately to pursue a historic mission: what I might call moral education—our responsibility both to our students and society. The Association of American Colleges and Universities terms this "core commitments," and calls on us to educate our students "for personal and social responsibility." This is the highest aim of liberal education. It is the culmination of our mission to service, to preparing our students with the skills and desire to contribute positively to our democratic society and to the greater world, to fostering a campus climate where speech is open, but where we can disagree—even passionately—without venom or hatred, and to ensuring that our students find in the classroom a safe and receptive environment in which to express, test, and challenge varying views.

A true liberal education encompasses far more than the breadth of knowledge and exposure to fields other than one's major that typically shape general education programs. That is certainly necessary, but liberal education transcends subject matter. Liberal education addresses both mind and heart. It is a set of experiences that give our students the tools they will need to think about complex issues and to deal with them as informed, ethical citizens. Liberal education helps our students deal with ambiguity and contradictions, helps them evaluate competing arguments and perspectives so that they will not have to fall back on the comfort—and distortion—of a binary, good/bad worldview.

Complexity characterizes our key social missions, as we seek to foster in our students respect and understanding of other cultures and viewpoints together with the skills they will need to move positively and effectively in a diverse and global society. I am most emphatically not talking about indoctrinating our students—presenting our values and asking them to take them as their own. Rather, I am talking about teaching our students *why* and *how* to think and reason about ethical and moral issues—not presenting them with answers, but developing their skills in finding their own way.

Liberal education prepares our students to act—and to do so in the context of values that take in the needs and concerns of others. Viewed in this context, the value of civically focused service learning is clear. It places our students in the arenas where ethics and efficacy need to join, where disciplinary boundaries are often irrelevant and integrative learning occurs naturally, and where students can gain a profound experience of their capacity—and responsibility—to effect positive change. As an antidote to cynicism and passivity, it is hard to top service learning.

Looking at the society into which they are graduating, our students might be excused for being cynical. From the front page to the business page to the sports section, headlines repeatedly reflect the ethical lapses of our society. This profound lack of integrity—the failure of a moral value system—is not restricted to one political party, to one religious group, to one ethnic group, or one gender group. It cuts across our society. In giving a final message to graduating students, I have asked them to seek one goal: to say no—say no to greed, say no to opportunism, say no to dishonesty, and decide that integrity—their own moral compasses—is what really matters.

If we accept that aim—and I believe we do—then service learning deserves a proud and prominent place in our curriculum. This series provides less a road map than a spur to creative course development for all faculty and administrators eager to adapt a powerful educational tool to a particular institution's nature, community, and student population.

Robert A. Corrigan
President, San Francisco State University
October 6, 2006

ABOUT THIS SERIES

Many service-learning practitioners are familiar with the comprehensive series of monographs on *Service-Learning in the Disciplines* produced and published by the American Association of Higher Education (AAHE) between 1997 and 2005 (The series is now published by Stylus Publishing, LLC). Each volume of the series focused on a specific discipline—accounting, biology, composition, and so on—and provided a rich collection of exemplary practices in service learning as constituted around a disciplinary theme. Edward Zlotkowski (1997–2002), then senior associate at AAHE and series editor for the monographs, wrote that in "winning faculty support for this [service-learning] work" it was important to recognize that faculty "define themselves largely in terms of [their] academic disciplines," and so it was logical to design a series around disciplinary themes. The AAHE series became a primary reference for faculty who were considering adopting service-learning pedagogy, and the community of service-learning practitioners have much for which to thank the editors and contributors to those volumes. Other resources that were discipline specific—such as collections of syllabi—also helped to promote service learning to the level of the widespread acceptance it enjoys today on both the national and international stages.

Over the past few years, as the civic engagement movement has gained momentum, as educators have taken on the challenge of producing graduates who are engaged civically and politically in their communities, there has been a growing reexamination of service learning as the means for producing "civic learning" outcomes, that is, the combination of knowledge, skills, and disposition to make a difference in the civic life of our communities. The ubiquitous three-element Venn diagram—three interlocking circles representing enhanced academic learning, meaningful community service, and civic learning—that defines the field of service learning at its intersection (Howard, 2001), continues to do so, but there has been a marked redirection of emphasis from academic learning to civic. Nonetheless, as John Saltmarsh points out in his 2004 white paper for Campus Compact, *The Civic Purpose of Higher Education: A Focus on Civic Learning,* service learning is "the most potent method for achieving civic learning if civic learning outcomes are a part of curricular goals" (p. 7).

In parallel to this shift in emphasis, a second, related movement within higher education, *integrative learning,* has begun to take hold. As characterized by the American Association of Colleges and Universities (AACU) in partnership with the Carnegie Foundation for the Advancement of Teaching (Huber & Hutchings, 2004), integrative learning encompasses practices such as thematic first-year experiences, learning circles, interdisciplinary studies, capstone experiences, and other initiatives to foster students' ability to integrate concepts "across courses, over time, and between campus and community life" (p. 13). These two educational reform movements—civic engagement and integrative learning—provide the motivation for the creation of the current series, *Service Learning for Civic Engagement.* Each volume of the series will focus on a specific social issue—gender and power, race and immigration, community health, and so forth—and then solicit contributions from faculty *across* disciplines who can provide insight into how they have motivated their students to engage in learning that extends beyond the boundaries of disciplinary goals. In some cases chapter contributors will be faculty within the "obvious" discipline relevant to a particular issue (e.g., women's studies faculty utilize service learning in the pursuit of knowledge on gender issues), but each volume will include multiple chapters from other disciplines as well. As each volume illustrates, when faculty step outside the normal confines of disciplinary learning, they can provide profound, transformational experiences for their students. Thus, the volume on gender issues includes examples from philosophy, psychology, ethnic studies, and more, and the volume on social justice includes contributions from communications, engineering, nutrition science, and so on.

It is also our intention to design each book as a collective whole. Each volume illustrates an array of approaches to examining a community issue, and we hope that, by exploring examples across the disciplines, faculty will be inspired to develop their own concepts for courses that combine academic and civic learning.

Over the past 10 years, service learning has enjoyed tremendous support throughout the California State University (CSU), from which most of our contributors have been recruited. The 23 campuses of the CSU form the largest university system in the country, with 405,000 students enrolled each year. Through strategic efforts and targeted funding, the CSU has created a systemwide network of service-learning offices with a center on each campus, a coordinating office at the chancellor's office, statewide conferences and initiatives, and a wide variety of service-learning courses and community-based research. In 2005 alone more than 1,800 service-learning courses provided opportunities for 65,000 students to participate. California, now one of four states designated minority-majority (i.e., a state in which a majority of the population differs from the national majority) by the U.S. Census Bureau, is rich in ethnic diversity and is home to great cities as well as vast rural areas. Virtually every societal issue challenges Californians, and our universities have pledged to use our resources to develop innovative ways to address them. It is this mixture of diversity and innovation that has created an environment for the success of service learning in the CSU represented in this series.

Gerald S. Eisman
CSU Service-Learning Faculty Scholar
July 19, 2006

References

Howard, J. (2001). *Service learning course design workbook.* Ann Arbor, MI: OCSL Press.

Huber, M. T., & Hutchings, P. (2004). *Integrative learning: Mapping the terrain.* The Academy in Transition. Washington, DC: Association of American Colleges and Universities.

Saltmarsh, J. (2004). *The civic purpose of higher education: A focus on civic learning.* Unpublished white paper for Campus Compact.

Zlotkowski, E. (1997–2002). (Ed.). *AAHE series on service-learning in the disciplines.* Washington, DC: American Association for Higher Education.

INTRODUCTION

In the academic world, there has been an ongoing debate about the meaning of democracy as it pertains to the issue of inequality. In discussing this issue, David Cooper, in his article "Academic Professionalism and the Betrayal of the Land-Grant Tradition" (1999), argues that "professionalism, along with an entire cultural complex evoked by the mystique of professionalization, long ago displaced a vigorous if oversimplified democratic ideology as the driving force behind American land-grant colleges" (p. 776). Ira Shor, in his book *Freire for the Classroom* (1987), proposes that this conservative educational policy has "imposed depressing programs of careerism . . . discouraged creativity . . . invited gifted teachers to leave the profession, while dissuading students from thinking of education as an exciting career" (p. 9).

Rather than blaming the victim, Shor proposes that much of the crisis in education has a structural basis and is produced by an authoritarian ideology. To address this crisis, Shor proposes a participatory education and critical pedagogy coupled with egalitarian policies in schools and society (1992, p. 13).

There are different ways to define the concepts of diversity and democracy. The American Association of Colleges and Universities, in the publication *The Drama of Diversity and Democracy*, defines democracy as "the ideal that all human beings have equal value, deserve equal respect, and should be given equal opportunity to fully participate in the life and direction of the society" (1995, p. 9). At the same time, the publication also proposes that when diversity is "characterized by patterned inequity and the marginalization of specific groups—it can signify unequal access to political, economic, social, and cultural power."

Shor proposes that these inequalities are not separated from the issue of power and that the development of a classroom culture with debate and critical study is part of the advancement of a more democratic society. In the creation of this "border culture," Shor proposes that a democratic discourse can be achieved where the students and the teachers are on a more equal status as learners and teachers (1992, p. 203).

In this context, the way we run our classrooms and the way we connect those classrooms to our communities can have a lot to say about whether our teaching and learning practices are advancing a more diverse, socially just, and democratic culture. These practices should not be contradictory to the pedagogy, research, and action that we implement alongside our community partners.

In this volume, we explore multiple examples of how to connect classrooms to communities through service learning and participatory research to teach issues of social justice. At the same time, the various chapters provide examples of how collaborations between students, faculty, and community partners are creating models of democratic spaces (on campus and off campus) where the students are teachers and the teachers are students. Our purpose, in this volume, is to provide examples of how service learning can be integrated into courses addressing social justice issues. At the same time, it is about demonstrating the power of service learning in advancing a course content that is community based and socially engaged.

The volume has five sections: section one, "Foundations of Service Learning and Social Justice"; section two, "The Day Labor Project"; section three, "Social Policy and Homelessness"; section four, "International Projects"; and section five, "Culture and Equity."

In section one, the volume's chapters focus on some of the overarching pedagogical strategies in service learning as applied to social justice.

Stan Oden and Amar Casey's "Advancing Service Learning as a Transformative Method for Social Justice Work" explores diverse examples of the use of service learning pedagogy for teaching about social justice issues. They examine the connections between the social movements of the 1960s and 1970s to social justice issues and service-learning models incorporating a transformative curriculum. They challenge the "charity" type of service learning employed by some nonprofit organizations with an analysis of the "social change" type of community service carried out by the Black Panther Party in the past and community organizations in the present.

David Schulz's "Stimulating Social Justice Theory for Service-Learning Practice" presents thoughtful and engaging discussions on theories of social justice, diverse uses of the concept, and the shifting expectations of educators. At the same time, he links these theoretical discussions of justice with examples from service-learning courses in communication studies.

Christine Popok's "Reflections on Service Learning as a Pedagogical

Strategy in Composition" provides an analysis of how an engaged pedagogy can be used in teaching social justice as part of classes in the field of composition. She presents service-learning strategies that combine feminist theory and pedagogical practices based on Paulo Freire's perspectives of combining action and reflection to advance a praxis based on community and political action.

The second section, titled "The Day Labor Project," focuses on service learning and social justice projects carried out in collaboration with day labor workers at a day labor center in the city of Pomona.

José Z. Calderón and Gilbert Cadena's "Linking Critical Democratic Pedagogy, Multiculturalism, and Service Learning to a Project-Based Approach" provides practical examples of the bridges being built between campus and community partners, the fusion of various pedagogical methods, and the advancement of social justice outcomes in the process. The chapter is an important contribution to the literature and provides inspiring examples of how to involve students using a project-based approach.

Edward Clancy follows the project-based approach by innovatively involving engineering students and day laborers in developing a day laborer safety program. This article shows how research, service, and action can help in reducing the common injuries that day laborers are prone to encounter at their daily jobs in the informal economy.

Susan Algert's "Community-Based Scholarship: Nutrition Students Learn Spanish in the Classroom and at the City of Pomona Day Labor Center" offers another innovative example of how a service-learning project, with a social justice angle, can collaborate with a day laborer immigrant community and simultaneously advance the social awareness of students who will be entering the health industry.

In section three, the authors provide concrete examples of how service learning can be used in social justice projects involving the homeless, human services, and public policy.

Roberta Ann Johnson and Robert C. Chope's "Social Justice and Public Policy" provides some examples of the literature and traditional methods of teaching about the poor and homeless that often leaves out the social justice implications. As a contribution to the literature and experiential methods of teaching public policy, Johnson and Chope describe a public policy class that connected social justice themes in the classroom to the engagement of students in community sites involving the homeless.

Jill Pable's "Social Responsibility by Design: Interior Design, Graphic Design, and Photography Students' Close Encounter with Homelessness" presents a unique example of service learning where design and photography students connect their specialties with a homeless shelter. Her approach and description of the process make this chapter an important contribution to a type of service learning that places social responsibility in the forefront. The sustained relationship that is developed between the author, the class, and the shelter make for a compelling example.

Robert C. Chope and Rebecca L. Toporek's "Providing Human Services With a Social Justice Perspective" presents examples of how social justice principles and service-learning practices can be used in counseling, education, and human service provisions. The authors provide various concrete activity modules that encourage faculty and students to think about how their positions and experiences can advance social change possibilities in these areas.

Section four focuses on an international project that involves students outside of the comfort of their home country to tackle service learning and social justice issues on a global scale.

Betsy J. Blosser's "Service Learning in the World Community: Video Production in South America" describes a transnational service learning project in which video production students document their participation and collaboration with Latin American organizations that are working to eradicate poverty.

In section five, "Culture and Equity," the authors focus on examples of cultural exclusion and the service-learning approaches that are being implemented to reclaim history, to create multicultural awareness, and to advance institutional change.

Tasha Souza's "Creating Social Justice in the Classroom: Preparing Students for Diversity Through Service Learning" focuses on how the preparation of teachers needs to be coupled with the preparation of students to work in a diverse society and to have a multicultural education as part of their learning. The author presents an example of how service learning is carried out in a communications class and what can be done in preparing students and teachers to make connections among multiculturalism, critical pedagogy, and service learning.

Velia Garcia's "Social Justice and Community Service Learning in Chicano/Latino/Raza Studies" grounds the connections between service learning and social justice in the tradition and history of Chicana/o studies. The author provides examples of these connections from two interdisciplinary courses that are cross-listed between Raza studies and criminal justice studies. The author proposes that institutions that were once opposed to this work now embrace the linkages being made between service learning, social justice, civic engagement, and social action.

Edith Chen's "Reclaiming a Forgotten Past: The San Fernando Valley Japanese American Oral History and Photograph Collection Project" involves students in the use of service learning and participatory research to draw out the history of Japanese Americans in the San Fernando Valley between the 1910s and 1960s. The author links this important subject to the development of a class that partnered with the San Fernando Valley Japanese American Community Center. The work of the students in the class served a particular need in the Japanese American community to tell their story and to preserve their history.

Karren Baird-Olson's "Cultural Issues in American Indian Education" presents some revealing statistics on the small percentage of American Indian/Alaskan Native students in higher education and some of the reasons for the push-out rate of students in postsecondary schools. At the same time, the author presents some culturally relevant pedagogical approaches that use service learning in an American Indian studies program at a major urban teaching university to increase sensitivity and awareness about the significances of indigenous cultures and nations.

As we seek to develop models and examples of how service learning can serve social justice outcomes, it is important for us to look toward new ways of carrying out democratic forms of learning and curriculum building in our classrooms that connect to new models of building democratic participation in our communities. Our beginning to dialogue on these new models may help us to understand how the engagement of our student and community partnerships can move beyond volunteerism (or charity) to a level of civic engagement that advances social justice in our institutions and a democratic culture in civil society.

José Zapata Calderón
Michi and Walter Weglyn Endowed Chair in Multicultural Studies
California State Polytechnic University, Pomona
August 23, 2006

Activity/Methodology Table: *Race, Poverty, and Social Justice*

Chapter	Discipline	Service Activity	Methodology	Applications	Type of Partner	Size of Class
Chapter 1: Oden & Casey	Ethnic Studies	Public advocacy Political education	Participant observation Problem-based learning	Political science Sociology Community studies Environmental studies	Youth advocacy Cultural arts and education Freedom Bound Center, Inc.	10–20 students
Chapter 2: Schulz	Communication Studies/ Rhetoric	Mentoring at-risk high school students Tutoring Hmong refugees Analysis of workforce safety and solutions	(Re)defining social justice Hypo-testing definitions in classroom scenarios Class presenta-tion/reflection	Communications Philosophy English Mass communications	"The Bridge" Hmong Re-source Center Local high schools Salvation Army	25–30 students

(continues)

Activity/Methodology Table: Race, Poverty, and Social Justice
Continued

Chapter	Discipline	Service Activity	Methodology	Applications	Type of Partner	Size of Class
Chapter 3 Popok	Composition & Rhetoric	Tutoring Environmental Lesson planning Fundraising	One-on-one reciprocation Writing	Education Resource stewardship	California Conservation Corps First 5 of California Boys and Girls Club Westminster Free Clinic	20 students
Chapter 4: Calderón & Cadena	Ethnic Studies Multicultural Studies Chicano/a & Latino/a Studies	Immigration rights Grant writing Community outreach Historical research Language class	Critical pedagogy Project-based research Ethnography Social change service learning Student-centered learning	Sociology History Marketing Community organizing Labor studies Informal economy	Day Labor Center	12–24 students

Chapter	Discipline	Service Activity	Methodology	Applications	Type of Partner	Size of Class
Chapter 5: Clancy	Engineering	Analysis of workforce safety and solutions	Problem-based learning	Engineering Chemistry Construction Manufacturing	Pomona Day Labor Center	Small teams
Chapter 6: Stubblefield	Human Nutrition and Food Science	Nutrition education counseling and classes Outreach to community health centers and community partners	Developing culturally competent health care Health promotion in the community	Health education Social work	Pomona Economic Opportunity Center	10–15 students each quarter
Chapter 7: Johnson & Chope	Political Science/Public Policy, and Public Administration	Administrative assistance Policy implementation	Policy analysis	Service providers and advocacy groups for homeless population	Government agencies and NGOs	15–35 students
Chapter 8: Pable	Interior Design	Redesign of a homeless shelter	Problem-based learning	Interior design Graphic design Photography Fine arts	Sacramento Salvation Army Community Services Center	Small teams

(continues)

Activity/Methodology Table: *Race, Poverty, and Social Justice*
Continued

Chapter	Discipline	Service Activity	Methodology	Applications	Type of Partner	Size of Class
Chapter 9: Chope & Toporek	Psychology, Counseling, Human Resources, Social Work	Individual counseling in community agencies	Case studies Self-reflection exercises	Interviewing in human resources and counseling	Various community agencies working with human services	Up to 15 students
Chapter 10: Blosser	Mass Communication	Public service announcement/documentary Video production International experience	Video production	Fundraising Information dissemination Television	Peruvian NGO Brazilian NGO	12–28 students
Chapter 11: Souza	Communication Studies	Design and facilitate diversity workshops	Critical pedagogy Active learning	Education Multicultural studies	Middle school students	25 students

Chapter	Discipline	Service Activity	Methodology	Applications	Type of Partner	Size of Class
Chapter 12: Garcia	Raza Studies Criminal Justice Studies	Critical analysis of systematic processes of social inequality in the justice system Mentoring and tutoring Activist participation in alternative ethnic community-based program building	Activist research Mitigation Social action Social change Community development	Juvenile and criminal justice Social work Counseling Education Advocacy Community organizing	Prison Activist Resource Center Youth Guidance Center Project Rebound Public schools Centro Legal de La Raza, Maldef S.F. Day Labor Program	50 students
Chapter 13: Chen	Asian American Studies/ Sociology	Recapturing Japanese American history in the San Fernando Valley	Oral history Photograph collection Video recording	History Political science Women's studies Ethnic studies	San Fernando Valley Japanese American Community Center	10 students

(continues)

Activity/Methodology Table: *Race, Poverty, and Social Justice*
Continued

Chapter	Discipline	Service Activity	Methodology	Applications	Type of Partner	Size of Class
Chapter 14: Baird-Olson	Sociology/American Indian Studies and Criminology	Tour guide at indigenous museum Assisting with American Indian Film Festival Assisting traditional healer with working with incarcerated youth Preparing historical records	Social construction of knowledge Talking Circles Integration of affective and cognitive learning	Sociology/ Anthropology Cross-cultural counseling Political science/ History Social welfare Law	American Indian/First Nation agencies and organizations	12–18 students

CONTRIBUTORS

Susan Algert (chapter 6) is assistant professor of human nutrition and food sciences at California State Polytechnic University–Pomona. (salgert@csupomona.edu)

Karren Baird-Olson (chapter 14) is associate professor of American Indian studies and sociology at California State University–Northridge. (karren.bairdolson@csun.edu)

Betsy J. Blosser (chapter 10) is professor of broadcast and electronic communication arts at San Francisco State University. (bblosser@sfsu.edu)

Gilbert R. Cadena (chapter 4) is professor of ethnic and women's studies at California State Polytechnic University–Pomona. (grcadena@csupomona.edu)

José Zapata Calderón (volume editor, chapter 4) is professor of sociology and Chicano studies at Pitzer College. (Jose_Calderon@pitzer.edu)

Thomas Amar Casey (chapter 1) is a lecturer in Africana studies at San Francisco State University. (tbcasey@aol.com)

Edith Wen-Chu Chen (chapter 13) is associate professor of Asian American studies at California State University–Northridge. (edith.chen@csun.edu)

Robert C. Chope (chapters 7 and 9) is professor of counseling at San Francisco State University. (rcchope@sfsu.edu)

Edward V. Clancy (chapter 5) is professor of engineering at California State Polytechnic University–Pomona. (evclancy@csupomona.edu)

Robert A. Corrigan (Foreword) is the president of San Francisco State University. (president@sfsu.edu)

Gerald S. Eisman (series editor) is the acting director, Institute for Civic and Community Engagement, San Francisco State University. (geisman@sfsu.edu)

Velia Garcia (chapter 12) is associate professor of Raza studies at San Francisco State University. (veliag@sfsu.edu)

Roberta Ann Johnson (chapter 7) is professor of politics at the University of San Francisco. (johnsonr@usfca.edu)

Robert Stanley Oden (chapter 1) is assistant professor of government at California State University–Sacramento. (rso@csus.edu)

Jill Pable (chapter 8) is assistant professor of interior design at Florida State University. (jpable@fsu.edu)

Christine Popok (chapter 3) is a lecturer in business and economics and English at California State University–Channel Islands. (Christine.Popok@csuci.edu)

David Schulz (chapter 2) is head of the department of applied communication at Trinity Lutheran College. (David.Schulz@tlc.edu)

Tasha Souza (chapter 11) is associate professor of communication at Humboldt State University. (tjs16@humboldt.edu)

Rebecca L. Toporek (chapter 9) is assistant professor of counseling at San Francisco State University. (rtoporek@sfsu.edu)

SECTION ONE

FOUNDATIONS OF SERVICE LEARNING AND SOCIAL JUSTICE

ADVANCING SERVICE LEARNING AS A TRANSFORMATIVE METHOD FOR SOCIAL JUSTICE WORK

Robert Stanley Oden and Thomas Amar Casey

We all have a certain measure of responsibility to those who have made it possible for us to take advantage of the opportunities. The door is opened only so far. If some of us can squeeze through the crack of that door, then we owe it to those who have made those demands that the door be opened to use the knowledge or the skills that we acquire not only for ourselves but in the service of the community as well.

—Angela Davis, television interview,
February 10, 1998

This article explores both theoretical and empirical approaches to learning about issues of social justice, and suggests ways in which crucial issues can be addressed within academic frameworks while supporting movements for social change. This examination connects the study of contemporary social movements with experiential education models, which have informed various approaches to service learning. One of the models discussed in this article is a model of service learning used by the coauthors at the University of California–Santa Cruz in a program called Oakes Serves, from 1995 to 2003. In this model, critical macro and micro political sociological analysis of the Santa Cruz community and the broader society occurred in the classroom, which assisted in informing the service-learning volunteer work in community agencies for the Oakes Serves students. The approach used in that course serves as a bridge from the coauthors' experiences as Black Panther Party members to the Oakes Serves program, to a proposed curriculum that links approaches to social justice work in an academic service-learning setting.

Understanding social justice and doing social justice work are two separate and distinct activities. However, the linking of these elements brings about the potential for social change within communities that are in need. Many individuals and groups have tried to link the understanding and the practice of social justice through developing and applying the precepts of service learning. In service learning, particular needs are addressed, while an active process of education and reflection is also undertaken. The theory and practice of service learning has its roots primarily in the civil rights period, from 1954 to 1974. It was during this time that African Americans and their allies actively challenged the "Jim Crow" era as manifested in the political, economic, and social structure of the South. They peacefully changed the social dynamics using many techniques, including a wide range of direct actions and acts of civil disobedience. This was accomplished within organizational frameworks such as the Southern Christian Leadership Conference (SCLC), the Student Nonviolent Coordinating Committee (SNCC), and the Congress for Racial Equality (CORE), among others. A social revolution was created, one that broke the foundation of racial segregation in the South (Carson, 1992; Kelley &Lewis, 2000; King, 1967).

While this phenomenon was important in itself, it was only part of a continuous process of challenging the institutional racism, class exploitation, and repression that has existed in the United States since the founding of the country (Goldfield, 1997; Zinn, 1980). In the inner cities of the northern and western parts of the United States, police brutality and increased violence against Black youth helped contribute to the urban rebellions of the 1960s. This police brutality, combined with political and economic underrepresentation, created an atmosphere in the mid-1960s that spoke to the need for social change. These conditions produced extraordinary challenges for groups seeking social change. Facing these challenges was necessary to provide much-needed social justice and to address the multiple levels of oppression articulated clearly by Iris Marion Young in her 1990 book, *Justice and the Politics of Difference*:

Accordingly, I offer below an explication of five faces of oppression as a useful set of categories and distinctions which I believe is comprehensive, in the sense that it covers all the groups said by the new left social movements to be oppressed and all the ways they are oppressed. I derive the five faces of oppression from reflection on the conditions of these groups. Because different factors, or combination of factors, constitute the oppression of different groups, making their oppression irreducible, I believe it is not possible to give one essential definition to oppression. (p. 42)

Young argues that oppression has five faces or elements: exploitation, marginalization, powerlessness, cultural imperialism, and violence (Young, 1990). Each of these has real-life consequences for many in the United States. African Americans, Mexican Americans, Native Americans, Asian Americans, women, and many other groups have experienced, at some level of intensity, these five elements of oppression. These elements have directly curtailed the efforts by many to achieve a level of social justice, which, as Young (1990) states,

Should refer not only to distribution, but also the institutional conditions necessary for the development and exercise of individual capacities and collective communication and cooperation. Under this concept of justice, injustice refers primarily to two forms of disabling constraints, oppression and domination. (p. 38)

In the mid-1960s, one organization that emerged out of the civil rights movement was the Black Panther Party. Dr. Huey P. Newton and Bobby Seale formed the organization in October 1966 in Oakland, California (Newton, 1973; Seale, 1991). In many respects, this organization was in the vanguard as it challenged these "five faces of oppression" in the Black communities of the United States. During its zenith in the early 1970s, the Black Panther Party had more than 38 chapters and branches across the United States and several abroad, with a total membership of more than five thousand. Its leadership provided a vision and praxis for challenging the racial and political order in the United States. It did this by articulating Marxist-Leninist-Maoist approaches to revolutionary theory and also by creating a community service apparatus that challenged the race, class, and gender oppression in the inner cities across the nation.

The vision of the Black Panther Party was articulated in its "Ten-Point

Platform and Program" (see Appendix 1.A), which outlines the organization's political program. What made the Black Panther Party stand apart from the other organizations of its time was its commitment to "an immediate end to police brutality and murder of black people" (Point 7, Black Panther Party Ten-Point Platform). This stance directly confronted the historic issue of violence against members of the Black community. The Black Panther Party accomplished much, through a creative, active, political insurgency that captured the imagination of the Black community. The party focus was particularly on the impoverished, unemployed, and underserved members of the Black community. The Black Panther Party served this sector in the manner first articulated by Malcolm X: "by any means necessary."

This new approach to building a self-sustaining, revolutionary movement was rooted in a model of community service and political education. In another work of ours, *The Black Panther Party as a Service-Learning Innovator* (Oden & Casey, 2004), we indicate that as former Black Panther Party members we were continually being educated about the political ideology of the organization and the needs of the Black community. This political education was linked to the community service structure, the activities of which were particularly focused in the period from 1968 to 1976, and consisted of a variety of community services. These ranged from selling the *Black Panther Newspaper* to providing free breakfasts for children, to sickle-cell screening, to offering medical exams in free health clinics.

The Black Panther Party insisted on armed self-defense as an answer to the police violence against some in the Black community. The organization—both its membership and its leadership—had to deal with armed conflict with law enforcement, led by the FBI (Federal Bureau of Investigation). Through its director, J. Edgar Hoover, the FBI declared the Black Panther Party to be the "most dangerous threat to national security." Hoover secretly implemented COINTELPRO (Counter-Intelligence Program), which, in conjunction with the actions of other law enforcement entities, led to the deaths of some Black Panthers, the wounding of hundreds more, and the incarceration of many others, some of whom are still imprisoned or in exile. The Black Panther Party sparked controversy and mixed feelings, particularly concerning the relative value of self-defense versus nonviolence as tactical approaches to achieving social justice and eliminating the multiplicities of oppression and domination that have existed in the United States.

In 1970, Huey Newton, after serving two-and-a-half years in the San

Luis Obispo Men's Colony, began to de-emphasize the immediate need for armed struggle. Instead, he called for "establishing 'survival programs' to help the black community simply survive on a day-to-day basis" (Hilliard, 2006, p. 127). This shift in the Black Panther Party approach signaled an emphasis on community service as a means of attaining social justice and political change. It provided a link to contemporaneous approaches to service, such as those in academia, that implement service learning as a tool in helping to seek social justice. These approaches evolved from the Great Society programs of the 1960s, and were then funded in the 1970s through the VISTA-ACTION agency programs, which helped to create community service projects in poor communities in the United States (Jacoby, 1996). Later models of service learning emanated from various college campuses. These projects also included community-based approaches to service learning, which engage the affected community through the use of empowerment strategies that strengthen opportunities for social change. Many of these approaches have based their ideas on the Wingspread Principles (see appendix 1.B), which were formulated at a conference in Racine, Wisconsin, in 1989, through the collaboration of key service-learning theorists, as well as service-learning practitioners in the experiential education movement. These principles outline a direction that the service-learning community could use to plan, implement, and evaluate their programs. While these principles are essential to understanding the dynamics of service learning, it is important to link these approaches to the strategies for achieving social justice and social change used by the Black Panther Party many years earlier.

In a 2004 study conducted by the authors of this chapter, interviews were conducted with former leaders and members of the Black Panther Party, who were asked questions about the party's community service actions, which related to the Wingspread Principles. For example, number 4 in the Wingspread Principles states, "An effective program allows for those with needs to define those needs" (Jacoby, 1996, p. 30). Former Black Panther Party chief of staff David Hilliard discusses a similar approach:

> First the ideas would come from the community, sometimes, distinct and disconnected. But we would take these ideas and refine them and send them back to the community as their very own. That was the technique of these professional organizers. Always having this dialogue with the community. (Oden & Casey, 2004, p. 18)

It is important to explore the links between the Black Panther Party and service learning. This relationship is influenced by what others have articulated as the agency of the oppressed—to become conscious, or in Paulo Freire's term, "conscientizacao" (Freire, 1993, p. 19). Freire envisioned and experienced the necessity that the oppressed become the masters of their own transformation. He introduced pedagogical directions that included transformative processes for reaching liberation. Praxis for Freire is "reflection and action upon the world in order to transform it" (Freire, 1993, p. 3). Newton and Seale, in their creation of the Black Panther Party, developed an organization that was engaged with the language of the oppressed. They used that language in the form of political action to inform the masses of the Black community who were living in substandard conditions. The Black Panther Party, particularly through its formative years, 1968–1974, engaged its communities through acting out its principles of serving the Black community as a whole. This was done in the face of constant harassment, shootings, entrapments, and surveillance, and yet this organization was still able to go forward. The party was able to withstand for a brief time period the constant blows from the repressive state apparatus and leave a legacy of commitment to community service while seeking social transformation. While complete social transformation was not possible, the Black Panther Party praxis of education and service in relation to social justice work is crucial to examine. Their approach to community service is linked to current efforts, particularly in community-based service learning. Their model can inspire social activists in poor communities and in communities of color to use a social change approach involving education and service in order to work, as did the Black Panther Party, toward the elimination of the multiple levels of oppression and domination in the United States.

Community Service: A Tool for Black Liberation

The legacy of the Black Panther Party approach to service learning is not commonly drawn upon by most volunteer community and service-learning organizations. Many people work today to provide critically needed services, such as tutoring for students; food, clothing, and shelter for the homeless; and medical care for people with AIDS and other diseases. But they often use an approach that treats social symptoms, without addressing the root causes of the educational deficits, poverty conditions, and medical maladies.

Quite often, to resolve the cause of the problem requires a political solution, one that can range from social revolution to advocacy for public policy changes.

As was briefly indicated earlier, the Black Panther Party owes its own approach in part to the civil rights movement. The Black Panther Party was named after the Lowndes County, Alabama, Black Panther Party, which was a part of the civil rights movement through the Student Nonviolent Coordinating Committee (SNCC) (Carson, 1992), which used politically aware volunteers to register African Americans to vote and run for political office. The Freedom Riders were highly motivated volunteers who risked life and limb to challenge the apartheid system of the segregated South. This voluntary political activism of the civil rights era is chronicled in Robert Coles's (1993) classic book, *A Call to Service*. People who have been involved in the civil rights movement, or who are graduates of the Peace Corps or of VISTA, often speak earnestly of those past times in their lives. As happens with memories, the tough and difficult times, the petty or rancorous moments, the experiences of disappointment or outrage, the occasional sense of betrayal by people on one's own side, can give way to the hyperbole of a glorious past, of courage affirmed, a moral life lived to the fullest, compromises shunned, and utterly unassailable principles constantly upheld. Yet these times were undeniably characterized overall by a high degree of commitment and many significant successes.

The other significant influence on the Black Panther Party's approach to service learning was the Black Nationalist movement as personified by Malcolm X. The Black Panther Party directly emulated Malcolm X and the Nation of Islam's soapbox preaching. Also in line with the work of Malcolm X, the Black Panther Party held regularly scheduled meetings in which people would be educated about the Black Panther Party's position on a number of community issues. In fact, Malcolm X's militant stance against police brutality helped inspire the Black Panther Party to initiate its first voluntary patrols of the Oakland Police Department. The civil rights movement and the Black Nationalist movement both had impact locally, nationally, and internationally. Just as the Black Panther Party was implementing its survival programs and protesting police brutality, many of these same ideas were being played out in a different context. For example, in South Africa, Black Africans were engaged in a life-and-death struggle against the apartheid regime. One of the most eloquent opponents was Steven Biko, who had this to say about Black Power in the United States:

> Black Power is the preparation of a group for participation in an already
> established society, which is essentially a majority society. The Black people
> are merely saying that it is high time that they are not used as pawns by
> other pressure groups operating in American society. They want to put up
> the kind of candidates they like and be able to support them using their
> block of votes. (Biko, 1979, p. 112)

Not only were Biko and other antiapartheid activists aware of such political
concepts as Black Power in the United States, some of their organizational
approaches were eerily similar to those of the Black Panther Party. Steven
Biko, leader of the Black Consciousness movement in the 1970s, explains the
movement's approach in South Africa:

> The approach of BCP (Black Community Programs) is three pronged.
> First we engage in the form of direct community development projects,
> which are in the form of clinics, churches and so on. And then we engage
> in what we call home industries—these are economic projects in rural areas
> mainly, sometimes in urban areas as well, which are in the form of cottage
> industries, producing one article or other. And the main purpose here is to
> give employment to people, and also to offer some kind of technical train-
> ing in that particular skill, so that they can themselves go and live off that
> skill if they like. And thirdly we do leadership-training courses. (Biko, 1979,
> pp. 118–119)

Much like the Black Panther Party's political education classes linked to survival programs, such as the liberation schools and free breakfast programs,
the leadership training course of the BCP in South Africa was a vehicle
through which the Black Consciousness political perspective could be
taught. Moreover, the influence of the Black Panther party and its survival
programs continued to inspire people even after its general demise in and
around 1980. One institution that embraced the Black Panther Party concept
of "service to the people" was the University of California at Santa Cruz,
which in 1992 created the Oakes Serves service-learning program. The students in the program were given college credit for performing 8 to 10 hours
per week of community service and attending a 3-hour weekly seminar. Both
of the authors of this chapter have taught the Oakes Serves class, and have
utilized the class to increase the awareness of students regarding the political

implications of their community service. Issues such as racism, environmental awareness, and public policy have been successfully explored with students. Our students were encouraged to understand their community service within a larger societal framework. In addition, students shared their experiences with the class and kept a weekly journal. This allowed the students to get the most out of their community service, which in some cases led to profound personal transformations. As was true with the Black Panther Party, so it was true with the students of Oakes Serves—when political consciousness is combined with community service, it not only meets a need in the community, but it also helps the volunteers transform their ideas about their community and the world. Definitely a distinct minority among community service organizations, there are only a few that have embraced the concept of political education combined with service as practiced years ago by the Black Panther Party. The two organizations we would like to highlight are The Mentoring Center in Oakland and the Freedom Schools sponsored by the Children's Defense Fund nationwide.

Founded in 1991, The Mentoring Center (TMC) provides technical assistance and training to approximately 50 to 85 mentoring efforts, and direct mentor training to 1,700 to 2,500 volunteers and program staff annually (www.mentor.org). In particular, it is the direct mentoring approach that is unique at TMC, utilizing a Transformative Mentoring approach to serve highly at-risk youth. Transformative Mentoring/Intervention is an intentional, structured, systematic, and corrective intervention focused on personally transforming the attitude and mental framework of a disrupted human development cycle. It is an intense service delivery system. TMC's approach includes a group-mentoring program that is curriculum based and long term. The ultimate goal is to change the mentality in the youth that gives rise to destructive behavior. TMC's Transition/Transformative Curriculum is designed for: character development, spiritual development, life skills training, anger management, and employability skills (www.mentor.org).

In addition, the youth, most of whom are parolees from the California Youth Authority (CYA), are given an Afrocentric perspective on the history and development of the African American male mentality in America. The numerous youth who seemed destined for a life of crime and who have come through this program are called The Positive Mind Group, and have been transformed into college-bound and socially active contributors to the community. The Mentoring Center has been recognized nationwide for significant application of this social technology, Transformative Mentoring, which has given a new lease on life to so many at-risk youth. This program is a more developed and sophisticated version of the political education classes that the Black Panther Party offered years ago. Its focus and intent is the same: to enable Black men and women to become productive participants and social advocates on behalf of the Black community.

Another project that exemplifies the spirit of the Black Panther Party in its approach is the Children's Defense Fund's Freedom Schools. Children's Defense Fund (CDF) Freedom Schools are partnerships between the CDF and local community organizations. Churches, universities, and schools provide literacy-rich summer programs that serve children ages 5 to 18, for five to eight weeks and that are staffed by college-age interns. Freedom Schools integrate reading, conflict resolution, and social action in an activity-based curriculum that promotes social, cultural, and historical awareness. In the summer of 2005, Freedom Schools operated at more than 70 sites in over 20 states and 40 cities. Approximately 5,500 children were served, with 650 college-age youth participating as Servant Leader Interns (www.freedom-schools.org). This project has created an effective system in which the children achieve higher literacy, the interns are given instruction, and the local community is included in the process. Training coordinated by the CDF's national staff prepares these young leaders to provide an enriching experience for the children they serve and to be part of a future generation of Servant Leaders. The training promotes principles of Servant Leadership by fostering an understanding of the important connection between effective programs, public policy, community development, political advocacy, and coalition building (www.freedomschools.org). In addition, the local community is included in the educational process. Adults are encouraged to share their experiences, stories, and time with the children and college-age staff of the local program site. The community volunteers serve as role models who believe in the children and share with them the joys of learning.

The Freedom Schools are a continuation of the Liberation schools begun by the Black Panther Party over 30 years ago. They have taken the volunteer, free-school idea, as pioneered by the Black Panther Party, and institutionalized it into a free summer program that reaches far more children, more consistently, than the Black Panther party was ever able to. More important, the children and the young staff are being taught African American history of social change in a dynamic way that includes change agents from the local community.

Unfortunately, however, the programs mentioned above are the exceptions rather than the rule. Most service-learning projects lack a political awareness component. They are primarily focused on the service portion to the detriment of the learning portion. The result is that effective movements that can alter public policy are not being built. Most projects fight to survive on constantly dwindling funding sources. Meanwhile, the gains of the civil rights era and the Black political power era are being eroded. The social and political thrust, so evident during the days of the Black Panther Party, has been halted. What is needed is a conscious effort to emulate projects like The Mentoring Center and Freedom Schools, which directly link service to changing public policy as well as to creating change agents.

Framing Social Justice in Higher Education

Linking social justice with the processes of service learning requires designing a curriculum that provides insights into the macropolitical dynamics of oppression and domination, and connects those insights with individual and collective experiences of people in communities of need. An analysis of the societal issues that produce social inequality is essential to understanding the causes of and factors involved in oppression and domination. An example of how this was accomplished is the work of the Black Panther Party in the 1960s and 1970s. As a leading Black political organization, the Black Panther Party sought societal changes and, as discussed earlier, utilized the pedagogical approaches of Paulo Freire to empower people to become more active in the community, either as party or community leaders. This development of political consciousness was achieved partly through the political education classes that utilized texts from revolutionary Third World movements, as well as from the U.S. social movements. Within this pedagogical framework party members were encouraged to articulate their political aspirations and, through a disciplined organizational apparatus, were able to pursue empowerment strategies that were aligned with the organization's Ten-Point Platform and Program (see appendix 1.A).

Although a university- or college-based curriculum using service learning as a vehicle to understand issues in social justice would not be formulated through an organizational framework such as the Black Panther Party, a similar pedagogical approach can be useful. This approach should examine the multiplicity of elements that produce social injustice in the United States.

An analysis of social justice should incorporate an understanding of the macropolitical analysis of race, class, and gender formation in the United States. First, the racial history of the United States is beset with the doctrine of White supremacy (Brown et al., 2003; Goldfield, 1997; Roediger, 1994), which has constrained the inclusion of people of color, particularly African Americans, into U.S. society. An assessment of how race disproportionately affected people of color in historical and contemporary settings is essential to understanding the impact of race in our society. Second, an analysis of the historical and contemporary effects of class from a macrosocietal level is important in order to assess the economic and structural constraints that influence economic life chances. Within this framework, the relationship of economic private and public interests should be examined in areas such as the environment and consumerism. Third, any discussion of social justice needs to examine issues that reflect historical and contemporary forms of gender and sexual inequality. Linking these three categories in a framework to lay a foundation for understanding social inequality will enable a deeper understanding of the need for social justice.

As mentioned earlier, the coauthors taught a course at UC Santa Cruz that used the three categories previously presented. The course was taught in a quarter system lasting 10 weeks. While this limited time compressed the learning and service work, meaningful learning, reflection, and service were accomplished. The curriculum that is being proposed here is more in depth theoretically, and within a 15-week semester system the student's ability to perform social justice work will be greatly enhanced.

One of the goals of this article is to articulate the need for a course in social justice, using service learning as a framework for understanding the issues of race, class, and gender oppression, and providing community service opportunities that examine social justice in a reflective, educational environment. The objective of such a course is to offer service learning as a process for seeking social justice within university and college settings. The learning objectives and outcomes of this course are as follows:

1. Ability to assess and examine community need
2. Understanding of the historical contribution of the Black Panther Party, in both theory and practice, to the service-learning movement
3. Understanding of the strengths and weaknesses of the contemporary service-learning movement as it relates to social justice and social change

4. Provision of theoretical tools that might be utilized to analyze the effectiveness of current community service practices
5. Ability to analyze community power structure
6. Knowledge of community resources

These course objectives and outcomes provide a theoretical understanding and practical application of the issues of social injustice in the United States and globally. The intent of the course is to provide a curriculum that will connect theoretically the community service work that would be performed by service-learning students to broader issues of social justice.

The proposed course contains an in-class and a field component. The in-class component consists of a two-hour seminar; meeting once a week, the field component comprises volunteer community service work for approximately six hours per week. The course requires the reading of at least one text and a course reader within in a 15-week semester and follows the teaching model of Oakes Serves at UC Santa Cruz, which was used by the coauthors from 1995 to 2003. The Oakes Serves course was designed to provide undergraduates with service-learning experiences at a variety of sites, including schools, community agencies, and nonprofit organizations. Similarly, a course designed for the California State University system meets on a once-a-week basis over a 15-week semester. Various issues of race, class, and gender oppression are examined, and reflection sessions are held in class with instruction-led and peer-led exercises. The proposed UC Santa Cruz course uses as a primary text *Ideas for Action* (2003) by Cynthia Kaufman, which provides a multidimensional view of oppression and domination, in a number of categories, including race, class, and gender. Additionally, a social justice reader would be used, consisting of essays and articles examining social justice from different disciplines and social movements. The reader also highlights the best practices in social justice work in the United States and abroad.

The class is organized as a two-hour seminar meeting once a week, ideally with one hour focused on the theoretical explorations of social justice based on class material, and the second hour on reflection exercises and discussions regarding students' community service experiences. The proposed course outline follows:

Week 1. Course introduction, orientation to service-learning placements
Week 2. What is social justice, conceptual frameworks, and group exercises on learning social justice

Week 3. What is service learning, journal writing, and reflection exercises

Week 4. Capitalism and Class—Kaufman—Chapter 2–3, Course reader

Week 5. Globalization—Kaufman—Chapter 4, Course reader

Week 6. Racism—Kaufman—Chapter 5, Course reader

Week 7. Patriarchy—Kaufman—Chapter 6, Course reader

Week 8. Environment—Kaufman—Chapter 7, Course reader

Week 9. Role of Government—Kaufman—Chapter 8, Course reader

Week 10. Midterm

Week 11. Bureaucracy and Organizations—Kaufman—Chapter 9

Week 12. Media and Democracy—Kaufman—Chapter 10

Week 13. Politics of Empowerment—Kaufman—Chapter 11, Course reader

Week 14. Student and community reflection on service-learning volunteer work

Week 15. Final reflection paper due

This course is designed to link the theoretical understandings of social justice with the experiences that students encounter as volunteers working in the field. To facilitate the assessment of this linkage, several assessment tools are used to determine the level of knowledge derived by students as well as the level of social consciousness they derive from their experiences. Initially, students are given a preservice learning survey to assess their level of civic engagement, community service experience, and other related background. A postservice learning survey is given at the conclusion of the course. This data is important in order to assess the effectiveness of the service-learning experience. Other assessment tools include journals, for students to reflect, on a daily or weekly basis, on their community service experience and the relationship of that experience to course work. Journals are also used as a process for assessing competence in the community service work. Additionally, the journals form a basis for weekly oral reflection sessions, using multiple formats to facilitate discussion of students' community service work and its meaning in relation to social justice issues. Finally, students are required to complete a final reflection paper linking theoretical understandings of social justice with their actual experiences in social justice work. Another level of assessment is the development of a community service contract, an agreement between the service-learning participants and community partners. The contract includes the number of hours of volunteer work as well as its scope. There is a semester-ending session between community partners and students in class, where a wrap-up session would highlight the work and contact between community partners and students.

The course is designed to promote self-reflection, community education, and theoretical inquiry, thus providing students with a holistic approach to understanding social justice issues. More important, this course addresses those issues that encourage a transformative perspective on the critical issues of social justice.

Service Learning as a Transformative Experience

Ultimately, this chapter emphasizes that social justice work, framed in the experiences of SNCC organizers in the Mississippi Delta region registering African Americans to vote, the example of a Black Panther Party member in the Westside of Chicago feeding breakfast to the hungry, and the examples of other courageous social activists, are highly essential today. Within such experiences, the individuals involved can see their work as a life-transforming process. Individuals who participated in organizational structures that pushed for social change during the era of the civil rights movement were committed to social justice work for however long the struggle lasted. In the spirit of the Panthers and individuals such as Rosa Parks who took bold steps toward attaining social justice, this commitment can be conceived today in a service-learning framework.

The development of a cadre of students who are able to interact within a reflective framework of reciprocity and community service settings through the proposed service-learning curriculum, would contribute to a stream of social activism that would surely be effective in communities of need. Moreover, such a model could effectively transform the lives of the participating students as well as enrich the communities influenced by their efforts.

Appendix 1.A

Black Panther Party Ten-Point Platform and Program

October 1966

BLACK PANTHER PARTY PLATFORM AND PROGRAM

WHAT WE WANT

WHAT WE BELIEVE

1. **We want freedom. We want power to determine the destiny of our Black community.**

   We believe that Black people will not be free until we are able to determine our destiny.

2. **We want full employment for our people.**

   We believe that the federal government is responsible and obligated to find every man employment or a guaranteed income. We believe that if the white American businessmen will not give full employment, then the means of production should be taken from the businessmen and placed in the community so that the people of the community can organize and employ all of its people and give a high standard of living.

3. **We want an end to the robbery by the capitalist of our Black community.**

   We believe that this racist government has robbed us and now we are demanding the overdue debt of forty acres and two mules. Forty acres and two mules were promised 100 years ago as restitution for slave labor and mass murder of Black people. We will accept the payment in currency which will be distributed to our many communities. The Germans are now aiding the six million Jews. The American racist has taken part in the slaughter of over five million Black people; therefore we feel that this is a modest demand that we make.

4. **We want decent housing, fit for shelter of human beings.**

   We believe that if the white landlords will give decent housing to our Black community, then the housing and the land should be made into cooperatives so that our community, with government aid, can build and make decent housing for its people.

5. We want education for our people that exposes the true nature of this decadent society. We want education that teaches us our true history and our role in the present-day society.

We believe in an educational system that will give to our people a knowledge of self. If a man does not have knowledge of himself and his position in society and the world, then he has little chance to relate to anything else.

6. We want all Black men to be exempt from military service.

We believe that Black people should not be forced to fight in the military service to defend a racist government that does not protect us. We will not fight and kill other people of color in the world, who, like Black people, are being victimized by the white racist government of America. We will protect ourselves from the force and violence of the racist police and the racist military, by whatever means necessary.

7. We want an immediate end to POLICE BRUTALITY and MURDER of Black people.

We believe we can end police brutality in our Black community by organizing Black self-defense groups that are dedicated to defending our Black community from racist police oppression and brutality. The Second Amendment to the Constitution of the United States gives a right to bear arms. We therefore believe that all Black people should arm themselves for self-defense.

8. We want freedom for all Black men held in federal, state, county and city prisons and jails.

We believe that all Black people should be released from the many jails and prisons because they have not received a fair and impartial trial.

9. We want all Black people when brought to trial to be tried in court by a jury of their peer group or people from their Black communities, as defined by the Constitution of the United States.

We believe that the courts should follow the United States Constitution so that Black people will receive fair trials. The Fourteenth Amendment of the U.S. Constitution gives a man a right to be tried by his peer group. A peer is a person from a similar economic, social, religious, geographical, environmental, historical, and racial background. To do this the court will be

forced to select a jury from the Black community from which the Black de-
fendant came. We have been and are being tried by all-white juries that have
no understanding of the "average reasoning man" of the Black community.

10. **We want land, bread, housing, education, clothing, justice, and peace.
And as our major political objective, a United Nations–supervised plebi-
scite to be held throughout the Black colony, in which only Black colonial
subjects will be allowed to participate, for the purpose of determining the
will of Black people as to their national destiny.**

> When in the course of human events, it becomes necessary for one people
> to dissolve the political bands which have connected them with one an-
> other, and to assume, among the powers of the earth, the separate and
> equal station to which the laws of nature and nature's God entitle them, a
> decent respect to the opinions of mankind requires that they should declare
> the causes which impel them to the separation.

We hold these truths to be self-evident, that all men are created equal; that
they are endowed by their Creator with certain inalienable rights; that
among these are life, liberty, and the pursuit of happiness. That, to secure
these rights, governments are instituted among men, deriving their just powers from the consent of the governed; that, whenever any form of government becomes destructive to these ends, it is the right of the people to alter
or abolish it, and to institute a new government, laying its foundation on
such principles, and organizing its powers in such form, as to them shall
seem most likely to effect their safety and happiness. Prudence, indeed, will
dictate that governments long established should not be changed for light
and transient causes; and, accordingly, all experience hath shown, that man-
kind are more disposed to suffer, while evils are sufferable, than to right
themselves by abolishing the forms to which they are accustomed. But, when
a long train of abuses and usurpations, pursuing invariably the same object,
evinces a design to reduce them under absolute despotism, it is their right, it
is their duty, to throw off such government, and to provide new guards for
their future security.

Appendix 1.B

Wingspread Principles of Good Practice for Combining Service and Learning

Ellen Porter Honnet and Susan J. Poulsen, The Johnson Foundation, May 1989

- An effective program engages people in responsible and challenging actions for the common good.
- An effective program provides structured opportunities for people to reflect critically on their service experience.
- An effective program articulates clear service and learning goals for everyone involved.
- An effective program allows for those with needs to define those needs.
- An effective program clarifies the responsibilities of each person and organization involved.
- An effective program matches service providers and service needs through a process that recognizes changing circumstances.
- An effective program expects genuine, active, and sustained organizational commitment.
- An effective program includes training, supervision, monitoring, support, recognition, and evaluation to meet service and learning goals.
- An effective program ensures that the time commitment for service and learning is flexible, appropriate, and in the best interests of all involved. In order to be useful to all parties involved, some service activities require longer participation and/or a greater time commitment than others.
- An effective program is committed to program participation by and with diverse populations.

Reprinted with permission, The Johnson Foundation; http://www.johnson fdn.org/principles.html

References

Biko, S. (1979). *Black consciousness in South Africa*. New York: Vintage Books.

Brown, M., Carnoy, M., Currie, E., Duster, T., Oppenheimer, D. B., Shultz, M., & Wellman, D. (2003). *Whitewashing race*. Berkeley, CA: University of California Press.

Carson, C. (1992). *In struggle: SNCC and the Black awakening of the 1960s.*Cambridge, MA: Harvard University Press.

Coles, R. (1993). *A call to service.* Boston: Houghton Mifflin.

Davis, A. (1998, February 10). [Interview in] The two nations of Black America [Television episode]. *Frontline.* Boston: WGBH.

Freire, P. (1993, originally published 1970). *Pedagogy of the oppressed.* New York: Continuum.

Goldfield, M. (1997). *The color of politics.* New York: The New Press.

Hilliard, D. (2006). *Huey: Spirit of the panther.* New York: Thunder Mouth Press.

Jacoby, B. (1996). *Service learning in higher education.* San Francisco: Jossey-Bass.

Kaufman, C. (2003). *Ideas for action.* Cambridge, MA: South End Press.

Kelley, R. D. G., & Lewis, E. (2000). *A history of African Americans from 1880, Vol. II.* Oxford: Oxford University Press.

King, M. L. (1967). *Where do we go from here, chaos or community?* Boston: Beacon.

Newton, H. (1973). *Revolutionary suicide.* New York: Harcourt Brace Jovanovich.

Oden, R. S., & Casey, T. A. (2004). *Black Panther Party as a service-learning innovator.* Unpublished manuscript.

Roediger, D. (1994). *The wages of whiteness.* London: Verso.

Seale, B. (1991) *Seize the time.* Baltimore: Black Classic Press.

Young, I. M. (1990). *Justice and the politics of difference.* Princeton: Princeton University Press.

Zinn, H. (1980). *A people's history of the United States.* New York: Harper Collins.

2

STIMULATING SOCIAL JUSTICE THEORY FOR SERVICE-LEARNING PRACTICE

David Schulz

The last of those qualities which make a state
virtuous must be justice, if we only knew what
that was.

— Plato's *Republic*, Book IV, paragraph 16
(410 BCE/1937, 10th ed., p. 695)

"With liberty and justice for all," six familiar words of a morning mantra rehearsed throughout American schools and encapsulating an essential American precept. Justice is invoked in a wide array of cultural products from inscriptions on legal tender to cartoon caricatures. Social justice is so central to American political consciousness that pundits invoke its ideals across the political spectrum in support of their point of view. As David Miller (2001) points out, social justice has become an "animating ideal of democratic governments" (p. xi).

Increasingly, the general public has focused its attention on the social value of universities, particularly those that are funded with public monies. As Plater (1995) elaborates, "Communities now believe universities and colleges not only have an obligation to apply knowledge and expertise to the solution of problems, but they have to do so in a timely fashion with immediate and demonstrable results" (p. 32). The academy thus faces a continuing challenge to demonstrate the fruits of its labors. As Maureen Kenny (2002) and her colleagues remark, "Indeed, perhaps the most consistently identified 'problem' in higher education, as reflected in the comments and behavior of taxpayers, legislators, governing boards, funders, parents, students, and businesses is that the academy is not playing a visible role in contributing to the improvement of the lives of people in the community as their lives are lived on a day-to-day basis" (p. 3). And as Carol Vincent (2003) points out, "the educational system, through its organization and practices, is implicated in the realization of just or unjust social outcomes" (p. i).

This volume offers sites for reflecting on social justice. The contributors provide exemplary case studies useful for the design and implementation of social justice projects into one's own curriculum through service learning. Observations from my experiences incorporating social justice–infused service-learning assignments in speech communication courses are intended to help readers avoid potential roadblocks while maximizing the benefits of service learning. In particular, I draw from service-learning experiences in courses such as Persuasive Messages, Intercultural Communication, and Advanced Presentational Speaking. While the subject matter for these courses is different, each course asks students to demonstrate their mastery of course concepts through applied presentations both in the classroom and in the surrounding community.

Many of my courses begin with discussions, readings, and exercises that explore the meaning of the term *social justice*. Joining Miller, I believe that without an understanding of its first principles, justice can never be realized. To undertake this exploration, I have my students read and discuss a range of social and political philosophers, from ancient (Plato c. 427–347 BCE) to modern (John Rawls). Together we explore the importance of social justice as both an ideal worth pursuing and a pursuit worthy of repeated practice, beyond the semester and graduation. Contemplating Plato's query (p. 23) illuminates what we know of justice, how it relates to the social, and why this inquiry matters to the academy.

In what follows, I outline a contingent theory of social justice as well as offer general tactics for implementation. My experiences using service learning in communication studies courses offer readers both theoretical and community-based applications.

The Meaning of Social Justice

Over the years, opposing ideologues have leveraged the phrase "social justice" for radically different ends. During the 1930s, Father Coughlin, a famous radio demagogue, published the first periodical on social justice and headed the National Union for Social Justice. The anti-Semitic nature of

Coughlin's public addresses would, for many, seem to pervert the spirit of social justice. Similar examples abound today, including noted conservative Patrick Buchanan's (1998) book, *The Great Betrayal: How American Sovereignty and Social Justice Are Being Sacrificed to the Gods of the Global Economy.* Buchanan theorizes social justice in terms of a cost-benefit calculus that many would find inimical to the concept. On the other side of the ideological spectrum, many progressive groups conflate social justice with everything from environmental causes to animal rights. Through such conflations, well-intentioned supporters invite critics to caricature their causes as an unrealizable "cosmic justice" (see Sowell, 1999).

Justice has become something of an empty set, a referent pointing to so many different ideals and ideas that it has lost currency and shared meaning across communities. Both conservative and progressive policy makers claim allegiance to "social justice" because the phrase has political cache, but when pressed for what justice means, each offer drastically different accounts. Therefore it is useful to review historical theories of justice in order to appreciate the many layers of meaning attached to it. Such genealogy is not designed to affix a central meaning to the concept of social justice, but instead to demonstrate a general and minimalist (or thin) theoretical consensus of first principles.

Justice is not an object but an ideal that has invited contemplative reflection since humans organized themselves into societies. Generations of theorists have borrowed something from their predecessors' thoughts on the subject. In my rhetorical theory and persuasive messages course, for example, I begin each semester coaxing students to contemplate the first principles of justice. I frame theoretical discussions as ongoing conversations and encourage students to join these conversations in the hopes that they personalize justice in their semester projects.

From a communication studies context, social justice is an ongoing *process* that necessitates, even demands, vigilant attention to both its precepts and practices. If we are to avoid social justice becoming cliché, it is essential to invite students to see justice as an endless journey and not a destination. In order to help students comprehend social justice and possibilities for its continued practice it is important to reflect on the scale of our enterprise.

Classroom conversations about justice typically begin with some metaphor, analogy, story, or picture that supplies thinkers with a ready referent for a subject that eludes a simple grasp. When asking students what justice represents, I receive a wide range of responses reflecting cultural imagery, current events, and/or personal experiences. For example, when pressing students for what justice looks like in practice I receive replies such as "the American flag" and "scales balanced by a blindfolded woman." The image connotes a legal arena where justice is objectively adjudicated. Justice has also been envisioned as a sunlike symbol bringing light to dark places. Some African cultures use two interlocking diamonds to depict justice's essence, while other cultures picture justice as a torch.

Classroom consideration of such culturally prominent justice metaphors serves as entry portals in discussions with students. In communication courses (such as Rhetorical Theory and Persuasive Messages) I return to the Greeks in general and Plato in particular in order to provide students with the long-standing intellectual tradition informing our current conceptions of justice.

Plato's interest in and impact on theories of justice cannot be overstated. In Book I of *The Republic*, when he pits Socrates against Thrasymachus, Plato explores the *practice* of justice. Thrasymachus contends that the strong use of brute force establishes what is and what is not just. Justice becomes something *made*. Using Socrates as his mouthpiece, Plato refutes this characterization, advancing a metaphysical notion of justice as something *found*. Justice thus conceived develops into an *a priori*, existing *before* human society. It is not something seized through force but rather something *discovered* through contemplative thinkers and their ability to balance reason, spirit, and appetite. The many students who enter my Persuasive Messages course anticipating that they will learn persuasive skills for exerting power *over* audiences are reflecting Thrasymachus's view of justice. The cited Platonic dialogue provides a method of critiquing the "justice as force" worldview. Students are encouraged to conceptualize justice as something discovered through partnerships with others, and many students work to apply this conceptualization of justice in their semester projects. For example, a number of students in my Persuasive Messages class opted to partner with high school and community leaders in an anti-gang coalition. Service-learning projects have ranged from mentoring at-risk youth programs to the creation of a dynamic anti-gang lecture series that visits local high schools. Such projects foster unique perspectives on the impacts of social injustice when left unchecked, and they encourage students to devise persuasive strategies with at-risk youth to provide alternatives to gang life.

Plato is not the only earlier philosopher informing my students' understanding of social justice. A differing perspective was proffered by Epicurus (341–270 BCE), who denied the possibility of justice existing before or inside of the contemplative individual. Epicurus was one of the first thinkers to develop a theory of justice founded on the notion of a social contract. Rather than existing *before* humans, Epicurus suggested that people working in mutual associations *created* justice. He wrote, "Justice and injustice do not exist in relation to beings who have not been able to make a *compact* with the object of avoiding mutual harm" (Benn, 1967, p. 300). Here justice was conceptualized as an agreement between the state and individuals to neither harm nor be harmed. For Epicurus, justice amounted to a compact between the state and its citizens to guard against unjust actors and actions. The Epicurean view of justice provides us with an alternative to the Platonic idealized form of justice. Epicurus equips us with a vocabulary to discuss the contingent nature of justice that reflects the ever-changing compact between states and their citizens. Students have commented that such discussions help them see that justice can be proactive (versus reactive and punitive). Representative service-learning campaigns have included public debates where teams of students contemplate both sides of local issues in public forums and switch sides between debates to engender appreciation of both sides of enduring societal issues.

Another ancient voice informing students' view of justice is that of Aristotle (384–322 BCE), whose views cut a middle path between Plato and Epicurus. Aristotle wrote that justice consisted of treating equal parts equally and unequal parts unequally, with a third party (an impartial judge) considering parity. For Aristotle the concept of "blind justice" encapsulated the idea that justice is not a respecter of person, wealth, or status. Justice is an entitlement of citizenship. Aristotle extended the theory of justice in his *The Nicomachian Ethics* to include distributive justice writing:

> [E]quality for the people involved will be the same as for the things involved, since [in a just society] the relation between the people will be the same as the relation between the things involved. For if the people involved are not equal, they will not [justly] receive equal shares; indeed, whenever equals receive unequal shares, or unequals equal shares . . . that is the source of quarrels and accusations . . . (1980, p. 123)

In Aristotle we see emerge a concept of equality based on *fairness* that contemporary theorists (Hume, Rawls, and Miller, to name a few) develop more completely. David Miller (2001) synthesizes preceding theories into three essential components of social justice: need, desert, and equality. Theorists from Plato through Rawls contribute to a conversation suggesting members of civil society are entitled (desert) to the fair (equality) distribution of the basic goods necessary for survival (need). Important to remember is the *human* circumstances in discussing all three components of justice so as to keep our subject from becoming unwieldy in scope. Classroom discussion, directed readings, and/or individual papers incorporating each of these three characteristics promise to keep students and instructors focused on realizing some semblance of justice's *social* potential.

It is difficult to characterize social justice without some discussion of basic social *needs*. Needs are those vital components necessary for a person to subsist in society. We can (and should) differentiate needs from wants. Common standards for basic human needs exist, and many people often turn to Abraham Maslow's Hierarchy of Needs, focusing on the lower two levels (physiological and safety needs) as the minimum rights of citizenship in the United States. Whatever standard is used to assess minimal needs, it must be "recognized and applied across the whole society . . . ," says Miller. "[T]he best way to understand this is in terms of the set of functionings [*sic*] that together make up a minimally decent life for people in the society in question" (2001, p. 247). In my experience, there is always some student challenge to the idea of basic needs as a *right* of citizenship. The objection often goes something like "people's bad decisions should not entitle them to basic needs that hard-working Americans end up subsidizing." Such objections are valid and rich sites for further discussion. Directed readings and class debate can help students reflect on basic needs students often take for granted that remain unrealized for millions of Americans.

A second facet joining theories of social justice is consideration of how distribution of social resources (primarily economic) is determined, or the principle of *desert*. Used in different contexts, desert connotes a variety of meanings. In the context of social justice discussions desert concerns "how people are rewarded for the work they perform, taking work in its broadest sense to encompass productive activities such as innovation and management as well as labor" (Miller, 2001, p. 248). Desert theoretically corrects the arbitrary allocation of resources, providing an official justification for *why* resources are distributed as they are. Educators and students alike who ostensibly work for social justice cannot overlook the integral role of *how* and with what rationale resources are allocated. Desert reminds us that what joins diverse peoples together into a society is the tacit agreement about how the whole provides for its constituent parts. The cohesion of this fragile agreement is only as good as the rationale guiding the institutions commissioned to ensure social order. Prevailing logics of desert offer educators ways of interrogating institutions and practices in need of change. For example, the fact that women get paid less than men for the same work exemplifies a violation of desert. Discussions do not have to be abstract, esoteric, or lengthy. If our aims are to address issues such as homelessness, critical pedagogy, and cultural competency, then the principle of desert figures prominently in addressing how and why current unjust structures endure.

Equality is an equally crucial element of social justice. In terms of justice, equality is only possible when individuals are members of the "social." When members of a society are identifiable (generally through citizenship), then the equal distribution of legal, political, and social rights promised through membership can be assessed and corrected (Miller, 2001, p. 250). If we wish to confront racism, poverty, and many other societal problems, we must begin with a rubric of inalienable rights promised to all. As Miller (2001) puts it:

> [t]o achieve social justice we must have a political community in which citizens are treated as equals in an across-the-board way, in which public policy is geared toward meeting the intrinsic needs of every member, and in which the economy is framed and constrained in such a way that the income and other work-related benefits people receive correspond to their respective deserts. (p. 250)

When the above conditions (need, desert, and equality) are identified as unmet, we can begin to devise strategies for change.

Perhaps the most prominent contemporary thinker on the concept of justice was John Rawls (1921–2002). His many writings on justice serve as an entry point for contemporary thinkers. Rawls argued that human nature committed us to act justly by virtue of our interconnected and complementary basic *needs*. Through such insights Rawls contributed the most pragmatic theory of social justice, namely, that justice means distributing benefits equally to serve *common*, versus *individual*, needs. I find Rawl's theory of social justice most applicable in my Intercultural Communications course, where students' service-learning projects focus on devising ways to meet the basic needs of culturally diverse groups. For example, some students opt to complete their service-learning hours at a Hmong resource center in Modesto, California, called "The Bridge," where students provide tutoring services to Hmong refugees. Students are asked to deliver oral reports of their experiences to the class, sharing lessons of social justice learned through practicing theoretical precepts in the field. Other students opt to spend service-learning hours working at the United Samaritans or Salvation Army and report back newfound empathy for the area's most impoverished populations as well as a desire to work for the betterment of these populations.

Identification of the circumstances or contexts of social *injustice* is important for beginning conversations about the design and diagnoses of social justice campaigns. The *membership* we wish to reach may seem obvious, but without clearly specifying and listening to target audiences, students and instructors may focus on subjects falling outside the purview of the "social," or worse, unintentionally ignore the needs of their target audiences. For example, prior students have lobbied for the inclusion of animal protection programs for their term projects. Reminding students of the *social* (or human) component of social justice assists in delineating projects that are both doable and faithful to the concept.

Moreover, we must work with students to identify those *institutions* charged with applying social justice. Encouraging students to identify the places where they think justice *should* happen proves useful for the diagnosis and design of communication campaigns of social remedy. When students are encouraged to see the interlaced network of institutions surrounding them as well as the consequences of their relationship to these institutions, they are better equipped to interrupt injustice in meaningful ways.

The ability to identify *change agencies* within this network helps students develop navigational strategies both for their projects and for life after college. The university itself can be seen as an agency with the *propensity* to change other institutional structures out of step with the aims of social justice. Students become pilots maneuvering various instrumental means within these change agencies to overturn injustices in their communities. Requiring students to identify agencies of change introduced students in my persuasion class to public school administrators who assisted them in creating antigang communication campaigns. In their final presentations, students reported that these alliances proved invaluable both for their term projects and in discovering career options. Attention to these *circumstances* of social justice (audiences, institutions, and change agencies) allows us to foreground a general set of first principles that can help us differentiate social justice from other enterprises.

Coauthoring classroom-specific definitions of social justice further connects campaigns in social justice to disciplinary conventions and goals. One such definition, crafted from a communication perspective, might read something like this: "Social justice is an ongoing process that requires communicative engagement particularly in the diagnosis of social injustice, assessing prevailing rationales for such injustice, and devising communicative strategies for equitable redress." When students are invited to craft definitions calibrated to their curriculum they are better equipped to apply theory in pedagogically sound practices.

Personalized definitions such as these empower creators to perform their projects confidently, because underlying convictions are their own. For educators, such definitions develop into defendable mission statements for classroom lectures, written scholarship, and grant proposals. However, it is essential to tether social justice to a minimal set of first principles. As David Miller (2001) puts it, "No matter what else it requires justice minimally demands consistency in the treatment of individuals and groups" (p. 253).

Whatever criterion of just treatment is devised with our students, "it is an elementary requirement that any two people who resemble each other along the dimension that justice tracks must be treated in the same way" (Miller, 2001, p. 253). Equity, need, and merit are three central components of social justice that assist students in diagnosing the "ingredients" of social problems so that, in Freire's words, "fantasy" solutions might be avoided (Friere, 2000).

From Social Justice Theory to Service-Learning Practice

Having made clear the importance of social justice to the mission of the academy and having explored a variety of perspectives on the meaning of justice, we arrive at the question of *how* to make social justice *happen* in the university. A first step toward this end has already been explored in inviting students to coauthor their own definitions of social justice. At some point, theories and definitions of social justice beg to be put into practice. Here, service learning enters our discussion as the catalyst for activating social justice locally.

My pedagogical preoccupation with social justice springs from Cicero's twin concepts of *vita contemplativa* (thoughtful life) and *vita activa* (active life). Cicero believed that educators should produce citizen-scholars who practice their theories for the betterment of the republic. Engaging social justice through classroom discussion and actualizing it through service-learning projects performs Cicero's *vita contemplativa* and the *vita activa* simultaneously.

Moving from classroom practices to applications of social justice in the "real world" necessitates that scholars and students practice the things to which our natures are best adapted. Nature has best adapted educators to the disciplines where we teach, research, and write. All disciplines, from the hard sciences to the humanities, provide students with concepts for practical use. Service learning actualizes these concepts in real contexts.

Most books on service learning employ a four-step model. Students are first taught to conceptualize justice abstractly. Students move from abstractions to scenarios that test theories in controlled classroom experiences such as small-group activities. These experiences lead to the identification of concrete problems that service-learning projects are designed and implemented to remedy. Finally, some variety of feedback mechanism promotes critical reflectivity.

In my Intercultural Communication classroom we begin with theories of intercultural communication and personal definitions of social justice. Definitions and theories are then put into practice through role-play activities. One example is to have students read Peggy McIntosh's "White Privilege: Unpacking the Invisible Knapsack" (1997). After reading this short, seven-page essay, I pair students up and ask each group to formulate additional unseen advantages that contribute to social injustice. Each dyad shares its list with the class, and then we contemplate strategies for interrupting these injustices and creating alternatives.

From classroom role playing, students are invited to choose from a number of service-learning sites for their semester projects. After completing learning logs, students reflect on the theory and practice of intercultural communication in typed journal entries and classroom presentations. Through such activities, I ask students to see themselves and their peers as encyclopedias. Each student contains invaluable insights and experiences from which all can learn. I mandate a second level of reflection in the form of student responses to presentations, nudging students to move beyond the role of passive audience member and into the role of active cocreator of shared social justice experiences.

While service learning for social justice campaigns furnishes instructors a pedagogically sound way of offering students more than the basics, many remain wary of how to implement social justice into their curricula. Reservations about time trade-offs and lack of resources or institutional support, as well as liability concerns, can paralyze one from implementing service learning in his or her classes. During my first year as a new faculty member the *last* thing on my mind was finding a way to fit service learning into my three new class preparations. Thanks to some gentle prodding, I visited my campus's office of service learning and found, to my surprise, much of the work was already done. Gracious colleagues offered templates I retooled for my own curricular goals. The vast inventory of samples to draw from, combined with a supportive staff, made service learning irresistible. If similar support is absent, online resources and books such as this one provide groundwork for implementing service learning.

Perhaps the greatest barrier to widespread incorporation of service learning is skepticism that such endeavors amount to little more than "charity" work or, worse, "distractions" from core disciplinary principles and theories. Bhatti (2003) elaborates, "Recent research which has engaged with issues concerning social justice in education has emphasized the contradictory ways in which seemingly good intentions may be reflected in practice" (p. 67). At intervals throughout a semester I remind students that their service-learning projects are not to be confused with charity work that they might be already doing in their private lives. Instead of charity, I insist that students conceptualize their projects as professional partnerships that require the application of the complete array of tools available in their disciplinary toolboxes. Sometimes the final results of a service-learning project do not match a student's initial project proposal. I encourage students and those reading this to (re)consider such "failures" as important lessons for determining what does and does not work in community campaigns. Many students begin their presentations reporting that they "failed" to meet their initial objectives and then unpack lessons they and their colleagues can learn through shared experiences.

Most students, however, report enthusiasm for their service-learning experiences. Initial resistance to community service soon gives way to realizations of the short- and long-term benefits. In the short term, students see how course concepts and theories play out in the "real world" and thus begin to personalize course materials in ways that help them excel on quizzes and tests and in other courses. Moreover, students experience solidarity with their colleagues as they network and develop collaboration strategies essential to life after the academy. Many students report that their service-learning projects provided either career opportunities with the agencies they served or letters of recommendation from community partners.

Conclusion

Throughout this chapter I have discussed the twin forces of theory and practice informing my service-learning-for-social-justice communicative campaigns. Theories of social justice help launch classroom discussions and collaborative coauthoring of discipline-specific definitions. Using examples from my classrooms, I have endeavored to provide ways of beginning conversations about social justice with students while moving these discussions to the street for practical application through service learning. I have also provided examples of the importance of such programs as socially and educationally potent sites for developing partnerships between educators, students, and community members. Such partnerships hold the potential of maximizing each partner's interests while simultaneously positioning the university to answer its critics. As a theoretical ideal, social justice cannot activate itself. Rather it takes the concerted effort of interdependent stakeholders (community members, students, and instructors) to transform social justice theory into service-learning practice. Reflecting on student projects ranging from antigang awareness campaigns to Hmong refugee tutoring programs, I have provided examples of the types of projects available for implementing social justice into college curriculums. Service learning offers a proven method for activating social justice through partnerships that are at once both theoretically sound and socially beneficial. In the final analysis, learning through social justice service offers synergies between educators, students, and community stakeholders with spectacular results, if we keep our goals clear and make the first move of implementation into our pedagogical practice.

References

Aristotle (1980). *The Nicomachean ethics* (D. Ross, Trans.). Revised by J. L. Ackrill & J.O. Urmson. New York: Oxford University Press.

Bhatti, G. (2003). Social justice and non-traditional participants in higher education: A tale of "border crossing," instrumentalism and shift. In C. Vincent (Ed.), *Social justice, education, and identity*. New York: Routledge Palmer.

Benn, S. (1967). Justice. In P. Edwards (Ed.), *The encyclopedia of philosophy* (pp. 298– 302). New York: Macmillan.

Buchanan, P. J. (1998). *The great betrayal: How American sovereignty and social justice are being sacrificed to the gods of the global economy.* Canada: Little, Brown.

Freire, P. (2000). *Pedagogy of the oppressed* (30th anniversary ed.). New York: Continuum.

Kenny, M., et al. (2002). Promoting civil society through service: A view of the issues. In M. Kenny, L. K. Simon, K. Kiley-Brabeck, & R. M. Lerner (Eds.), *Learning to serve: Promoting civil society through service learning* (pp. 1–14). Norwell, MA: Kluwer Academic Publishers.

McIntosh, P. (1997). White privilege: Unpacking the invisible knapsack. In Bart Schneider (Ed.), *Race: An anthology in the first person* (pp. 120–126). New York: Crown.

Miller, D. M. (2001). *Principles of social justice.* Cambridge, MA: Harvard University Press.

Plater, W. M. (1995). Future work: Faculty time in the 21st century. *Change*, pp. 22–33.

Plato. (1937). *The dialogues of Plato* (10th ed.) (Benjamin Jowett, trans.). New York: Random House (original published 410 B.C.).

Rawls, J. (1971). *A theory of justice.* Cambridge, MA: Harvard University Press.

Sowell, T. (1999). *The quest for cosmic justice.* New York: The Free Press.

Vincent, C. (Ed.). (2003). *Social justice, education, and identity.* New York: Routledge Palmer.

3

REFLECTIONS ON SERVICE LEARNING AS A PEDAGOGICAL STRATEGY IN COMPOSITION

Christine Popok

To educate as the practice of freedom is a way of teaching that anyone can learn. That learning process comes easiest to those of us who teach who also believe that there is an aspect of our vocation that is sacred; who believe that our work is not merely to share information but to share in the intellectual and spiritual growth of our students. To teach in a manner that respects and cares for the souls of our students is essential if we are to provide the necessary conditions where learning can most deeply and intimately begin.

—bell hooks, *Teaching to Transgress: Education as the Practice of Freedom* (1994)

When I first started teaching First-Year Composition (FYC) at California State University–Channel Islands (CSUCI), I told students I wasn't as concerned with their subject selection as I was with observing and improving their writing skill. Now, after employing service-learning strategies for three years, I find that what students write about does matter. By planning service-based experiential learning assignments that emphasize environmental, social, and personal responsibility, I am a better writing teacher and they are better writers. And in the process, the community of learners benefits as well. In this chapter, I am enthusiastic about sharing some of the theory that has informed my pedagogy, some of the methods I have used in and out of the classroom, and some of the student responses and results from teaching FYC and service learning simultaneously.

Not only do these courses enhance student efficacy, by emphasizing praxis—the recursive combination of action and reflection (Freire & Macedo, 1987)—student writing improves as well. Service-learning pedagogy necessitates critical thinking and as such assists students in developing meaningful rhetorical skill that transfers to their later work. Involving a student in the community outside and within the university setting and asking that student to be attentive to academic and community audiences as the student grapples with an issue of social justice makes pedagogical sense. Critical reflection is central to the learning part of service.

My approach draws upon the work of bell hooks, distinguished professor of English at City College in New York, and Paulo Freire, Brazilian philosopher and educator, who stress that teaching should emerge from a joyful mission and that the most productive learning is born out of experience and dialogue versus lecture and testing. Although their work serves different populations with variant needs and literacy levels than those in FYC, utilizing an engaged pedagogy to teach writing has improved my efforts to "empower [students] to be better scholars, to live more fully in the world beyond the academe" (hooks, 1994). Service learning's effectiveness depends on the degree to which it requires the learner, student and faculty alike, to think his or her way through a new situation. Students often write of discovering a creative aspect of themselves while working with community partners; this newfound ability to rise to the task fosters an excitement for learning. By participating fully in the service-learning experience and critical reflection activities and essays, students can "develop the confidence to know that, when they really do have something important to say, they will be able to say it clearly, forcefully, and with a proper marshaling of evidence" (Beidler, 1997). In my experience, when students narrate and reflect on something and/or someone to whom they have a direct connection, the quality of their writing improves.

Learning Objectives

Digging into historical and present-day injustices bristles, and that reality makes it all the more important to uplift students with optimism for the work they are doing in and out of class. Service learning allows teacher, student, and community partner to witness recursively the differences that separate and the humanity that binds. Experiential pedagogy rivets us: "our capacity to generate excitement is deeply affected by our interest in one another" (hooks, 1994, p. 8). We work to encourage students to celebrate the goodness in humanity during a period in history when all news seems to be focused on our greedy and violent natures. Service learning provides an opportunity for students to do more than just sit and watch. Students who may have discriminated against and feared the Other write of a deeper understanding once they experience the Other in the one-on-one manner of service learning. Such humanistic goals are admittedly lofty, so to focus students on what I wish for them to learn, I have developed the following Learning Objectives for the required narrative/eflective service-learning essay and their problem/solution essay:

1. To become aware of community-based organization (CBO) missions and about career options for the public good
2. To write about a shared, firsthand experience and to narrate and reflect upon service learning before an audience of peers, professors, and community partners
3. To balance action and reflection
4. To analyze one's personal stake in social justice
5. To reflect on character development and self-actualization

I will examine each of these objectives in greater detail after explaining how power dynamics in the FYC classroom can facilitate service learning.

Power Dynamics in the FYC Classroom

For a course involving the exploration of issues of social justice to be effective, we must create an environment where students can challenge their fundamental values and beliefs about themselves, their communities, and their roles as responsible citizens. In this environment we abandon the "banking system" of education, in which the teacher possesses a priori knowledge to transfer from his or her brain to the student's, for a system where the student learns from his or her impact on an audience whether or not a piece of writing is effective for its purposes. Feminist and resistance theories as they relate to composition and rhetoric provide a framework for introducing service-learning pedagogy. These theoretical models prove useful in practice as they stress engaged, empowering classrooms that emphasize increased representation of disadvantaged groups. The student-centered classroom addresses issues of competition and inequality by attempting to transfer power from the instructor to the instructed, in discussions and workshops, and from those most proficient in English to those acquiring proficiency. By modeling respectful dialogue and attentive coaching on their essay drafts, students can learn to serve the community in a similar manner while employing their unique talents.

While a complete transfer is impossible, as each participant is aware on some level that the instructor has final authority, practices such as team holistic scoring can move a vast majority of that power out of the classroom. In the CSUCI Directed Self Placement (DSP) composition program, 80 percent of the students' work is scored, not by me, their teacher, but by my colleagues on the holistic scoring team. Decreasing the distinction between Grader and Graded sets a further tone of equality in and out of the classroom and facilitates engaged pedagogy, a critical component of service learning. It is precisely for this reason—to break down the barrier between Teacher and Taught—that I encourage my students to address me as Coach Christine. Shifting the classroom dynamics to a more democratic space further enhances the program. And since criticism is much more readily received if solicited, I encourage students in our workshops to ask me and their peers to respond to their specified needs with regard to their writing and their synthesizing of readings and service-learning experiences.

At CSUCI, all FYC classes prepare one narrative/reflective essay, and I insist on service learning for this assignment. Requiring each student to serve is a risky proposition in that not every student is going to be receptive or find him- or herself capable of providing meaningful service. I persist because I feel a responsibility to provide students an avenue for contemplating the effects of apathy toward injustices we strive to diminish in the twenty-first century. In *Opening Spaces* (2001), Hardin notes that students discover their "own negotiated positions . . . [through] a process of accepting or resisting values as they are re-inscribed through language and text" (p. 6) and, I would add, through experience and critical reflection as well.

So, how to reach those " 'resisting' students who did not want to learn new pedagogical processes, who did not want to be in a classroom that differed in any way from the "norm," as hooks accurately describes? I begin discussions in which I strive to break through student bias toward service learning by relating my ongoing confrontations with my social class, racial composite, sexual identity, education level, and citizenship. While reflecting on hooks, I challenge my own ability to value and serve each individual student and partnering organization client. Empathizing with students' difficulty in overcoming ingrained blinders, as they work toward critical consciousness, by openly discussing my own development represents a portion of my service to them. Experiential service learning has "been shown to contribute to a greater sense of civic responsibility in students" (Ehrlich, 2005, p. 1), and it has improved mine as well.

Writing Assignments and Learning Objectives

The key assignment is the Service-Learning Narrative/Reflective Essay with Research, which requires an initial research report on the organization for which the student performs service. Research from this report is then incorporated in the narrative/reflective essay. Students are evaluated on their ability to balance their narrative description about what they did with their critical reflections regarding the implications of their service and of the CBO's mission. Students are asked to reflect on questions such as "identity in the context of the community they serve" and whether or not "social justice is achievable." (A complete description of the assignment is provided in Appendix 3.A, p. 52.)

Through their experience, writing assignments, and class discussions, all students in the service-learning FYC class are expected to meet the learning objectives noted previously. In what follows, I will examine the preparation, methods, and results obtained thus far in achieving these objectives.

1. *To become aware of community-based organization missions and about career options for the public good.*
At CSUCI, the Office of Service Learning and Civic Engagement will send a representative to visit the class in order to walk students through an informational packet on this pedagogy's relevance to themselves, the community, and CSUCI's mission. Often, a second-year student who was in the FYC student's shoes one year ago will also visit class to share and respond to

questions. Each semester, I offer a variety of service activities with community-based organizations (CBOs) that have varying missions and schedules in order to enhance student agency. Representatives of the CBOs are invited to attend class to familiarize students with their clients and their specific need.

After selecting the community partner that best suits their interests and calendars, students complete a Student Learning Plan. This plan requires students to explain in their own words what they will be doing at CBO sites, why they will be doing it, and what learning objectives they aspire to fulfill in so doing. Throughout the semester we do oral and written reflection exercises that allow me to more fully know each of my students individually. Through reflection, we can identify and discuss their concerns, strengths, weaknesses, and so on. Student-centered pedagogy facilitates their discovery of their assets and can alleviate concerns they may have about their ability to be effective in addressing community needs.

Frequently, students choose sites that will provide them with experiences geared toward their career goals. A female CSUCI student who aspires to be a high school mathematics teacher and who lived in Simi Valley during the 2003 fire writes of her experience tutoring at the California Conservation Corps (CCC): "This organization came to Simi Valley after the fires . . . [and repaired] the hillsides surrounding my home." Her gratitude for their work was reflected in her desire to reciprocate by helping CCC members prepare for a variety of exams. She notes, "I was anxious to give back to this organization," and in so doing, she received additional "experience toward my career of teaching" (Long, 2005). Through service learning Ms. Long enhanced her understanding of this organization, its members, and her skills in her desired career. Another who is studying to be a high school teacher and who continually returned to serve the CCC beyond the requirement for my course explains, "while teaching students different subjects, I was teaching myself how to teach" (Heller, 2005). CSUCI students who sometimes are reluctant to serve CCC members who are their age or older learn from their peers and from their experiences that the effort is meaningful.

For those students who wished to continue in their service learning in the spring of 2006, in addition to the required Service-Learning Narrative/ Reflective Essay, I also invited students to write problem/solution essays based on optional service-learning experiences. The students who chose that option are serving at the Westminster Free Clinic and writing about the disparity in medical care for the unemployed, day laborers, and migrant farm workers of primarily Hispanic ethnicity; serving the Boys and Girls Club and writing about juvenile delinquency issues; and serving the RAIN Project, a homeless shelter adjacent to our campus, and writing about poverty, mental health, and addiction.

Working together at CBO sites allows students to build strong, potentially lifelong relationships with each other and the community. Many students who are compelled to continue their development as servants join clubs like Rotaract, take other service-learning courses, and work with faith-based organizations on and off campus. Several students are now employed by the community-based organization they served in their FYC class. In an effort to match students' talents, interests, and areas for growth with community needs, I offer students as many options for service learning as I am able in any given semester. Research shows that students will be more engaged with the experiential learning and produce higher quality writing if they choose which organization with which to serve rather than my identifying a specific community issue for students to address. Of course, my role is to mentor them through this process by working at sites with students, facilitating class discussions and writers' workshops, and selecting relevant readings for student writing and discussion.

2. *To write about a shared, firsthand experience and to narrate and reflect upon service learning before an audience of peers, professors, and community partners.*
    Following the analysis of various service-learning strategies in composition (Julier, 2001), I assign service-learning activities outside class and plan time for critical reflection about them in class. In discussions and in their essays, I have found "service-learning experiences give students ways to confront and find language for both the differences among people and the common ground that enables them to work together" (Julier, 2001, p. 141). Asking students to reflect in writing about shared experiences serving the community facilitates their comprehension of social justice discourse.
    I engage students with Remen's ideas as they relate to their service. First, I ask students to write about a time someone fixed, helped, and served them. We discuss Remen's distinctions: To *fix* is to see the other as damaged, to *help* is to see the other as weak, but to *serve* is to stretch one's talents and perceptions to meet the need expressed by another (Remen, 1996). After we

have discussed these terms in that personal context, I ask them to write about which of these activities best describes their experience in the community related to the composition course. This analysis of service-learning discourse encourages students to approach their assignments by addressing real community needs as opposed to their perceptions about what the community wants. Students are asked to contextualize their writing to analyze critically, rather than to just accept and cope with the status quo.

Reading about peers' prior experiences with community partners prepares students for their own. Students' essays narrating and reflecting on service-learning experiences appear in a campus publication, *Island Voices*, which is used by the composition faculty as a primary textbook, providing valuable modeling for first-year students.

Students' reflection essays sometimes reveal the depth to which the experience impacted their feelings, and that honest expression inspires peers to open up and experience their own strength in vulnerability. A male Caucasian CSUCI student wrote after researching the CCC, "People in the Corps volunteer their time for the benefit of my environment. So now that it has come time for me to volunteer as a tutor to CCC members, I am more than happy to offer" (Henrich, 2005, p. 1). After his tutoring a CCC student, he went on to write, "I also felt something that surprised me: shame. I felt ashamed of my background, my prosperity" (p. 3). More affluent students learn they have advantages not readily available to those we assist in the community, and this realization aids their understanding of inequality.

A central goal for service-learning pedagogy in composition is the advancement of personal efficacy, from knowing that social injustice exists to knowing how one may diminish it in one's sphere of influence. Learning to communicate effectively by sharing and receiving feedback on essay drafts from their peers and me, and eventually a final draft with the community partner if they choose, enhances understanding of the power of writing. I strive to provide students with a meaningful writing task coupled with a personally and socially significant experience. Students often are motivated by those they serve, and recipients of the service often report receiving a much appreciated mentor.

Significant evidence exists that the service-learning experience enhances students' writing ability in ways that would be difficult to approach in a traditional classroom. A spring 2006 student, Parissa Keshavarzian, prepared written deliverables under the direction of community partners, what Nora

Bacon calls "Community Service Writing" (Bacon, 1994, p. 53). The West-minster Free Clinic asked her to prepare an article about diabetes for their newsletter. She brainstormed a creative approach, writing a story about a Hispanic family recognizing their mother had advanced symptoms. Through the story, she explicates early warning signs to encourage readers to visit the clinic earlier when the disease is easier to treat. This added layer of audience allows the student to discover varying purposes for, and genres of, writing.

3. *To balance action and reflection.*

When service learning is most effective, both the provider and the recipient of service progress in their understanding of the other for having met the task with openness and creativity. In relating Freire's impact on her, hooks defines his efforts as "a crucial example of how a privileged critical thinker approaches sharing knowledge and resources with those who are in need" (hooks, 1994, p. 53). She goes on to emphasize the importance of simultaneous reciprocity, and I am able to relate these concepts to students through experiential service learning.

A Hispanic student whose parents immigrated illegally to the United States writes about tutoring a student who joined the CCC to escape gang life in Chicago, "My heart poured out to her. I just wanted to do anything and everything possible to help her make it to a university" (Boggs, 2005, p. 3). In working toward the CCC member's goals, this CSUCI student received the ability to empathize. She writes of her feelings toward the woman she tutored: "I did not feel pity. . . . I know she had it way worse than I did, but I could relate to her to some degree" (Boggs, 2005, p. 3). Her action of serving this individual as she turned her life around aided the student's reflection about her own identity and the plight and strength of others.

In the spirit of reciprocity, I always stress that the work we do in the community must benefit our community partners: We have evidence that it does. After sending student essays, of those who gave written permission to do so, to community partners, I received qualitative evidence that students are meeting community partners' needs and providing meaningful feedback.

Student essays "were a great evaluative tool for what we did right to make the experience meaningful to the student, and where we need to improve," reported the executive director of Pleasant Valley Neighborhood for Learning, a First 5 program that prepares children 0 to 5 for kindergarten. "I look forward to our continued partnership" (J. Cook-Tate, director, Pleasant

Valley Neighborhood for Learning, e-mail interview, January 9, 2006). From student essays, this community partner learned that student volunteers prefer working directly with the children and developing lesson plans as opposed to assisting behind the scenes. Students also have reflected on their role in making the service experience more productive by being proactive in communicating how they think they will be best able to serve while remaining receptive to the needs of the community partner.

The instructor for the California Conservation Corps writes,

> As a result of this relationship, my students have embraced what it means to serve their community, and look for innovative ways in order to do so. In addition, my students have the benefit of one-on-one tutoring in the high school core subjects, resulting in better test scores on the Calif. High School Exit Exam, the ASVAB (military entrance exam), as well as benchmark gains on the CASAS and TABE tests. My students have also greatly benefited from the relationships that have developed in light of tutoring/ mentoring. Because they have worked so closely with university students, some have come to the understanding that they can achieve higher education also. I have even had a few enroll as undergraduates at CSUCI. (C. Vanderlaan, instructor, California Conservation Corps of Camarillo, e-mail interview, January 12, 2006)

Ms. Vanderlaan expresses her appreciation for the service her organization receives and offers feedback regarding how I can improve in preparing students for their tutoring service. By maintaining open dialogue, we are developing a brief training session for students who will tutor at the CCC in the future.

Three years ago, Ms. Vanderlaan shared with me her goal of bridging the gap between the CCC and our university, which share the same campus, and this achievement (university enrollment) is the praxis for which we, as educators, strive. She and I knew hypothetically that CSUCI students could be mentors to CCC students; all we do is provide that hypothesis an opportunity for action. Greenleaf asks, regarding the effectiveness of service, "Do those being served grow as persons: do they, while being served, become healthier, wiser, freer, more autonomous, more likely themselves to become servants" (Greenleaf, 1998, p. 43). Based on CBO representatives' responses to my inquiries concerning assessment of service-learning pedagogy's effectiveness for their clients, I would say our efforts are worth it, and we are just scratching the surface in terms of continuous improvement. The efficacy of both groups of students improved as a result of service learning, and more often than not they honed in on the reciprocal benefits they received from each other.

Reflection tends to be the more difficult aspect of this assignment, but students do improve in this area when peers and I ask them to expand upon statements like "it changed me forever" with concrete examples of what they mean by that platitude.

4. *To analyze one's personal stake in social justice.*

I stress to my students that the composition assignments offer more than just charity work. It is one thing to tell students they should get involved; it's another to give them a firsthand reason to do so. Humanistic elements of service learning, paired with public policy information that students find through their own research and class discussions, allows them to draw their own political conclusions and to make their own decisions about political activism. My strategy is to provide community projects coupled with sociopolitical and socioeconomic questions during workshops on drafts of their reflective essays.

For example, to prepare students for working with underserved populations, I lead them through an analysis about property taxes and how most primary and secondary schools are funded. We discuss property values in areas where most CCC students come from, as opposed to neighborhoods where most CSUCI students grew up. This discussion aids in their understanding about the disparity in wealth and resources within the same cities. I mention stories CCC students have shared about their backgrounds in an effort to diminish "widely held assumptions that blacks, other minorities . . . are poor and unemployed because they want to be" (hooks, 1994, p. 29). Students learn to shed light on misconceptions by tutoring CCC students one-on-one and often by hearing each person's individual history. I assist my students for whom critical reflection is seemingly impossible by asking them probing questions based in theory about their stylistic choices, synthesis, critical thought processes, and logical reasoning to "make a writer aware of the forces at play" (Bartholomae, 1995, p. 66). Such forces in the United States have been given more attention in the wake of Hurricane Katrina, and several students chose for their service learning to assist in CSUCI's Katrina Relief campaign, which raised funds for the Red Cross's efforts in the region.

I also bring feminist theory and pedagogical practice to the course to facilitate understanding that the struggles for civil rights are not only something we study in historical texts, but something we continue to work toward today. We discuss in class the broader application of feminism in that the movement seeks equality for all disadvantaged, underrepresented groups. We also discuss through the work of Terry Tempest Williams (2004) and other Eco-feminist writers that the disadvantaged group need not be human.

My colleague Environmental Science Resource Management Assistant Professor Don Rodriguez and I linked our English and ESRM courses and focused service-learning activities and reflections around local environmental issues. These activities lead to reflections about ways those in power exploit the environment. We discuss stewardship versus ownership of resources, riches, power, people, and so on. While building square-foot-gardening boxes while serving University Preparation School at CSU Channel Islands, one student learned about "growing [organic] quality vegetables in less space" (Fliesler, 2005, p. 5). His classmate who wrote about his gratitude for the friendship the project cultivated with his peer added, "Ideally, teaching children about organic farming will help these kids to learn healthier consumption habits" (Pimentel, 2005, p. 4). These students learn about environmental responsibility, business ethics, and political injustice through their service and their research. Instead of writing another typically uninteresting essay about childhood obesity being on the rise, students who participated in service-learning activities wrote about what they observed, and what they contributed toward the local community in an attempt to correct the problem.

This same student who aspires to teach grades K–12 after graduating went on to critically analyze marketing rhetoric in the processed food industry: "[s]acred words like pure, natural and healthy are featured on packaging [where the] majority of ingredients are unidentifiable . . ." (Pimentel, 2005, p. 5). He discussed his skepticism with regard to corporate aims and decided to plant his own organic garden as a result of being empowered to stand against the popular culture with regard to food choices. He adds, "These children are at ages where lifelong habits develop, and with the health education they are receiving, corporations like McDonald's will struggle when a greater number of consumers are conscious of the benefits of truly healthy, nutritious whole foods" (Pimentel, 2005, p. 10). Based on discussions between us, I am confident that this project enhanced his commitment to his profession as a mission-based social justice endeavor rather than just a job to put food on his table.

While Mr. Pimentel reflected on social justice as it related to his lifestyle and his future career, another CSUCI student who had attended "mostly white Catholic schools" (Haag, 2005, p. 2) reflected on the insight his research and service afforded him with regard to economics. He tutored a CCC member of Jamaican decent, Martin, who was just becoming literate. After learning about people his age who have not received basic education he writes, "The California Conservation Corps has a noble calling, but they lack the funds to offer a complete curriculum that satisfies the need out there. That's where volunteers come in; we need to help those without the resources to live up to their potential" (Haag, 2005, p. 3). I doubt he will forget how Martin illustrated for him that American school systems often fail those from lower socioeconomic strata. My student also experienced Martin's intelligence and determination, and I believe that may change his and others' perceptions about racial stereotypes.

I shared with these classes how they encouraged me that stereotypes about them are not fair. In my experience, these students don't just care about podcasts and parties. When shown a little faith in their ability to engage with social injustice and how it affects us all, more often than not students have risen to the occasion (and then they can hopefully go download and get down with more social responsibility). Service learning in FYC allows me to open students' eyes to the problems of the world while providing them an avenue for hope.

5. *To reflect on character development and self-actualization.*

I can relate to hooks's consternation at "complaints like, 'I thought this was supposed to be an English class, why are we talking so much about feminism?'" (hooks, 1994, p. 42), as my students will sometimes begin their essays with the same confusion: *What does service have to do with composition?* Questions like this lead to a classroom discussion about Aristotelian methods and the dual goals of a service-learning-focused FYC assignment. Service learning returns FYC to the roots of classical rhetoricians by preparing students for civic affairs rather than emphasizing only fitness for academic discourse (Schilb, 1996). And, like hooks, I have had "my students who bitch endlessly contact me at a later date to talk about how much that experience meant to them" (hooks, 1994, p. 42). I empathize with my students who struggle with this assignment, as I continue to experience the sublime anguish of growth that educating oneself about social injustice brings. Ignorance of one's own ugly bias is blissful; recognition of it stings! Yet, it's a "historical moment when one begins to think critically about the self and identity in relation to one's political circumstance" (hooks, 1994, p. 47). The students who do write about assisting others (and themselves) in transgressing racial, ethnic, economic, social, and educational boundaries motivates me such that others' negativity won't wear me down.

Even though initially some students express reservations about service learning, what we do in and out of the classroom can prepare them. I encourage them to speak and write honestly about their attitudes toward service and those they serve; students who demonstrate their writing skill and who despise the experience can still earn a top score.

With regard to personal growth, a student who selected the Boys and Girls Club of Camarillo as his service site researched the club's mission, "to inspire and enable all young people, especially those from disadvantaged circumstances, to realize their full potential as productive, responsible and caring citizens." In his essay he discusses his reciprocal desire for the attainment of character and notes, "I am still learning these things as a young adult and maybe I could help" (Mortimer, 2005, p. 1). The children benefited from the presence of a playful, attentive adult male, and as the witty title of his essay, "The Not-So-Snot-Nosed Kids," reveals, he benefited from pressing past his initial reservations to appreciating his service-learning experience. He expressed satisfaction with himself both in being receptive to the children in need of his care and in following through on a commitment that at first gave him pause.

Another former student who continued his service by traveling to Guatemala with dentists from the United States asked me to read his essay (he voluntarily wrote one that wasn't assigned!) about his experience. His pathos is compelling as he describes what he felt about "the diseased, crime ridden, beautiful, humbling *calles* and *avenidas* of Guatemala City. I wept for what I could not control" (K. Morford, CSUCI student, e-mail interview, November 25, 2005). Later, he writes with a great deal of respect for the villagers' culture about his being invited to dine in their hut, "we were all one family. The village welcomed us into their arms and embraced us with this huge honor." He explains the empathy this service gave him when he writes, "Bonding with a group of people makes you really feel human compassion on a level that you can never experience any other way." He received a first-hand educational experience about international poverty, and he gave. "[W]e performed all kinds of procedures from extractions to cleanings to root canals. . . . we helped over 358 children. In total, over 600 procedures were executed." And he concludes, "When I look back on my experience, I know that it changed my life forever. Selfishness will never be my problem" (K. Morford, CSUCI student, e-mail interview, November 25, 2005). This trip took place in October 2005. And through my continued contact with this student in the CSUCI Rotaract Club, I bear witness to the fact that his potentially platitudinous statement bears concrete fruit. He is actively engaged in developing service projects with other Rotaract Clubs in our community and across the globe. Additionally, he continues to use his own resources to travel to regions in need of his assistance.

His exposure to international injustice spurred him to be active in alleviating the effects of poverty in the United States. He chose to spend winter break serving hurricane victims in the Gulf. In January 2006 he wrote to me, "We feed about 1,200 people a day, so I work 15-hour days, every day! EXHAUSTING! But it is the greatest feeling in the world when the residents come up to you in the food line and they start crying because we are here helping them who have nothing . . ." (K. Morford, CSUCI student, e-mail interview, January 7, 2006). While there, he participated in protests to protect homes from being torn down to build parks. He is returning to New Orleans during spring break. Not every student responds in such a dramatic, life-altering way to the seed of service-learning activity in their composition class, but he continues to inform his classmates with his dedication. He also informs the community by making presentations to Rotary International and other community service organizations. He relates to me often how thrilled he is with his newfound passion. On the other end of the spectrum is the student who has not yet been self-motivated to enhance her efficacy.

Early one semester, this student confided in me that she suffered from depression and had a serious drinking problem. For the first few weeks, if she came to class she was angry and resistant to learning and participating. After her first experience serving another who came from a much more complicated background than she, and who had made it through drug rehabilitation, this student then told me she quit drinking. Cultural anthropologist and Pulitzer Prize–winning author Ernest Becker notes in *Denial of Death,* "[Medard] Boss says that the terrible guilt feelings of the depressed person are existential, that is, they represent the failure to live one's own life, to fulfill one's own potential" (1973, p. 213). This same student continued to serve far beyond the course requirement and has expressed interest in taking additional service-learning courses. Becker (1973) adds about the importance of usefulness:

> When does the person have the most trouble with his self-esteem? Precisely when his heroic transcendence of his fate is most in doubt, when he doubts his own immortality, the abiding value of his life; when he is not convinced that his having lived really makes any cosmic difference. (pp. 209–210)

While more severe, clinical cases of depression cannot be alleviated without professional intervention, milder cases related to the isolation and insecurity of adjusting to academic standards and social norms may benefit from the sense of community that service learning provides. Because service learning promotes agency, it improves work–life balance and aids those engaged with it by advocating hopeful change. Service learning helped this individual move from self-destruction toward self-actualization.

When service learning achieves reciprocity, all parties achieve a greater sense of their value to humanity. Another way to consider this notion comes from Paul Loeb's collection *The Impossible Will Take a Little While*, "Being politically active is for the citizens of a democracy maybe the best way of speaking to God and hearing Her answer: You exist" (Kushner, 2004, p. 170). As Abraham H. Maslow reminds us, we are all aware that, on some level, reaching our full potential does not have to do with satisfying bacchanal urges, or with achieving honors and monetary success; rather, self-actualization is the apex for which we should reach (in Jarvis, 2005).

Critical Reflections of a Teacher-Servant

A while back I wrote in the margin of *Teaching to Transgress*, next to hooks's words quoted at the beginning of this chapter, *why else do it?* My story that I candidly share with my students (I'm never afraid to play the fool if I think they can learn from it) is of just one small woman doing deceptively small things, but what if all profit-minded accountants and bomb-builders (both former careers of mine) decided instead to serve others? All the supposed accomplishments I achieved prior to advancing service-learning pedagogy

now seem worse than just insignificant; they were jaded by self-interest, ignorance, and a grimy pride. That arrogance is replaced with humility, and I'm
pleased with where my journey has led. Service-learning strategies have
helped me in constructing an identity that's more authentic with regard to
my self-concept. I am a coach who serves her students, the university, and
the community.

hooks writes, "It has not been easy for me to do the work I do and reside
in the academy, but one is inspired to persevere by the witness of others"
(hooks, 1994, p. 56). I too am encouraged by mentors who are teacher-
servants. Seeing Terry Tempest Williams (2005) weep for the suffering she
experienced while serving in Rwanda inspires me to continue to make my
work more effective. Williams and hooks remind us that we are better educators when we too strive for self-improvement with regard to character and
compassion for others. When their message is at the heart of my service-
learning strategies, the work flows with an almost effortless joy. As students
and faculty give back to their communities, they equip disadvantaged groups
in their ability to succeed and in turn become givers themselves. Intuitively
and concretely, service learning aids in countering social injustice, developing character, and increasing agency in writing.

My desire is that my reflections might inspire students to face their fears
and prejudices with regard to socioeconomic class, race, and educational
ability. Service learning makes students aware of social injustices and which
programs/organizations they can aid in their community in an attempt to
alleviate its problems. We contribute to the CSU's mission, and service learning focuses my efforts in that context. Through service-learning pedagogy, I
am learning not to discriminate based on a student's facility with Standard
Formal English, but rather to serve each in reaching her or his full potential
as "responsible citizens in a democracy" by "providing opportunities for individuals to develop intellectually, personally and professionally" (CSU Mission, available at http://www.calstate.edu/PA/info/mission.shtml).

Appendix 3.A
Assignment for Service-Learning Activity From Syllabus

Service-Learning Narrative/Reflective Essay With Research

Students will choose one of several Service Learning options. Your Service
Learning Community Partner must be approved by me and must be an official CSUCI/Community Partnership. All students will complete and turn in

a Student Learning Plan as well as their Narrative/Reflective essay. Students will engage respectfully with these partners and their clients as representatives of CSUCI, demonstrating professionalism and leadership. In workshops and at home you will be working through several drafts of this essay. In the first draft, vividly describe the experience physically, emotionally, spiritually, and intellectually: What did you and others say? What reactions did you observe? You'll need to be very observant in order to do a good job on the narrative aspects of the essay. You will need to scan or insert a picture from this experience into your essay, so bring a camera. In the second draft, you will develop your thoughts by analyzing your response to and impressions of this experience. You will reflect on Service Learning and how it affected your perceptions of the University's surrounding community. You will comment on whether your thinking about the experience has changed since you began writing about it. Reflect on your initial reactions to the visit and on what you think and feel in retrospect, as you write. What surprised, excited, puzzled, troubled, angered, or simply interested you? What reasons might there be for the way things are? What kinds of solutions can you imagine for some of the problems you see? What questions might you ask someone the next time you go? What might you want to check out through further research? As you prepare revised drafts of this essay, return to the Learning Outcomes for the course and for Service Learning (below) to analyze your synthesis of the experiences more fully.

1. Learning Outcomes
   a. Consider your personal connection to the Characteristics of a CSUCI Graduate: *Informed* (about human society and natural world), *Empowered* (to evaluate problems, take action, and communicate opinions), *Creative* (with independent thinking), *Dedicated* (to social justice and responsible participation). Did your Service Learning experience bring new insight as to what is expected from you in the academy?
   b. Contemplate your identity in the context of the community you serve and the service you provide. Can/should a person operate without a community focus?
   c. Demonstrate your understanding of the term *efficacy*, particularly as it relates to writing. Can words lead to action? What happens when there is action without reflection? Or, reflection without action?

    d. Consider the term *apathy*. Is social justice achievable? Does democracy always result in a dissatisfied minority?

    e. Evaluate how critical thought may be enhanced by personal involvement.

    f. Discover personal contribution (assets you bring) to the experience. How does service benefit the student, the organization, and your university?

References

Bacon, N. (1994, Spring). Community service and writing instruction. *National Society for Experiential Education Quarterly*, pp. 14, 27.

Bartholomae, D. (1995, February). Writing with teachers: A conversation with Peter Elbow. *College Composition and Communication, 46*, 1.

Becker, E. (1973). *The denial of death*. New York: The Free Press.

Beidler, P. C. (1997). Chapter 1: What makes a good teacher? In J. K. Roth (Ed.), *Inspiring teaching, Carnegie Professors of the Year speak* (pp. 14–22). Bolton, MA: Anker.

Boggs, A. (2005). *Red*. CSUCI student essay, Camarillo, CA.

Ehrlich, T. (2005, July). Service-learning in undergraduate education: Where is it going? *Carnegie Perspectives, 19*. Retrieved July 2005 from http://www.carnegiefoundation.org

Fliesler, M. (2005). *Building a garden one box at a time*. CSUCI student essay, Camarillo, CA.

Freire, P., & Macedo, D. (1987). *Literacy: Reading the word and the world*. New York: Bergin.

Greenleaf, R. K. (1998). *The power of servant leadership*. San Francisco: Berrett-Koehler.

Haag, T. (2005). *Clandestine courage*. CSUCI student essay, Camarillo, CA.

Hardin, J. M. (2001). *Opening spaces: Critical pedagogy and resistance theory in composition*. Albany: State University of New York Press.

Heller, A. (2005). *Going back*. CSUCI student essay, Camarillo, CA.

Henrich, J. (2005). *The satisfaction of volunteering*. CSUCI student essay, Camarillo, CA.

hooks, b. (1994). *Teaching to transgress: Education as the practice of freedom*. New York: Routledge.

Jarvis, M. (2005). *The psychology of effective learning and teaching*. Cheltenham: Nelson Thornes.

Julier, L. (2001). *Community service pedagogy. A guide to composition pedagogies*. New York: Oxford University Press.

Kushner, T. (2004). Despair is a lie we tell ourselves. In P. Loeb (Ed.), *The impossible will take a little while*. New York: Basic Books.

Long, A. (2005). *Teaching conservation*. CSUCI student essay, Camarillo, CA.

Mortimer, H. (2005). *The not-so-snot-nosed kids*. CSUCI student essay, Camarillo, CA.

Pimentel, J. (2005). *Alternative education: Focusing on typically ignored aspects of education and life*. CSUCI student essay, Camarillo, CA.

Remen, R. N. (1996, Spring). In the service of life. *Noetic Sciences Review, 37*, 24–25.

Schilb, J. (1996). *Between the lines: Relating composition theory and literary theory*. Portsmouth, NH: Boynton/Cook.

Williams, T. T. (2004). *The open space of democracy*. Great Barrington, MA: The Orion Society.

Williams, T. T. (2005, November 8). *The open space of democracy*. Public lecture at California State University–Channel Islands, Camarillo.

SECTION TWO

THE DAY LABOR PROJECT

José Z. Calderón

The Pomona Day Labor Center: Connecting Local Action to Global Issues

A s multinational corporations move across the world to find cheap labor, there is also a movement of immigrants from third world countries to more developed ones (Sutcliffe, 1993, pp. 84–107). The response in European countries and the United States has been twofold: on the one hand, the companies (and even some government officials) see the need for immigrants to fill employment voids (particularly when these countries are faced with an aging population). On the other hand, these countries do not want to acknowledge immigrants as human beings with basic human rights. There are "open borders" for multinational corporations when it comes to investment, trade, and moving jobs (Sutcliffe, 1998). However, when it comes to the free migration of immigrants, the meaning of democracy does not exist. That is why there is a backlash to this meaning of democracy where a growth in international investment has meant increasing unemployment and the forced removal of the peasantry from their rural lands to the urban cities (Gonzalez, 2001; Robinson, 2003, pp. 253–258).

In the fall of 2005, I taught a class at Cal Poly Pomona University that grappled with the question of how to create a democratic space in the classroom and facilitate that same democratic culture in various service-learning projects with new immigrants at a nearby day labor center.

The class Ethnic Immigration, taught as part of my position as the Michi and Walter Weglyn Endowed Chair in Multicultural Studies, aimed at examining how Latino and multiracial communities were being transformed through economic restructuring locally and globally. It sought to bring the issues of community building and participation in the informal economy to life through a service-learning collaborative with a day labor center in Pomona (PDLC).

In order to immediately introduce students to the history of the site that they would be working in, I had the students read a paper, "Action Research and Strategies in the Pomona Day Labor Center" (Calderón, Foster, & Rodríguez, 2005). I made this paper "real," by taking the students to a meeting with the day laborers. Here, the students had the opportunity to hear about the lives of the immigrant workers and also to hear about what needs the workers had. It was out of this discussion on "needs" that the students organized themselves to work alongside the day laborers on various projects. Using readings by Kenneth Reardon (1998), Douglas Porpora (1999), Orlando Fals-Borda (Fals-Borda & Rahman, 1991), John Wallace (2000), and Doris Hamner (2002), I sought to instill a pedagogy of learning that aimed at involving all the participants as both students and teachers. Hence, in addition to working alongside the day laborers in implementing English classes, health workshops, and immigration rights research projects, the students also developed a dialogue on immigration issues that tapped the problem-solving capacities of all the participants.

In the classroom, we discussed how the spread of capital and transnational corporations is resulting in an uprooting of the peasantry and a forced migration of workers across borders where their labor is used by the new lords of finance, investment, and real estate interests (Feagin, 1998; Hondagenu-Sotelo, 2001; Sampio, 2002; Velez-Ibanez, 2002).

Moving beyond service, a group of students and day laborers began to carry out research on the question of why countries throughout the world enjoy the use of cheap immigrant labor but refuse to allow the laborers basic human rights. In providing initial answers to this question, the students relied on their class readings and library research, while the workers developed their analyses from Spanish newspapers and their lived experiences.

This class was an example of connecting history to civic engagement for social change. In order for the students to get engaged, they first had to know some of this country's history when it came to issues involving immigration. In addition to the other readings mentioned in this introduction, we used the book *Harvest of Empire* by Juan Gonzalez (2001) to understand how the

United States' "success was due in large measure to the unique brand of representative democracy, the spirit of bold enterprise, the respect for individual liberty, and the rugged devotion to hard work that characterized so many of American settlers" (p. 269). At the same time, my syllabus also included literature on one of Gonzales's other contentions that "there was another aspect to that success . . . the details of which most Americans knew nothing about, but which was always carried out in their name. It was a vicious and relentless drive for territorial expansion, conquest, and subjugation of Native Americans, African slaves, Latin Americans, and others . . . one that our leaders justified as Manifest Destiny for us" (2001, p. 270).

Through connecting the readings to participatory service and research, the students were more equipped to understand the contemporary debates over immigration, free trade, globalization, and the many myths that have been created regarding the immigrant's taking of jobs, importing disease and crime, and stealing of social services.

The students' involvement at the Pomona Day Labor Center engaged other Cal Poly faculty from multiple disciplines in developing service-learning classes according to the needs of the day laborers. Hence, Carlos Navarrete, professor in the Computer Information Systems Department, involved his students in projects to buy computers for the center and to train day laborers in using the Internet. So many workers came to use the Internet to contact their families in Latin America that the center had to establish time limits for the day laborers' use of the computers. Professor Jen Bracy engaged her graphic design students in collaborative discussions with the day laborers to develop a logo design for the Pomona Day Labor Center. The logo design is now used in all the literature used to market the center's activities. Two professors in the Ethnic and Women's Studies Department, Estela Ballon and Terri Gomez, consistently sent students to join in the weekly worker meetings and to help in teaching English classes. Professor Richard Santillan and I taught a class focusing on day laborers in the spring of 2006 that resulted in a pictorial and art exhibit on the lives of immigrants, a research project on the media's treatment of immigrant issues, and an updated English language curriculum for future day laborer classes.

This section includes articles by other Cal Poly Pomona faculty members who carried out interdisciplinary service learning and participatory research projects specifically focused on the issues of immigration, nutrition, and health safety.

Conclusion

In many of our institutions, there is still a tendency to separate the content of the curriculum and practice of service learning in our communities. The best type of learning is where the reading materials in the classroom are helping the students to learn about the history of the communities that they are working with. The two should help build on each other.

In addition to the content of the curriculum, we have to question the dominant traditional style of teaching in the classroom that often has left out the voice of the student. If we are serious about creating a diverse and engaged democracy, we have to begin where we have the most influence. Our classrooms can be examples of top-down decision making, or they can be spaces where the students are free to share their perspectives, to question the literature, and to use research methodologies that are carried out alongside the community.

This is deliberate on my part. In working with immigrants, students carry out service but they also attend weekly meetings with the workers. It is in these meetings that dialogue occurs and where the issues that the workers are concerned about come to the forefront. It is here where action research is used in finding solutions to these problems. It is here where the practice of democracy, just like in the classroom, advances to the level of civic engagement. It is here where the immigrant and student participants join together in common actions to raise their voices and to ensure that their voices are heard.

With this framework, the practice of critical pedagogy and a democratic student-centered classroom join with a participant-centered site in implementing a deliberate framework of service that advances a culture of social change steeped in the voices of all the participants.

In my Ethnic Immigration class, as students learned about new ways of building democratic forms in the classroom and the community, they sought to learn from the day laborers that they came in contact with weekly. Moving from their readings to weekly interactions based on service with the day laborers, they moved to the level of carrying out common action research projects based on the issues that emerged from the concerns of the participants. As the two groups interacted, both sought to find an avenue to have their voices heard and to affect social policy.

As we seek to develop models and examples of participatory service and research, it is important for us to look toward new ways of carrying out democratic forms of learning and curriculum building in our classrooms that connect to new models of building democratic participation in our communities. Our beginning to dialogue on these new models may help us to understand how the engagement of our student and community partnerships can move beyond volunteerism (or charity) to a level of civic engagement and the advancement of a more democratic and socially just culture in civil society.

References

Calderón, J., Foster, S., & Rodríguez, S. (2005). Organizing immigrant workers: Action research and strategies in the Pomona Day Labor Center. In E. C. Ochoa & G. L. Ochoa (Eds.), *Latino L. A.: Transformations, communities, and activism.* Tucson: Arizona State University Press.

Fals-Borda, O., & Rahman, M. A. (1991). *Action and knowledge: Breaking the monopoly with participatory action research.* New York: Apex Press.

Feagin, J. (1998). *The new urban paradigm.* Lanham, MD: Rowman & Littlefield.

Gonzalez, J. (2001). *Harvest of empire.* New York: Penguin Books.

Hamner, D. M. (2002). *Building bridges.* Boston: Allyn and Bacon.

Hondagneu-Sotelo, P. (2001). *Domestica: Immigrant workers cleaning and caring in the shadows of affluence.* Berkeley: University of California Press.

Porpora, D. V. (1999). Action research: The highest stage of service learning? In J. Ostrow & S. Enos (Eds.), *Cultivating the social imagination.* Washington, DC: American Association of Higher Education.

Reardon, K. M. (1998). Participatory action research as service learning. *New Directions for Teaching and Learning, 73,* 57–64.

Robinson, W. I. (2003). *Transnational conflicts: Central America, social change and globalization.* New York: Verso.

Sampaio, A. (2002). Transforming Chicana/o and Latina/o politics: Globalization and the formation of transnational resistance in the United States and Chiapas. In C. Valez-Ibanez (Ed.), *Transnational Latina/o communities: Politics, processes and cultures* (pp. 47–71). Boston: Rowman & Littlefield.

Sutcliffe, B. (1993). Immigration and the world economy. In D. Baker, G. Epstein, J. Graham, & J. Nembhard (Eds.), *Creating a new world economy: Forces of change and plans for action.* Philadelphia: Temple University Press.

Sutcliffe, B. (1998). Freedom to move in the age of globalization. In D. Baker, G. Epstein, & R. Pollin (Eds.), *Globalization and progressive economic policy*. New York: Cambridge University Press.

Velez-Ibanez, C. (2002). Reconceptualizing Latina/o studies and the study of Latina/o subjects. In C. Valez-Ibanez (Ed.), *Transnational Latina/o communities: Politics, processes and cultures* (pp. 39–45). Boston: Rowman & Littlefield.

Wallace, J. (2000). A popular education model for college in community. *American Behavioral Scientist, 43*(5), 756–757.

4

LINKING CRITICAL DEMOCRATIC PEDAGOGY, MULTICULTURALISM, AND SERVICE LEARNING TO A PROJECT-BASED APPROACH

José Z. Calderón and Gilbert R. Cadena

As colleges become more diverse, new strategies are being developed to reflect the changing communities around them. The use of creative project-based methodologies in developing connections between critical democratic pedagogy, service learning, and multiculturalism are seen as new models for meeting the needs of a diverse student body as well as ensuring the involvement of the community in that process (Judkins & LaHurd, 1999; Wallace, 2000). This article provides examples of these linkages in classes taught by the authors during the academic year 2004–2005, in the diverse settings of California State Polytechnic University–Pomona (Cal Poly Pomona) and the city of Pomona.[1]

In collaborating to build connections between critical democratic pedagogy, service learning, and multiculturalism, the authors sought to apply an approach that could overcome the limits of a quarter system.[2] In this process, the authors collaborated in designing and implementing courses that celebrated the contributions of individuals and groups who have been marginalized or excluded from mainstream historical texts. At the same time, as part of these courses, the authors developed dialogue around specific readings that connected to the issues being faced by local communities. This analysis and dialogue was followed up with the application of a service-learning pedagogy that was collectively developed alongside community partners using various participatory action and research (PAR) methodologies (Mora & Diaz, 2004). Ultimately, this led to some form of action in the classroom and in the community that resulted in various community-building outcomes.

Projects that involved the students and faculty from various classes connected the classes and the class content. This project approach used the readings in the classroom to help inform the students about the work that they were carrying out in the community.[3] At the same time it allowed for collaboration between faculty, students, and community partners.

The project-based approach, as developed by Randy Stoecker in his book *Research Methods for Community Change*, develops out of a perspective of trying to understand the participants "we are working with, what is happening to them, and what they can do about the problems that are affecting them" (Stoecker, 2005, p. 5). This type of participatory research and involvement emerges from a question that comes from the participants themselves regarding a problem that they would like to resolve. In this process, the participants follow some of the basic steps that are part of the project-based approach. That is, they begin by discussing a problem, analyzing how they will deal with the problem, implementing a plan of action, carrying out the action, and evaluating the results.

Although the authors developed the intersections between these different aspects in each class, the article is divided into sections that accentuate the application of critical democratic pedagogy in relation to the *matricula* service project as part of the Ethnic Immigration and Chicano/Latino Contemporary Issues classes, the project-based research approach in the Grant Writing and Christmas Parade projects in the Community and Culture and Community Service-Learning classes, and the emphasis on multiculturalism in the Agbayani and Alternative Spring Break projects as part of the Rural and Urban Social Movements and Community Service Learning classes.

Critical Democratic Pedagogy and the Matricula Service-Learning Project

In our classes, we practice what Ira Shor, in his book *Empowering Education*, calls a critical democratic pedagogy for self and social change. This approach works to develop a student-centered classroom that involves both the teachers and students in the "habits of inquiry and critical curiosity about society, power, inequality, and change" (Shor, 1992, p. 15). At the same time, it follows with the critical-holistic paradigm that is based on empowering community participants to "help themselves by raising their level of consciousness about their problems and the societal causes and remedies available" (Wright, 2000, p. 816). Hence, this approach combines the creation of a democratic space for dialogue and inquiry in the classroom as part of working alongside community participants to advance models of "social action and social change for the purpose of achieving social justice" (Strand et al., 2003, p. 8). This type of service learning requires faculty to challenge their traditional control of the classroom and to have confidence that their students will empower themselves to complete their projects. With preparation and experience, faculty contributes to the structure of service-learning projects while simultaneously recognizing the role that students and community partners have in developing their specific interests and outcomes (Dardar, 2002; Horton & Freire, 1990; Shor, 1992). Although this type of pedagogy inherently includes ambiguity and uncertainty, the stress and benefits are ultimately created and shared by the students and community partners involved in the process.

In the fall quarter we taught two courses that exemplified this approach. In the courses, Ethnic Immigration (see Appendix 4.A) and Chicano/Latino Contemporary Issues, we structured our classes as "learning circles" that promoted dialogue and critical thinking about the assigned readings. We used the "critical democratic pedagogy" approach that placed topical issues and academic themes in the context of the lived experiences of the students. Simultaneously, we involved the students in choosing service-learning sites that best fit their interests and the themes of the classes.[4]

From our classes, students learned material that helped them to understand the plight of immigrant workers, which helped them to carry out their particular service-learning projects. One student, for example, reflected on the meaning of participation as tied to the ideas of Paulo Freire:

> Community involvement can be very deceiving when people do not grasp an understanding or passion for what they are doing. The important part is not to simply give your time as a form of volunteering but instead giving your thoughts and efforts into creating change within that organization or

movement. I like how Paulo Freire proposed, in *Pedagogy of the Oppressed*, that the solution for the oppressed is not to "integrate" them into the structure of oppression, but to transform the structure so that they can become "beings for themselves." (Rocio Navarro, major in Gender, Ethnicity, Multicultural Studies, and Sociology)

At the same time, a group of students attended Friday morning meetings at the Pomona Day Labor Center. At these meetings, the workers and students held discussions on developing new employment opportunities and dealing with employers who refused to pay the workers. The Mexican Consulate contacted the Pomona Day Labor Center and proposed the idea of holding a consular mobile-clinic service day for the purpose of having immigrants apply for and obtain consular-approved identification cards (called *matriculas*); one of the Friday meetings was devoted to organizing this project. In this meeting, the workers and students discussed the importance of obtaining a *matricula consular* card that was officially recognized by the Mexican government and various cities and law enforcement agencies throughout the country. Further, they discussed the "need" to have a *matricula* card to help them to open bank accounts, cash checks, send remittances abroad, and to defend their human rights.

From this initial meeting, our students began the process of creating a larger coalition by reaching out to community-based groups and churches in the region. Meeting at the Cal Poly Pomona Downtown Center, the coalition included students from the classes of the two authors, representatives from the Mexican Consulate, students from the Claremont Colleges, the Inland Valley/San Gabriel Valley Latino/a Roundtable, the Latino Chamber of Commerce, Our Lady of Assumption Church, Our Lady of Guadalupe Church, and the Pomona Day Labor Center.

As part of their participation, our students joined various committees where they worked alongside other members of the coalition in providing logistical support to the Mexican Consulate: writing press releases, obtaining donations, distributing leaflets at churches, and recruiting students to plan day care activities. As the organizing developed, students summarized their experiences in the classroom and implemented outreach contact to other groups on campus.

The success of the organizing effort was best exemplified by the 300 immigrants who were already standing in line at four in the morning.[5] Ultimately, out of 1,000 immigrants that showed up to apply, 550 applicants were able to obtain their *matricula* identification card on the same day. Just as impressive were the organizing efforts of the students from our classes who used the medium of art to involve the children of the immigrants in sketching, drawing, and face painting. Other students helped in creating a festival atmosphere to the service day. Eddie Cortez, mayor of Pomona, and Angelica Sanbrano, director of the immigrant rights organization CARECEN, spoke on the need to build coalitions that could advance the successful legalization and integration of all immigrant families in the United States.

After the event, the workers and students evaluated the project and summarized that the organizational effort had gone beyond any of their expectations. The large turnout, they proposed, showed how hungry immigrant families were for having some type of identification that would make it easier to survive in U.S. society. Although both the students and day laborers described the day as a means of service to the immigrant community, they also characterized it as one more tool for the workers to defend themselves.

In this context, the *matricula* card took on a special significance, immigrant workers being treated as human beings. The meaning that the workers attached to the *matricula* card was one of human rights, and therefore it was viewed as a material act in the process of obtaining social justice. Nationally, although nine states are accepting the *matricula* card, there has been stated opposition to the use of the card by various political representatives, government officials, and political organizations. Nevertheless, in a vote of 222 to 177, the U.S. House of Representatives voted in September 2004 to support the use of the *matricula consular* to open bank accounts (Immigrants' Rights Update, 2004). While pro-immigrant groups support the *matricula* as a means of advancing democratic rights for new immigrants, those opposed to its use see it as one more obstacle in the battle to curtail "illegal" immigration and to ensure national security.

Overall, the *matricula* service day represented a larger struggle as to whether immigrant workers, and especially undocumented workers, will have access to some of the same basic democratic and human rights that other citizens have. The creation of a project for these basic rights began with an environment in the classroom where dialogue broke down barriers of authority between the students and professors. It was further advanced with readings that introduced students to the underlying reasons why immigrants were being forced out of their homelands to be used as cheap labor in the more developed countries. This practice was reinforced with the Friday meetings at the day labor center where day laborers raised their concerns and the students listened. In the process, the workers and students expanded a democratic space that came to include a coalition of community groups. In the end, the *matricula* service day created another democratic space for hundreds of immigrant workers who saw the *matricula* as part of one more step in gaining more equality and a voice in U.S. society.

Project-Based Research in Grant Writing and Christmas Parade Projects

In the winter academic quarter, the authors involved their students in collaborations that used aspects of the project-based research approach. This approach, part of implementing a community-based research strategy, involves students, faculty, and community members in social change projects based on finding alternative solutions to community problems (Strand et al., 1993).

In implementing this approach, Professor Calderón and a group of students met with the Pomona day laborers at one of their weekly Friday meetings to discuss the obstacles that the workers were confronting in their efforts to develop their own day laborer advocacy organization.

One of the day laborers, Samuel, explained that the workers had formed an organization of day laborers that had begun to meet on Wednesday evenings. Another worker expressed that the workers had also elected a group of four officers for the organization but that they were having difficulties in making agendas, implementing rules, ensuring minutes, and facilitating the meetings. After analyzing the problem, the workers proposed that the officers and members of the group needed more training in how to run an organization. At the same time, the workers insisted that no one had the time to get trained. They settled on the idea of finding resources for one of the day labor leaders to get trained so that he could, in turn, train the others. In the course of this discussion, Professor Calderón and the students were tapped as a resource for writing a grant proposal with the specific purpose of hiring and training a day laborer organizer. This was an example where the workers and students engaged in a discussion about a problem of significant importance to the day labor center and worked together to find a mutual solution and plan of action. Together, the workers, the professor, and the students proposed that it would be beneficial to write a proposal to hire an organizer from the ranks of the day laborers themselves. The workers proposed that this individual could be trained by IDEPSCA, a southern California popular education organization, or by the National Day Laborer Network. The process of writing a grant proposal began out of an identified need. In this process, the students carried out service-learning projects at the center, attended the weekly Friday meetings of the workers, and worked with Professor Calderón in writing a grant proposal with the input of the workers. Reflecting on the experience of writing a grant alongside the workers, one of our students commented:

> I did not know how to draft a grant, but the other students did not know either, so it was a learning process for all of us. In the grant we focused on how the services provided at the center promote social change at the level of empowering workers. It has been a great learning experience and an opportunity to realize that an individual can make a difference and be a part of social justice, not only for immigrants, but for all humanity. I have been inspired to continue work with the organization and in the future to do volunteer work overseas. I have also learned firsthand the reasons why immigrants come to this country and that the myths about immigrants are false. (Analisa Alvarez, major in sociology)

By the end of the quarter, a grant proposal was written to the Liberty Hill Foundation that led to two seed grants totaling $20,000. The seed grants laid the foundation for the hiring and training of a day laborer organizer and the development of a day laborer advocacy organization. The final phase included the direct involvement of the workers in telling their stories to the foundation representatives who carried out interviews as part of the final phase of the review process.

As described through this example, the collaborative and participatory nature of project-based research does not fit into a traditional model where the purpose is primarily to serve the interests of the expert. Research as action brings the community participants to the center stage of the process by sharing their experiences, deepening the understanding of their experiences through dialogue, and reflecting on those experiences as a means of developing a plan of action for change (Stoecker, 2005). While service is part of the research process, the difference is that this type of research is "trying to create some difference in real people's lives, and the research exists in the service of that effort" (Stoecker, 2005, p. 8). In this type of research, "the outcomes of the project, not the results of the research, are most important. The research is important but only in the context of the project" (Stoecker, 2005, p. 14).

Another good example of a project that emerged out of a problem and involved all the steps in a project-based research approach was the Day Laborer Christmas Parade Project, which involved students from our classes in the fall quarter.

Panchito, a 75-year-old day laborer, brought a "research question" to a weekly meeting of the day laborers and students. After citing a letter to the editor that referred to day laborers as "criminals," he asked the day laborers and students, "Why do they hate us? We work hard and don't bother anyone, but why do they hate us?" Various workers responded from their own experiences. One worker responded that some of the parishioners at his church, although Latino, truly believed that immigrants were taking the jobs away from residents. Another worker proposed that it was the fault of the politicians who always blamed the immigrants for any downturns in the economy. A heated dialogue developed when one worker suggested that the day laborers were to blame "because you are not as smart as the white man." This last assertion was completely discounted by all the day laborers present. Eventually, the workers agreed that the media and the politicians portrayed the day laborers as taking jobs and services away from the residents. They agreed that this was contrary to their own experiences of being needed by many employers, taking the jobs that no one else wanted, and contributing much to the economy through their work and payment of taxes.

After sharing and analyzing their experiences, the workers and students discussed a plan for reaching out to the community at large. One worker proposed the idea of marching in the annual Pomona Christmas Parade. At first, the idea was laughed at by the other workers. One of the students from our classes questioned whether the action would be perceived as a protest against the parade. The mood became more serious when one of the workers, a known day-labor carpenter, responded that this was the season of Christmas and that "Jesus was a carpenter like myself." When this worker spoke, the eyes of all the other workers lit up, and one after the other offered to bring their tools. As the workers deepened their analysis for reaching out, the students joined in the excitement by volunteering to make a leaflet describing the day labor center, explaining the reasons why the day laborers were marching, and collaborating on a banner that could be carried at the front of the procession. The leaflet, passed out to thousands of spectators on the parade route, included a summary of the day laborers' conclusions as to why they were marching:

> As day laborers, we are walking in the Christmas parade asking the residents of Pomona to open their hearts in the spirit of the holidays. Remembering that Joseph and Mary walked door to door at this time of year, we are walking, tools in hand, searching for an open door in the form of jobs—so that we can provide for our families. We ask you to open your hearts by providing work and we are grateful for your support.

On the day of the parade, forty-five workers turned out in their work clothes holding hammers, saws, paintbrushes, shovels, rakes, and other tools.[6] Two workers carried a banner in the front of the procession that read "Pomona Day Labor Center." Eight students divided up 4,000 leaflets and began to pass them out to the spectators as the day laborers made their way down the street. The success of the action was expressed in the applause that the workers received from the crowds gathered throughout the route of the parade. A month after the parade, when workers and students gathered to evaluate the results of the action, day laborer Eduardo Nuno summarized that the march and leafleting were very positive and had resulted in a sharp increase in the number of jobs for workers.

Similarly, a Latina first-generation student shared the positive lessons that she had learned from her participation:

> I learned that when a community is united and organized, a more effective change can occur. This has helped me to appreciate my community more. The laborers that I have met and spoken with do not have an academic education or speak English. Despite their limited education, they are very wise and have proved to me their wisdom and knowledge of life and how to be a leader in the community. (Maria Guzman, major in sociology)

As shown by this action, the nontraditional character of research can emerge in forms that are nonacademic but help to advance unique bridges of civic and democratic participation. In this example, a community-based research style emerged where a problem was identified, a solution was agreed upon, a plan was implemented, and there was an evaluation of the results in the end.

Multiculturalism and the Agbayani and Alternative Spring Break Projects

The challenge in our classes was also to ensure multiculturalism as a key aspect of the readings, projects, and actions. We began by finding spaces for practicing a type of multiculturalism that could involve our students in "shifting" their "center of thinking so as to include previously silenced voices" and to implement projects that could place at center stage the experiences of oppressed groups that have been historically excluded by the "power and privilege" of others (Andersen & Collins, 2004, pp. 15–17).

One project that emerged from our classes in social movements and community service learning involved 25 students learning about the role that Filipino farm workers played in the development of the United Farm Workers (UFW) Union in California. In this example, after students read about the history of Cesar Chavez and the United Farm Workers (UFW) movement, our students visited the sites and met with the leaders that they had read about. As part of an "Alternative Spring Break" in La Paz (Keene, California), the students stayed at Agbayani Village, a retirement housing complex for elderly retired Filipino farm workers, located in Delano.[7] The 60-unit village is named after Paulo Agbayani, a Filipino farm worker who died on the picket line in 1967 (Scharlin & Villanueva, 1994). The village was constructed brick by brick through the labor of students and farm workers between 1969 and 1974. At one time, 61 Filipino farm workers who had been evicted from the labor camps during the 1965 grape strike lived in the complex (Ferris & Sandoval, 1997).

Today, all the Filipinos have passed away and their new replacements are primarily Mexican-origin retired farm workers. Agbayani also has a memorial room set aside where Cesar Chavez slept during his 36-day fast in 1988. The experience of our students sleeping there was itself an education on the history of the farm worker movement and the coalitions that developed between diverse ethnic groups. At the same time, our students had the opportunity to listen to the stories of the farm worker movement from Cesar Chavez's bodyguards, a Filipino and former mayor of Delano, a farmworker woman who had been wounded on the picket line, and the contemporary leaders of the United Farm Worker's Union. One of our students, a female Latina senior, explained that the experience of meeting these leaders had helped her to understand their "passion for what they did" and "the pitfalls that they had to face" (Andrea Serrata, major in gender, ethnicity, and multicultural studies). Another student, of mixed Asian Pacific and Latina background, reflected that the experience had taught her the significance of the farm worker's history in promoting unity among diverse groups: "One of the largest issues that arose in the Civil Rights Movement was the inability for the people to respect that the movement was not only a movement based on people of color but also included women's struggles and gay rights" (Amy Tam, major in sociology and gender, ethnicity, and multicultural studies).

In the course of carrying out service projects, our students were introduced to a room at Agbayani decorated with numerous pictures of the Filipino elderly who had lived in the complex. These pictures were not organized in any sequence and lacked any historical labeling or content. The director of the center, an elderly farm worker woman who had been a leader in the first strikes called by the UFW in the early 1970s, explained the role of the Filipino farm workers while pointing to each picture. In an ensuing discussion with the students, the director raised the need to frame and label the pictures of the Filipino farm workers with a history of each individual's contributions to the farm worker movement. In order to implement service that came out of this need, the students measured the size of each photograph. They took the measurements back with them and developed a plan for returning and framing some of the pictures.

When the students returned to Cal Poly, they took the lead in organizing a Cesar Chavez commemoration week that included a panel on the history of the Filipino farm workers, a Cesar Chavez breakfast honoring UFW cofounder Dolores Huerta, a city proclamation, and a four-mile pilgrimage walk from Pomona city hall to Cesar Chavez park.[8] One of the Filipino students who participated in the Alternative Spring Break returned from La Paz and formed the Agbayani Organizing Committee to help follow through on the picture framing historical project. In advancing the commitments made to this project, students from our spring classes in Rural and Urban Social Movements and Community Service Learning returned to Agbayani in the spring quarter to document more stories about the Filipino elders, to frame their pictures, and to mount them on the village's walls.[9]

As shown through the Alternative Spring Break and Agbayani project, the practice of multiculturalism and participatory research can be combined out of something as tangible as the framing of pictures and the researching of the histories of those in the pictures. Other forms that followed with this methodology included the use of skits, drumming, and "teatro" presentations. On the last evening of the Alternative Spring Break, the students summarized their experiences at La Paz through *teatro* presentations to the farm worker community. They also used the arts of drumming, music, and dance as a form of reciprocity and as a means of sharing their traditional and nontraditional multicultural talents with the larger UFW community.

Conclusion

Overall, this chapter has presented examples of campus and community collaborations that have resulted in the diagnosing and implementation of creative plans of action to achieve diverse forms of social justice and social change outcomes.

Through the application of the project-based approach, the authors and their students worked alongside day laborers, farm workers, and community-based organizations in defining the specific problems being confronted and implementing service-learning projects to find alternatives to those problems or issues.

In analyzing the participatory outcomes as lessons learned, the results of these projects have advanced the concept of "multiple layering": the intersection between various classes, professors, campus organizations, and community partners working on simultaneous projects. This chapter has highlighted some examples of these intersections, whose successes were achieved through the synergy of several campus entities including faculty from the Ethnic and Women's Studies Department, professional staff from the Cesar Chavez Center, students from various classes, members from the Weglyn Endowed Chair committee, and student leaders from various campus organizations. Off campus, the coalition efforts have involved collaboration with various community partners ranging from the San Gabriel/Pomona Valley Latino Roundtable and the United Farm Worker's Union to the Mexican Consulate, Park West High School, and the Pomona City Council.

In addition to creating models of social change, these collaborations with immigrant and farm workers have brought to center stage the culture and history of those that have been excluded. This has been accomplished through the consistent and conscious use of cultural productions (such as music, theater, dance, photography, signage, and banner making) to achieve social justice outcomes that have contributed to the faculty and students' passion for service learning. After being involved in many of the various projects, student Manà Guzman commented on this increased passion:

> Through my participation . . . I have also acquired leadership skills, self-confidence, political and social awareness of the injustices occurring in my communities. My commitment to my community has grown because of my knowledge and belief that anything is possible. My desire to go back and help my community stems from my passion and strength in the belief that the unity of a people, of an organized group of committed people, can fight for a common cause.

Overall, the collaborative work on common projects, as described in this chapter, has contributed to a type of dialogic democratic teaching and learning that has engaged the students and community participants in building diverse coalitions, tapping unheard voices, and creating a culture of action for social justice and social change.

Appendix 4.A
Course Syllabus: Ethnic Immigration

Ethnic Immigration
Ews 350
Fall Quarter
Professor: José Z. Calderón

Description of Course

This course examines the socioeconomic and political factors which are shaping the development of local and global immigration policies and practices. In particular, the class will focus on the two largest groups in the region: Latino and Asian Pacific Immigrants.

The course will examine how these groups and multiracial communities are being transformed through economic restructuring locally and globally. The issues of community building and participation in the informal economy will also be examined (particularly through concrete examples from the professor's research and organizing work in the cities of Monterey Park and Pomona). As part of the class, students will work in service-learning sites and practice aspects of participatory research as part of connecting to the theme(s) of the course.

Readings

Ethnic Immigration Reader (Available at Ask Copy and Printing, 3530 Temple Ave. #D, in Pomona)

Grading

Grades Will Be Allocated as Follows:

Research Proposal	5%
Participation	15%
Essay Exams	25%
Cultural Group Presentation	10%
Cultural Praxis Journal	20%
Final Paper and Presentation	25%

1. **Research Proposal.** A proposal at the beginning of the quarter that includes a description of the service-learning project where you will carry out participatory research, the arrangements you have made to carry out your project, when and how you will begin, and whether there are any ethical issues you will confront. (5% of final grade)

2. **Participation.** Weekly attendance at the seminar and two hours per week of fieldwork at a community site are required for the course. 15% of your final grade will be based on your fieldwork at the site, class attendance, completion of the readings for each class, and your participation in weekly discussions.

3. **Take-Home Essay Exams.** The take-home exams will be based on assigned readings, class discussions, and presentations. (25% of final grade)

4. **Cultural Group Presentation.** The class will be divided into cultural groups. Each group will focus on a particular issue decided by the group but related to one of the sections in the syllabus. The group should identify major themes for the presentation and collectively develop them into a class

presentation which uses a creative medium or combinations of mediums (e.g., video, theater, art, music, collage, dance, rap, poetry, etc.). The presentation should include (1) an introduction with the primary objectives of the presentation, (2) transitions between the primary points, (3) connections between the themes/concepts in the readings and community or lived experience, and (4) a conclusion that summarizes the main points. Remember, the class presentation will be carried out collectively in a group. Connections to your fieldwork are welcomed for this presentation. *Do not* merely summarize the argument of the author(s) but develop your own thinking and criticality about what the author(s) is/are saying. The class and groups will be consulted on a team grade using a handout of "criteria" for grading the presentation. (10% of final grade)

5. **Cultural Praxis Journal.** The journal will include descriptive field notes of your step-by-step observations of the site, the participants, and the activities taking place at your site. *To help you stay on top of your journal writing, you will receive "questions" that should be addressed in your field note journal.* When the journal is turned in, it should include *minimally* the responses to these questions. You should use the readings to help inform and frame your work (integrate your experiences from your weekly service-learning activity to the concepts, theories, and examples that we are studying in the classroom). The purpose of the journal is to give you data that you can use as a foundation for your final paper and a means of connecting theory with practice. It is not the particular conclusions that you reach but the process you demonstrate in reaching them that is the goal of the weekly journal. Your journal will be collected at different times during the quarter and turned in with your final paper. A total grade average for journal entries will count for 20% of your grade.

In terms of a site for research and participation, it must be connected in some way to immigrant and immigration issues. The proposal is that this class primarily focus on a local site where students can meet and interact with immigrant workers: the Pomona Day Labor Center (1682 West Mission Blvd. in Pomona). There are some possible projects that students can work on, including (1) ESL (teaching English to day laborers), (2) computer classes (teaching computer programs to day laborers), (3) Health Project (organizing of informational materials, educational forums, outreach to health clinics, and a "medical check-up day" in partnership with local medical interns and doctors), (4) Community Garden development, (5) mural and exhibit development, (6) job development project in collaboration with the day labor center and the City of Pomona, (7) leadership development project (meetings of workers on Friday and the development of a worker organization), (8) Dia de los Muertos Project (working with day laborers to have their own altar at the college event), and (9) fund-raising project (organizing a car wash for day laborer emergency funds). Students should look at spending at least 2–3 hours per week at their community-based site and organizing their specific project.

6. Final Research Paper and Presentation

a. Paper—Utilize the field notes from your site and literature (at least six references that include reading materials from the class and/or outside readings) to write your final paper. All students will write a final paper (10–12 pages long) that connects the findings from your field notes to the readings, theories, concepts, and issues discussed in the class. As you adopt the role of a participant observer, it is important that you examine the research findings of other researchers in regard to your particular issue or topic. Any generalizations that you make concerning the potential impact of any issue on your particular site should be based on or related to our readings in this class or to the works of other urban or community sociologists who have studied similar issues. Review the literature that is available on the issue and where your research fits into that literature. USE YOUR READINGS. The readings for this class are meant to serve as examples of how research on immigration issues is carried out and written up.

b. Presentation—During the final week of class, students will present a five-minute summary presentation on the results of their research project. The presentation should include a description of the site; the primary issue, problem, or argument developed out of the research; the literature related to the topic; the methodology used; the data gathered; and conclusions reached from the findings. (Paper and Presentation: 25% of final grade)

Notes

1. Cal Poly Pomona is located about 30 miles east of Los Angeles. The city of Pomona represents some of the demographic changes taking place throughout California. The city of Pomona has grown from 131,723 in 1990 to 149,473 in the year

2000, a 13.5% change. The population changes between 1990 and 2000 have resulted in Latinos growing in numbers from 54.3% (77,776) to 64.5% (96,370), the population of Asian Pacific Islanders increasing from 6.9% (9,846) to 7.2% (10,765), African Americans decreasing from 14.4% (19,013) to 9.6% (14,398), and Euro-Americans decreasing from 25.6% (36,687) to 17% (25,348) (U.S. Bureau of the Census, 1990, 2000). Cal Poly Pomona is considered one of the most diverse campuses in the United States, with 40% Asian and Pacific Islander, 26% Latino, 4% African American, less than 1% Native American, and 30% Euro-American, Middle Eastern, and others. The mission statement of the university reflects a commitment to connect "theory and practice in all disciplines" and to prepare students "for lifelong learning, leadership, and careers in a changing multicultural world" (Cal Poly Pomona Catalog, 2003, p. 14). This campus and city setting in southern California provides an important context for creating multiethnic partnerships and projects.

2. Some of the obstacles in developing service learning classes and cultivating community partnerships in CSU campuses on the quarter system include the 10-week quarter, a high percentage of students working more than 20 hours per week, and a commuter campus environment. Faculty members also have a course load of three classes per quarter with ongoing pressure to increase their full-time equivalent (FTE). To help overcome these barriers, the Offices of Community Service Learning on each CSU campus are attempting to assist faculty, community partners, and students in institutionalizing service learning throughout the curriculum and providing needed support.

3. Some of the readings, in addition to introducing students to community-based research approaches, also included traditional methodologies for gathering and coding field notes, writing final papers, developing senior capstone projects, and presenting at service-learning and academic association conferences.

4. Students had a choice of suggested sites and projects. Ultimately, this included 12 students from the Chicano/Latino Contemporary Issues class and 12 from the Ethnic Immigration class who worked on the *matricula* service-learning project.

5. The *matricula* service day took place October 9, 2004.

6. The parade took place on December 4, 2004.

7. The Alternative Spring Break was held in La Paz and Delano, California, March 18–21, 2005.

8. Various planning meetings were held at Agbayani Village and La Paz with the students, where they made commitments to continue working in all these service-learning projects during the spring quarter.

9. Presently, students are continuing to carry out research on this history and have already returned to Delano to frame more of the remaining pictures.

References

Andersen, M. L., & Collins, P. H. (2004). *Race, class, and gender*. Belmont, CA: Wadsworth.

Cal Poly Pomona Catalog 2003–2005. (2003). Pomona, CA: California State Polytechnic University.

Dardar, A. (2002). *Reinventing Paulo Freire: A pedagogy of love.* Boulder, CO: Westview Press.

Ferris, S., & Sandoval, R. (1997). *The fight in the fields: Cesar Chavez and the Farmworkers Movement.* Orlando, FL: Paradigm Productions.

Horton, M., & Freire, P. (1990). *We make the road by walking: Conversations on education and social change.* Philadelphia: Temple University Press.

Immigrants' Rights Update (2004, September 21). Vol. 18, No. 6.

Judkins, B. M., & LaHurd, R. A. (1999). Addressing the changing demographics of academia and society. *American Behavioral Scientist, 42*(5), 786–789.

Mora, J., & Diaz, D. R. (2004). *Latino social policy: A participatory research model.* Binghamton, NY: The Haworth Press.

Scharlin, C., & Villanueva, L. V. (1994). *Philip Vera Cruz: A personal history of Filipino immigrants and the farmworkers movement.* Los Angeles: UCLA Labor Center, Institute of Industrial Relations.

Shor, I. (1992). *Empowering education: Critical teaching for social change.* Chicago: The University of Chicago Press.

Stoecker, R. (2005). *Research methods for community change: A project-based approach.* Thousand Oaks, CA: Sage.

Strand, K., Marullo, S., Cutforth, N., Stoecker, R., & Donahue, P. (2003). *Community-based research and higher education.* San Francisco: Jossey-Bass.

U.S. Bureau of the Census. (1990, 2000). *Statistical Abstract.* Washington, DC.

Wallace, J. (2000). A popular education model for college in community. *American Behavioral Scientist, 43*(5), 756–766.

Wright, M. G. M. (2000). A critical-holistic paradigm for an interdependent world. *American Behavioral Scientist, 43*(5), 808–824.

5

DESIGNING A SAFETY
PROGRAM FOR DAY LABORERS

The Forgotten Workers

Edward V. Clancy

Safety Engineering and Service Learning

To the uninitiated, the subject of safety engineering can seem like a dull affair. The standard textbook-based course covers fundamental principles of hazard reduction and occupational safety and a dizzying array of state and federal laws and regulations. To the engineering student, anxious to apply his or her newly acquired engineering skills to challenges requiring innovation and creativity, the required course in safety principles and practice appears to be yet one more hurdle to cross before being released into the real world of engineering.

Perhaps what is missing for these students is an understanding of just how important safety rules are and how these rules and practices came to be a central part of every project. As engineering faculty we are well trained in the fundamentals of physics and material science that underlie our discipline, in the skills and knowledge of how to apply these fundamentals to project design and implementation, and in how to train and test our students to see how well they have acquired an understanding of the discipline. What we are less than well trained to do is to instill in our students an understanding of the history of struggle over issues of safety in the workplace, and an understanding of how these issues involve a basic question of social justice regarding those at the bottom rung of the social strata who are forced to toil in an environment in which their health, and often their lives, is placed at risk.

Service learning can play a significant role in the deep education of an engineer. Beyond honing their skills in project management, beyond learning how to apply knowledge of safety techniques and devices, students who experience firsthand the purpose of these principles and practices of safety engineering come away incorporating the real meaning of the course—that safety saves lives—into their core beliefs.

I am fortunate to teach at an institution, the California State Polytechnic University–Pomona (Cal Poly Pomona), whose motto "learning by doing" is genuinely applied. Throughout the engineering program, in fact throughout the university, courses are designed around experiential learning. Our graduates have a reputation for being the kind of "hands-on" engineers that many employers look for in today's marketplace. We are also fortunate that the university president, Dr. J. Michael Ortiz, has challenged faculty and students to become more involved in the local community.

Pomona is one of the cities that make up the vast Los Angeles megalopolis. Located 30 miles east of downtown L.A., Pomona attracts many recent immigrants, mostly from south of the border, who come to the U.S. seeking opportunities to work in order to support their families. Many find their way to the Pomona Day Labor Center (PDLC), where temporary work arrangements can be negotiated.

The day labor market is an extremely effective mechanism for bringing together prospective employers and seekers of work.[1] For many workers, day labor is a chance to gain a foothold in the urban economy. For others, it is a first job in the United States, or a last chance at securing some type of employment. For still others, it represents an opportunity to earn some income when temporarily laid off from a job in the formal economy or a viable alternative to wage employment that pays poorly. Employers of day laborers similarly benefit from this market. The simplicity of hiring a day laborer, almost instantaneously as needed, to help you with a household improvement job or repair activity is an important attraction for homeowners and other employers alike. The market is extremely attractive to construction subcontractors who aim to replace a regular employee who has called in sick or has been fired. The employers recruiting on the street corner typically are subcontractors who rely on day laborers because labor needs are variable. Employers of day laborers range from bonded, insured, and state licensed contractors to fly-by-night landscapers and demolition operators.

Beyond the basic factors of supply and demand, day laborers are a pliable labor force that can be used to undertake tasks not easily or willingly performed by workers in the general economy. And therein lies the rub: day laborers engage in occupations that are among the most dangerous in the United States.

The bulk of employment at the PDLC is for physical labor in construction, landscaping, or moving. Construction is considered the single most dangerous trade in the country, with one in five workers in high-risk fields like roofing or sheet metal suffering a work-related injury or illness each year. The yearly fatality rate for roofers is six times higher than for the average of all other jobs; for the lowest skilled job classification, construction laborer, the position commonly occupied by day laborers, the death rate is eight times higher than for the average job. The major causes of injury and death are falls and burns. In 2000, 23 percent of fatal occupational injuries to foreign-born workers occurred to workers in construction trades (Brown, Domenzain, & Villoria-Siegert, 2002).

Federal regulations set strict guidelines for high-risk work situations such as roofing, requiring gloves, masks, and extensive fall-protection systems such as harnesses. The regulations also set stringent standards for ladders and scaffolding, but for day laborers these regulations are widely ignored. Although laws protecting them in the event of fraud or injury nominally cover undocumented workers, exercising these rights is difficult. Day laborers are reluctant to contact authorities and are limited by language barriers and low levels of education and of legal sophistication. For some, it is difficult to mount a potentially protracted suit while transient and homeless. Economic pressures also make day laborers reluctant to leave a job and can make injured workers feel that they must continue to work despite their injuries.

At our first visit to the PDLC we heard directly of incidents that made these statistics all too real. One recent account was about a day laborer who had fallen from a roof. The worker had no health insurance and sustained injuries to both his legs. Another account was about a worker who had died when he fell into a pool with a leaf blower machine on his back. The worker was unable to swim and drowned in the backyard pool of a home where he was working as a gardener. These stories convinced me that the PDLC was an ideal candidate for a community partner for a safety-engineering capstone class. Today, all Cal Poly Pomona students are required to complete a capstone that brings together the lessons learned in their earlier classes. Where better for students to learn how to apply engineering principles that could make a difference!

Capstone Course in Safety Engineering

Engineering 461/462 is a yearlong sequence built around a specific project. In 2005 we launched our first engineering capstone course covering safety at Pomona Day Labor Center (see Appendix 5.A for course syllabus). Six engineering technology students signed up for the initial project. These students had taken a previous course in safety engineering and were all seniors. I challenged them to use the principles discussed in the course and apply them to the PDLC. Each student worked on an average of 16 hours per week in the class. Weekly time logs were required and students were also required to keep a log of their reflections on the project.

A safety-engineering program starts with evaluation of the workplace. The safety engineer tries first to eliminate any hazard that might cause injuries. If hazards cannot be eliminated the engineer tries to reduce the possibility of injuries by education or by engineering a method that will reduce the possibility of injury. The safety professional must visit the workplace and interview workers. He or she must study completely the type of task that workers are performing.

The PDLC had a weekly management meeting on Friday mornings, and the students met there weekly. The students quickly learned that day laborers engage in occupations that are among the most dangerous in the United States, and a variety of social factors related to their undocumented temporary laborer status tend to increase their risk for work injury. These factors include inadequate training and experience, substandard safety equipment, and economic pressures that limit their capacity to avoid hazardous workplaces. The students quickly understood that these day laborers went to work each day without training and were getting injured at alarming rates. Through direct interviews of the laborers, they learned that most had not been educated on the importance of safety at their job sites. Many workers did not realize how easily a piece of wood could get in their eye, or how long durations of loud noise could lead to permanent ear damage if ear plugs are not worn.

The students came to understand how safety education could change the workers' ideas on the importance of safety. The lack of safety education is partly caused by the public's unwillingness to work with and inform day laborers. Many people are so busy and consumed with their own lives that they do not have time to educate these laborers. Through the interviews with the day laborers, the students started to bond with them. They began to express a palpable excitement about taking on the challenge of educating the workers on safety and ways to protect themselves.

The majority of the day laborers do not speak English, and many of the employers do not speak Spanish, so there is often a considerable language barrier to overcome. The students broadened their project to include the development of Spanish safety brochures and Spanish safety videos to help overcome the language conflict.

In interviewing the day laborers, the students found that many did not consider safety issues to be a high priority. This came as a real surprise to the students, and it was a problem that required a solution. The students took on the challenge of changing attitudes and created a Safety Awareness campaign. They developed a training program, which showed that wearing the safety equipment would show respect for themselves, their families, and other people around them. This concept of respect was something that the workers caught hold of. They realized that it was important what other people thought of them. The workers found out for themselves that safety equipment could make them look more professional, and thereby more employable. They started to equate personal safety equipment with respect. The students were successful in changing their perception of the use of personal safety equipment. They were particularly proud of the large banner that they hung across the Center that read, "Safety First—Your Family Is Counting on You!"

The students used the training sessions to talk to the laborers about unsafe working conditions. Many of the day laborers identified what was lacking at employer work sites: safety items such as appropriate machine guards, gloves, safety glasses, dust masks and respirators, ear plugs, and eye-flush stations. Many laborers added that, even when equipment was provided by an employer to help protect them from injury, there was frequently no instruction given about the equipment's proper use.

The students realized that personal safety equipment must be made available in order to reduce the hazards of these work environments. They sought funds from the PDLC but learned that the Center had none available

for the purchase of this equipment. The students had become a highly motivated team that had the safety-engineering knowledge to reduce the injury
rate, but no money to do the job. Undaunted, they decided to develop a
management plan and time schedule to get the funds needed for this project.

Medical Exams and Safety Kits

The students enlisted the help of a team of medical interns and students
from the physical therapy department at Western University, a private college of osteopathic medicine and medical school located in downtown Pomona. The Western team came to the PDLC and conducted physical
examinations of the workers. The injury data from the medical exams indicated that 59 percent of the PDLC workers had been injured on the job.
This was an unacceptably high rate of injuries, especially since most of them
can be eliminated with safety education, training, and the use of personal
safety equipment.

The safety-engineering students used this opportunity to survey the doctors and physical therapists on the type of injuries the workers were incur-
ring. The engineering students compiled the exam data and then matched
the types of injury to safety equipment such as eye- and hearing-protection
equipment. The information became the basis for designing a safety kit that
would be provided to each day laborer. The results dictated a specific focus
on prevention of injury to the ears, eyes, hands, back, and skin. Each kit
included a pair of safety glasses, a breathing apparatus, ear plugs, a pair of
leather gloves, a mini flashlight, a safety-visible vest, Band-Aids, infection
ointments, and an accident report card.

The students even designed and developed a fanny pack in which to
carry the safety kit. As with every aspect of this project, the students sought
input from the workers on the design of the safety pack. The conversations
produced a style that the workers found manly and acceptable, and embla-
zoned on its face was the PDLC logo. Sensitivity to workers' values and views
proved crucial to the success of the project and boosted attendance at the
weekly training sessions.

The acquisition of the safety material was made possible through grants
and donations from various companies and safety associations that the students had approached. Over the course of one semester, we received more
than $4,000 in cash and donations for the program.

In safety training sessions at the PDLC, each piece of equipment was presented along with an explanation of how and when to wear and use it properly. The students taught classes on 10 Saturday mornings to workers on eye protection, reducing back injuries, hearing loss, hazardous and toxic chemicals, documentation needed if you get injured, and other topics selected by the workers. Course material developed by the students was made available on the Web so that future groups of workers could go online and learn the material.

The students held a graduation ceremony for day laborers who completed the 10-week training. The laborers were excited to receive a certificate indicating their successful completion of the course. For many of them, this was the first training they had ever received. Quizzes were developed by the students and administered each week to provide feedback to the group in order to evaluate if the workers were getting the intended outcome from each training session.

Learning Outcomes

Service learning can be used to produce a variety of learning outcomes. In engineering it has most often been used for problem-based learning to develop disciplined skills of project design and implementation. But the safety-engineering course demonstrated to me that so much more could be learned including values, more skills, and knowledge that we would want any engineering graduate to possess.

The students developed skills not only in engineering and project management, but also in communication and public speaking, skills that were required for the success of the project. They learned applied research skills through the analysis of both the survey and medical examinations. The students learned teamwork and the value of hard work. They became fully committed to the project from the start, bonding with each other and the day laborers as well. And most important, they learned how safety engineering made a difference in the lives of laborers who needed it most. It was a lesson that they will certainly carry throughout their professional lives.

I found the experience to be quite rewarding and satisfying for me as well. After the yearlong project ended, we went out for dinner to celebrate and debrief, and I asked the students why they had become involved. I was surprised when I heard the same response from so many of them. As one student put it, "I wanted to get involved so that I could help someone because my grandmother told me stories about her family's struggle to survive when they first came to this country."

Then it hit me. These students were at most two generations from being immigrants themselves. What a remarkable educational system we have here in California. We educate families of immigrants and, within one or two generations, create technically competent college graduates. These are people who make this country great; they work hard, pay taxes, and support this county. When we look at the day laborers, we should realize that an engineer, doctor, or teacher is only one or two generations away!

I had never felt as attached to my students as when they refreshed my memory. Why shouldn't their stories of their grandmothers resonate with me? After all, I remember hearing similar stories about the struggles of my immigrant grandparents. You see, I too am only two generations removed. This is a country of immigrants. We all share a common past.

Appendix 5.A

Course Syllabus: Safety Engineering at the Day Labor Center

Safety Engineering at the Day Labor Center
ETT 461/462 S
Service Capstone Project
Campus: California State Polytechnic University
Department: Engineering Technology Department

Course Description

This course covers the fundamental principles and techniques of safety engineering as applied to day laborers. Topics include State and federal regulations and Laws, Fundamental Concepts and terms of the profession, Mechanical, Electrical Hazards and Hazard Reduction. Fire Protection, Pressure and Heat and Cold problems will be discussed. Hazardous waste and personnel protection equipment will be emphasized. Presentations and research of safety topics will be performed at the Day Labor Center in Pomona.

Grading

Website Project   30 Points
Project—Demonstration Bag 30 points
Research Reflection Journal   20 Points
Portfolio Assignment   20 points

A (89–100)   B (80–88)   C (70–79)   F (below 70)

Purpose

Safety engineering encompasses a wide range of disciplines. This service-learning safety course is designed to provide the student with the practical experience of examining a job (day labor) and then designing and implementing a safety program that will reduce accidents and encourage a safety culture among workers.

Service Goals

1. The goal of this project is to assist in developing a safety culture within the Day Labor Center. The benefits will include fewer injuries to workers and improved productivity.
   a. A bag of safety equipment will be developed. The bag will demonstrate to laborers what safety equipment they should have to prevent injury (e.g., hard hat, safety glasses, etc.)
2. The students will gain firsthand understanding of how to conduct a safety meeting.
3. To provide an opportunity for construction and mechanical engineering technology students to bridge the classroom experience to the community through a service project. These students had all taken a safety-engineering course. This capstone course will enable them to develop appropriate training material for day laborers, hand-outs, and website material so that a safety culture will take route at the Day Labor Center.

Community-Based Component

Students in the class will visit the Day Labor Center in Pomona and interview day laborers and center personnel. The students will understand the types of jobs day laborers do and document their present understanding of safety procedures.

Challenges

- Day laborers may have communication problems and not be familiar with safety rules, equipment, and regulations.
- The cost of safety equipment might be prohibitive for day laborers. Therefore, a low-cost demonstration kit must be developed. The students must develop a link between safety and productivity for the day laborer to understand.
- Assessment tools of the safety program must be developed to measure program effectiveness.
- Spanish is the language that must be used for training material.

Requirements

1. Portfolio Assignment that covers the project.
2. Research Reflection journal (e-mail is required).
3. Draft report.
4. Final report.
5. Presentation to day laborers.
6. Develop a list of future safety projects for the center.
7. Develop training material.
8. Develop safety equipment bag.
9. Conduct safety training at center.

Materials

Anton, T. J. (1989). *Occupation safety and health management* (2nd ed.). New York: McGraw-Hill.

Brauer, R. L. (1994). *Safety and health for engineers.* New York: Wiley & Sons.

Covan, J. (1995). *Safety engineering.* New York: Wiley & Sons.

Goetsch, D. L. (2002). *Occupational safety and health for technologists, engineers, and managers* (4th ed.). Upper Saddle River, NJ: Prentice Hall.

Louvar, J. F., & Louvar, B. D. (1998). *Health and environmental risk analysis.* Upper Saddle River, NJ: Prentice Hall.

Wentz, C. A. (1998). *Safety, health, and environmental protection.* New York: Mc-Graw-Hill.

Notes

1. Loue, S., & Bunce, A. (1999). The assessment of immigration status in health research. National Center for Health Statistics. *Vital Health Stat 2*(127), p. 140.

Reference

Brown, M. P., Domenzain, A., & Villoria-Siegert, N. (2002, December). *Voices from the margins: Immigrant workers' perceptions of health and safety in the workplace.* Los Angeles: UCLA Labor Occupational Safety and Health Program.

6

COMMUNITY-BASED SCHOLARSHIP

Nutrition Students Learn Spanish in the Classroom and
at the City of Pomona Day Labor Center

Susan Algert

Social environments lacking basic resources—
healthy food, safe housing, living wage jobs,
decent schools, supportive social networks, access to health care and other public and private
goods and services—present the highest public
health risk for serious illness and premature death.

—L. M. Anderson, J. E. Fielding, M. Fullilove,
S. C. Scrimshaw, V. G. Carande-Kulis, and
the Task Force on Community Preventive
Services (2003)

Community Health Model

The discipline of public health and health promotion increasingly
recognizes that there is a relationship between social determinants
of health and health outcomes that may be responsive to community interventions employing culturally sensitive health care professionals
(Anderson, Scrimshaw, et al., 2003; Institute of Medicine, 2001).

According to the Task Force on Community Preventive Services (Department of Health and Human Services), understanding patterns of health or disease requires focus not only on personal behaviors and biologic traits but also on characteristics of the social and physical environments that offer or limit opportunities for health (Anderson, Scrimshaw, et al., 2003). The model for linking the social environment to health (see Figure 6.1) is based on the fundamental premise that access to societal resources determines community outcomes.

The model delineates the societal resources that a population relies upon to maintain health, including social and political institutions, the built environment, economic systems, socioeconomic status, and culture. The level of access to societal resources determines community health outcomes. Patterns

FIGURE 6.1
Community guide's social environment and health model.

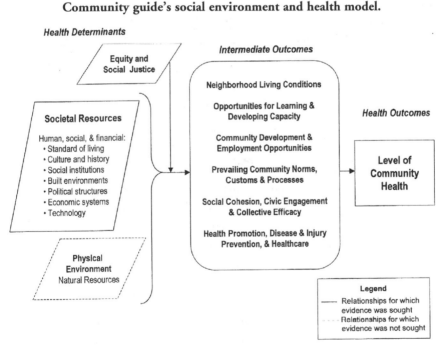

From "Methods for Conducting Systemic Reviews of the Evidence of Effectiveness and Economic Efficiency of Interventions to Promote Healthy Social Environments," by L. M. Anderson, J. E. Fielding, M. Fullilove, S. C. Scrimshaw, V. G. Carande-Kulis, and Task Force on Community Preventive Services, 2003, *American Journal of Preventative Medicine, 24*(3S), pp. 25–31.

of exposure to risk vary across income groups and are associated with basic access to resources and health outcomes in a community. According to the model, six intermediate outcomes in the social environment are associated with community health outcomes.

Variables that can influence health outcomes include community interventions to train students in *culturally competent* health care. The goal of culturally competent care is to ensure that appropriate services are provided to clients across all income and ethnic groups. Inability to communicate with a health care provider creates barriers in access to care, questions quality of care provided, and decreases likelihood of appropriate follow-up. Lack of common language and understanding of cultural norms can result in diagnostic errors and inappropriate treatment (Mutha, Allen, & Welch, 2002). Thus, cultural competence is a tool to improve quality of health care including health outcomes and a way to reduce disparities in utilization of procedures across ethnic groups.

According to the U.S. Census 2000, the foreign-born population of the United States was estimated to be 28.4 million, approximately half of whom speak some Spanish (Lopez, 2003). Additionally, approximately half of all Mexican immigrants in California have difficulty speaking English (U.S. Census Bureau, 2004). Clearly, there is a rapidly increasing need for Spanish-speaking health care practitioners in the United States and California.

Community Partner—The Pomona Day Labor Center

In 1997 college students, community advocates, a faculty member from Pitzer College, day laborers, and the City of Pomona joined together to establish an official site, the Pomona Day Labor Center (PDLC), from which day laborers could negotiate employment and obtain skills such as ESL classes and computer training. A participatory model of education and communication was implemented at PDLC that led to the launch of several projects designed to empower the workers to speak out and act on issues they identify as important. For example, the health projects, initiated with the help of students from Pitzer, included eye and dental exams.

The workers at PDLC were also interested in learning more about how to make healthy food choices, given the demands and variability of their employment. As a professor in the Human Nutrition and Food Science (HNFS) department at Cal Poly Pomona, I learned of this interest through the campus's Office of Community Service Learning. I initially met with PDLC organizers to discuss the feasibility of setting up a series of educational sessions on healthful food choices to be taught by HNFS students in Spanish during the summer and fall of 2005. Follow-up meetings were scheduled with the day laborers, students, day labor center staff, and myself to determine the topics of greatest interest to the men.

Spanish and Nutrition Course

Thus was launched the Spanish for Nutritionists service-learning course as an attempt to meet the increasing need to train culturally competent dietitians. The purpose of this project was for students in HNFS to partner with workers at the Center in order to address their health and nutrition concerns and to develop and implement a Spanish language curriculum focused on training culturally competent nutrition students.

Culturally competent health care includes making services available in the language spoken by patients and recognizing and accommodating the cultural beliefs and practices of diverse communities (Anderson & Meyers, 2006). In addition, the Campinha-Bacote model of cultural competency[1] focuses on the need for health care providers to skillfully engage with patients or clients and apply knowledge and skills in each encounter (Campinha-Bacote, 1998). The five overlapping dimensions of the model—Cultural Awareness, Cultural Skill, Cultural Desire, Cultural Knowledge, and Cultural Encounters—define the process of cultural competence and form the basis for educating students.

The underlying premise of this project was that societal conditions or social determinants affecting health can potentially be altered by social and health programs. Social determinants of health include social relationships such as positions in social hierarchy, differential treatment of social groups, and social networks. The goal of this project was to have students and day laborers work together to address issues of proper diet and disease prevention that would provide both short- and long-term benefits for the men. This mutually beneficial relationship enabled students to enhance their Spanish speaking skills and helped workers increase their knowledge of proper diet and nutrition. An additional outcome was that students working to achieve cultural awareness through participation in community-building programs became more aware of situations of racism and inequality that exist in larger society.

Service-Learning Experience

Teachers and students served together in the community in planning and implementing the nutrition education sessions. Students did not just sit at a desk learning Spanish vocabulary and phrases relevant to health promotion; they worked hands-on in teams with classmates in the community. Students visited the Economic Opportunity Center on two different occasions to conduct a needs assessment and discuss nutrition topics of interest with the men before planning their educational sessions. Consistent with the participatory model of communication and education, both sessions were conducted in an informal group setting and focused on discussions and a problem-solving approach to the nutrition and health concerns raised by the men.

The discussion brought up several concerns of the men, including food safety and sanitation, food choices while at work, long-term health risk for heart disease and diabetes, fluid intake and dehydration, and fast-food choices. The men discussed how most often their food choices while at work are very limited. Typically, an employer will take them to a fast-food restaurant or provide them with food on-site, or sometimes not even allow them a break to eat. Several workers reported becoming ill after eating food that had not been refrigerated properly or had been reheated after sitting out the day before. Healthy and sanitary food choices available for purchase from the food truck that passed by the Center twice daily were also very limited.

Several of the men reported having a family history of diabetes, hypertension, or heart disease. Many indicated that they felt that the traditional Mexican diet or foods that they had left behind at home were much healthier and less processed than the mainstream American diet. In fact, research has shown that less acculturated Mexican Americans experience more positive health outcomes than their more acculturated counterparts due to the consumption of a traditional Mexican diet and use of less alcohol and tobacco (Algert & Brezezinski, 1998; Hayes-Bautista, 2003; Markides & Eschbach, 2005). Students decided to address the following topics in their presentations to the PDLC workers as a result of their meetings: (1) healthy fast-food choices, (2) beverages, sodas, and drinks in relation to dehydration, (3) food safety and refrigeration, and (4) fiber and diabetes.

Learning Objectives and Outcomes

Service-Learning Objectives and Outcomes

Exemplary service learning provides benefits to both sides of the partnership. In addition to doing work that will benefit the community participants in the program, a complementary goal is that those who are learning about service experience positive changes in their knowledge, skills, attitudes, and/or behaviors (Furco & Billig, 2002). Thus, the bidirectional relationship between students and the community groups they serve is characterized by reciprocity. Students provide service to community participants and are rewarded with an enhanced educational experience. With these mutual goals in mind, the following were established as the skills, values, and knowledge to be obtained by HNFS students in their service-learning work at the Economic Opportunity Center:

- Cultural competency
- Cross-cultural/bilingual or trilingual communication skills
- An ethic of caring
- How to apply professional skills for the betterment of society
- How individuals in public health act in socially responsible ways

Learning Objectives and Outcomes Specific to the Spanish for Nutritionists Course

The Human Nutrition and Food Science department contracted with Mari Mendoza, RD, to help develop the curriculum in Spanish for our students. Ms. Mendoza is an employee who teaches Spanish to employees with the Special Supplemental Nutrition Program for Women, Infants, and Children. Ms. Mendoza has extensive experience in developing and teaching nutrition education in Spanish to pregnant and breast-feeding women and children. She has worked closely with the instructor during the yearlong course, to create course materials that meet specific objectives and course requirements (see Appendix 6.A for the syllabus). Learning objectives and outcomes established for the yearlong Spanish course for Nutrition majors include the following:

- Ability to translate health education materials from Spanish to English

- Ability to conduct basic diet interview in Spanish
- Proficiency in food and nutrition vocabulary in Spanish
- Proficiency in key food and nutrition phrases in Spanish
- Ability to communicate food and nutrition issues to native Spanish speakers in a group setting
- Ability to communicate food and nutrition issues to native Spanish speakers one-on-one

Teaching and Learning Process

The course is designed to be student centered; that is, each student establishes his or her own individual learning plan at the beginning of each quarter. Students state what they would like to accomplish by the end of the quarter for each of the learning objectives and outcomes listed above (see Appendix 6.B for Individual Learning Plan Form). The course is able to accommodate students with varying levels of proficiency in Spanish by allowing them to establish individual learning plans. Reflective class discussions of progress in teaching and teaching outcomes are also used as part of the learning process.

Class Organization

The course was held for two hours per week. Students received CDs with Spanish dialogues to listen to and study on the following topics: shopping for traditional Mexican foods, cooking traditional foods, how to conduct a diet interview, counseling for a healthy diet, and a visit to the doctor's office. Each CD also contained vocabulary words and key phrases.

During class time the students practiced the content of the dialogues by speaking to each other one-on-one in Spanish and covered basic to intermediate-level grammar. A limited amount of class time was allotted for students to develop one-hour presentations or workshops on topics determined by the workers. Many students designed original educational materials in addition to developing the class content in Spanish. The content of the course was designed to complement the content of a course being taught during the same quarter on cultural foods. Several students in the Spanish course were also in the cultural foods course, so that while they were studying dialogues on Mexican dishes and cooking in Spanish they were learning about traditional food practices in Mexico.

Students were tested in class on intermediate and advanced grammar, vocabulary words featured in the dialogues, and the ability to converse in Spanish on nutrition topics.

Students gave two group presentations to men at the Economic Opportunity Center during the 10-week quarter. Topics covered in the presentations at the PDLC included healthful food choices during work, beverage choices and the importance of hydration, and high-fiber and snack choices. Each presentation was accompanied by a selection of fresh fruits and healthy snacks.

Feedback from students about their experiences included informal reflections after the completion of each of the classes. Also, students completed a summative evaluation form for the class at the end of the quarter (see Appendix 6.C for the evaluation form).

Assessment

Classroom

Four forms of formative and summative assessment were used to measure success of the program in meeting service-learning and course objectives, including the following:

1. *Diagnostic test of current level of knowledge and experience in speaking Spanish.* An eight-page diagnostic test was given at beginning of the quarter and repeated as the final at the end of the quarter.
2. *Students' assessment of their current level of comfort with the six skills emphasized in class* (see evaluation form in Appendix 6.C). At the beginning and at end of quarter, students rated their own skills on a scale of 1 to 4 (with 1 being extremely comfortable and 4 being uncomfortable). Students completing the assessment reported an improvement in their ability to conduct a diet interview, increased proficiency in food and nutrition vocabulary/key phrases, and an increase in translation skills. Increases in the level of comfort with speaking Spanish varied greatly depending on the level of students' knowledge when they entered the course. Students who were more

proficient in Spanish to begin with made greater or more rapid progress in becoming comfortable with their ability to speak.

3. *Progress in achieving goals established in each student's individual learning plan.* Progress was assessed by the student and instructor at the
end of the quarter. The course grade was determined according to
the student's ability to meet his or her own learning objectives.

4. *Course evaluation conducted at the end of the quarter* (see Appendix
6.C). Student feedback indicated that students found the opportunities to practice speaking Spanish one-on-one or in groups in class to
be most valuable. Students felt that time spent planning presentations for the Economic Opportunity Center during class time was
less productive. Students recognized and valued the need to cover
basic grammar and nutrition vocabulary. The class seemed to be very
well received and students found it to be a rewarding and valuable
experience.

Workers at the Economic Opportunity Center

A formal evaluation regarding the knowledge the workers acquired from the
student presentations in the form of a survey or questionnaire was not gathered. Obviously, it would have been very helpful, and an evaluation will be
done in the future. However, we received very positive feedback from the
workers as to the value of the information-sharing meetings and discussions.
Students were able to learn about the backgrounds of the workers—both of
their pasts in Mexico and of their current lives the United States—through
the open-ended questions, discussions, and group meetings. Students
learned to recognize and value traditional Mexican and Latino culture
through their interactions with the PDLC workers, and the workers appreciated learning about healthful food choices from the students.

Future Directions and Outcomes

Classroom

Enrollment in the Spanish for Nutritionists course has expanded from 2 students during the summer to 6 students for the fall quarter and 10 students
for the winter quarter. Two students who are advanced native speakers assist
by speaking Spanish one-on-one with six intermediate students. As the

instructor, I have worked with two entry-level students who are already bilingual in English and Vietnamese or Chinese and have a desire to become trilingual.

Community

Short-term benefits for the PDLC workers included learning about healthful food choices. Most important, however, the HNFS department at Cal Poly and the PDLC have been able to establish a long-term mutually supportive relationship that can be expanded in the future. Although the official 10-week service-learning course ended with Fall Quarter 2006, students remain committed to providing the PDLC workers with information and assistance in improving their nutritional health and quality of life. Long-term plans include exploring ways to improve the overall health of the day laborers, who often have little control over the type and amount of food purchased during periods of employment. The workers can also benefit from assistance in navigating the health care system to learn about disease prevention and health promotion.

The community partner with whom the students will be teaching nutrition in Spanish during Winter Quarter 2006 is the Senior Nutrition Program in Pomona. Topics for group presentations developed by students include healthful diets for seniors, assessment of seniors for nutritional risk and healthful diet, and exercise for prevention of diabetes. Students will also be conducting one-on-one nutritional assessments in Spanish with seniors.

This program can be replicated in the health care field in any area of specialization including nursing or medical schools. Dialogues can be copied and used to train students or can be customized to meet the needs of their specific community partner. This is a wonderful opportunity for students to learn from members of the community about culturally relevant health care and larger issues of disparities and inequality in health outcomes and access to resources. The program can lay a foundation for exploring a range of issues—from small ones, such as learning more about healthful food choices available from the food truck that passes by the PDLC two times a day, to larger issues of social justice that affect the nutrition decisions of day laborers. Through this program, students can investigate how the lack of personal funds and resources and the limitations of day labor employment (including the power of employers) affect workers' daily nutrition intake and their food choices each day. Students will discover that by working directly with the day laborers and local food servers they can make a difference.

Appendix 6.A

Course Syllabus: Spanish for Nutrition Majors

Spanish for Nutrition Majors
FN 499
Cal Poly Pomona Human Nutrition and Food Science Department
Winter 2006 Class: MW 10–10:50 a.m.
Instructor: Susan Algert, PhD, RD
Office phone: 869-5226   E-mail: salgert@csupomona.edu
Office hours: T 10:30–12 p.m.; WF 11–12 p.m.
Office: Bldg. 2-103

Course description: Students will increase proficiency in dialogues, vocabulary, and grammar related to nutrition counseling in Spanish.

Course objectives: After successfully completing this course, students will be able to:

1. Translate nutrition education materials from Spanish to English and vice versa.
2. Master 5 to 6 dialogues on conducting dietary interviews and nutrition counseling in Spanish.
3. Demonstrate an increased proficiency in vocabulary and key phrases related to nutrition counseling in Spanish.
4. Practice dietary interviews and/or counseling sessions with native Spanish speakers in a community setting.

Knowledge and skills:

1. Ability to translate health education materials from Spanish to English.
2. Ability to conduct a basic diet interview in Spanish.
3. Proficiency in food and nutrition vocabulary in Spanish.
4. Proficiency in key food and nutrition phrases in Spanish.
5. Ability to communicate food and nutrition issues to native Spanish speakers in a group setting.
6. Ability to communicate food and nutrition issues to native Spanish speakers one-on-one.

Readings/workbooks: HNFS Department workbook and dialogues.

Grading: Based on ability to meet goals established in individual learning plan.

Entry-level or new students: You will be assigned a topic to present to the seniors at the community center—probably either heart disease or diabetes treatment and prevention.

Week	Topic	Assignments
1	*Assessment*: vocabulary, key phrases, Basic grammar Write individual learning plan for quarter *Dialogue*: doctor's office visit	Complete assessment as homework; turn in by 1/6 Beginning or intermediate WIC manual
2	*Dialogue/vocab*: foods, diet interview *Dialogue/vocab*: diabetes or heart disease nutrition lesson	Tests, quizzes on diet interview and foods, grammar
3	*Dialogue*: continue practice of diet interviews; prepare presentation in Spanish for Senior Center *Dialogue/vocab*: diabetes or heart disease nutrition lesson	Test/quiz on food and diet interview vocab/key phrases, grammar Prepare presentation and handouts in Spanish
4	Presentation to fellow students (practice) and seniors in pairs *Dialogue/vocab*: reading a food label nutrition lesson	Self-evaluation and pre-post test for audience
5	*Dialogue*: nutritional assessment of adult, DETERMINE checklist	Practice vocab/key phrases and grammar
6	*Dialogue*: Counseling session for senior at nutritional risk	Practice vocab/key phrases and grammar
7	Practice diet interview and counseling sessions	Individual nutritional assessment of seniors at center
8	Practice diet interview and counseling sessions	Individual nutritional assessment of seniors at center
9	Practice and prepare for final presentations	Review dialogues and vocab
10	Presentation of nutritional assessment of senior to class	

Intermediate: Students will choose topic that they want to present at Senior Center; emphasis on small group practice during class time.

Advanced: Work with Mari Mendoza (via e-mail) on advanced nutrition vocab/grammar.

Week	Topic	Assignments
1	*Assessment*: vocabulary, key phrases, Basic grammar Write individual learning plan for quarter *Review dialogue*: doctor's office visit	Complete assessment as homework; turn in by 1/6 Workbook lessons Advanced WIC manual
2	*Dialogue/vocab*: diabetes or heart disease nutrition lesson; practice counseling session in class	Test or quiz on diabetes or heart disease; choose original topic for presentation
3	*Dialogues*: continue practice of diet interviews; prepare presentation in Spanish for Senior Center *Dialogue/vocab*: diabetes or heart disease nutrition lesson	Prepare for presentation at Senior Center with partner; develop handout
4	Presentation to fellow students (practice) and seniors in pairs *Dialogue/vocab*: reading a food label nutrition lesson	Self-evaluation and pre-post test for audience
5	*Dialogue*: nutritional assessment of adult, DETERMINE checklist	Practice vocab/key phrases and grammar
6	*Dialogue*: counseling session for senior at nutritional risk	Practice vocab/key phrases and grammar
7	Practice diet interview and counseling sessions	Individual nutritional assessment of seniors at center
8	Practice diet interview and counseling sessions	Individual nutritional assessment of seniors at center
9	Practice and prepare for final presentations	Review dialogues and vocab
10	Presentation of nutritional assessment of senior to class	

Appendix 6.B
Individual Learning Plan Form

FN 499 Winter 2005   Professor Algert
Name: ————————————   Date: —————————

Individual Learning Plan
Knowledge and Skills

1. Ability to translate health education materials from Spanish to English
    Current level (beginning, intermediate, advanced): —————————
    Plan for progress: ——————————————————————.
    Activities: ———————————————————————————

2. Ability to conduct a basic diet interview in Spanish
    Current level (beginning, intermediate, advanced): —————————
    Plan for progress: ——————————————————————
    Activities: ———————————————————————————

3. Proficiency in food and nutrition vocabulary in Spanish
    Current level (beginning, intermediate, advanced): —————————
    Plan for progress: ——————————————————————
    Activities: ———————————————————————————

4. Proficiency in key food and nutrition phrases in Spanish
    Current level (beginning, intermediate, advanced): —————————
    Plan for progress: ——————————————————————
    Activities: ———————————————————————————

5. Ability to communicate food and nutrition issues to native Spanish speakers in a group setting
    Current level (beginning, intermediate, advanced): —————————
    Plan for progress: ——————————————————————
    Activities: ———————————————————————————

6. Ability to communicate food and nutrition issues to native Spanish speakers one-on-one
    Current level (beginning, intermediate, advanced) —————————
    Plan for progress: ——————————————————————
    Activities: ———————————————————————————

Appendix 6.C

Summative Evaluation Form

CALIFORNIA STATE POLYTECHNIC UNIVERSITY, POMONA
HUMAN NUTRITION AND FOOD SCIENCE DEPARTMENT

KNOWLEDGE AND SKILL EVALUATION –

FN 499 Fall Quarter—Spanish for Nutritionists

Name: _____

Knowledge/Skill Statement	Extremely Comfortable	Moderately Comfortable	Somewhat Uncomfortable	Uncomfortable
Ability to translate health education materials from Spanish to English				
Ability to conduct a basic diet interview in Spanish				
Proficiency in food and nutrition vocabulary in Spanish				
Proficiency in key food and nutrition phrases in Spanish				
Ability to communicate food and nutrition issues to native Spanish speakers in a group setting				
Ability to communicate food and nutrition issues to native Spanish speakers one-on-one				

Note

1. A description of the model can be found at www.transculturalcare.net/ Cultural_Competence_Model.htm

References

Algert, S., & Brezezinski, E. (1998). *Mexican American food practices, customs and holidays*. Chicago: American Dietetic Association. One of a series of booklets describing ethnic and regional food practices developed by the American Diabetes/ American Dietetic Associations.

Anderson, L. M., Fielding, J. E., Fullilove, M., Scrimshaw, S. C., Carande-Kulis, V. G., & Task Force on Community Preventive Services. (2003). Methods for conducting systemic reviews of the evidence of effectiveness and economic efficiency of interventions to promote healthy social environments. *American Journal of Preventative Medicine, 24*(3S), 25–31.

Anderson, L. M., & Meyers, B. (2006). Improving access to culturally competent health care systems. Retrieved May 12, 2006, from Guide to Community Preventive Services Web site, http://www.thecommunityguide.org/social/soc-int-competent-system.pdf

Anderson, L. M., Scrimshaw, S. C., Fullilove, M. T., Fielding, J. E., et al. (2003). The Community Guide's model for linking the social environment to health. *American Journal of Preventative Medicine, 24*(3S), 12–20.

Campinha-Bacote, J. (1998). *The process of competence in the delivery of health care services: A culturally competent model of care*. Cincinnati: Transcultural CARE Associates.

Furco, A., & Billig, S. (Eds.). (2002). *Service-learning: The essence of the pedagogy*. Charlotte, NC: Information Age Publishing.

Hayes-Bautista, D. E., Hsu, P., Perez, A., & Kahramanian, M. I. *The Latino health landscape: California and Los Angeles*. University of California, Los Angeles Center for the Study of Latino Health and Culture.

Institute of Medicine (U.S.), Committee on Capitalizing Research on Social Science and Behavioral Research to Improve the Public's Health, Division of Health Promotion and Disease Prevention. (2001). *Promoting health: Intervention strategies from social and behavioral research*. Washington, DC: National Academy Press.

Lopez, A. (2003). California's use of English and other languages. Census 2000 summary, Center for Comparative Studies on Race and Ethnicity, Stanford University. Retrieved May 12, 2006 from http://ccsre.stanford.edu/reports/report_14.pdf.

Markides, K. S., & Eschbach, K. (2005). Aging, migration and mortality: Current status of research on the Hispanic paradox [Special issue II]. *Journals of Gerontology 60B*, 68–75.

Mutha, S., Allen, M. A., & Welch, M. (2002). *Toward culturally competent care: A toolbox for teaching communication strategies.* San Francisco: University of California, Center for Health Professions.

U.S. Census Bureau. (2004). *Fact sheet: California, 2004, American Community Survey data profile highlights.* Available from the U.S. Census Bureau at http://sss.census.gov/acs/www/index.html

SECTION THREE

SOCIAL POLICY
AND HOMELESSNESS

7

SOCIAL JUSTICE AND
PUBLIC POLICY

Roberta Ann Johnson and Robert C. Chope

Social justice means moving towards a society
where all hungry are fed, all sick are cared for,
the environment is treasured, and we treat each
other with love and compassion. Not an easy
goal, for sure, but certainly one worth giving our
lives for!
            —Medea Benjamin, cofounder Global
      Exchange and Code Pink (in Kikuchi, 2005)

P ublic policy classes are offered across the country at every major postsecondary educational institution. The vast majority of undergraduate courses provide an overview of what public policy is and what it
does along with a focused analysis of one or more specific policy areas such
as health care, civil rights, housing, or transportation. A plethora of textbooks are available for faculty to choose from in addressing any specific area
of policy.

Though social justice ideals are embraced by most educators, it is all too
often the case that when these courses are taught in a traditional classroom
setting, students are exposed to issues of inequity or injustice only as an ab-
straction, as idealized definitions along with supporting data. How can we
as educators develop in our students a fundamental belief in fairness, the
commitment to protecting those least able to protect themselves, the knowledge of the level of privilege that most of us possess and take for granted,
and the belief in equitable distribution of the vast resources of this wealthy

nation? And most important, how can we teach them both the role that public policy often plays in sustaining inequality and the skills and motivation to change the course of policy to build a better world?

We make the case here that the service-learning experience within a public policy course can have a profound impact on the development of students' sense of social justice in ways that are rarely obtained in courses without an experiential component. We will demonstrate how a service-learning experience can reinforce class lessons and engage students on a very personal level with social justice issues. Offering a service-learning component allows students to be exposed to the often oppressive conditions that many disenfranchised people face and develops in them a true understanding of the meaning of public policy to the health and welfare of the underprivileged.

The Traditional Public Policy Course

Social justice is not generally on the radar screen of most faculty preparing courses on public policy, and it is not a prominent issue in most public policy textbooks; however, there is, in fact, a wide variety of books on hand for different public policy classes. Available are dozens of environmental public policy books (Bryner, 1995; Switzer, 1994; Vig & Kraft, 1997), books specializing on aging and public policy (Rich & Baum, 1986), illegal drug policy (Sharp, 1994), gun control (Spitzer, 1995), and AIDS (Theodoulou, 1996). There are even public policy books on garbage (Melosi, 1981) and on the tobacco industry and smoking (Fritschler & Hoefler, 1996). There are also many books organized as collections of policy areas (Cochran et al., 1990; Cochran & Malone, 1995; Hird, 1995; Rushefsky, 1990).

Some frameworks for public policy courses can be especially intriguing. Among the more captivating themes explored are "time and public policy," where the author examines "the manner by which time impinges upon public policy . . ." and "values and public policy" (Smith, 1988, pp. 1, 2). Another author presents "ethical considerations underlying public controversies" (Mills, 1992, p. v). But the framework offered by most public policy classes (and books) is less exotic and fits into one of two categories: public policy analysis or public policy process.

Public policies can be analyzed in a prescriptive way, sometimes resulting in formal recommendations and public policy proposals (Heineman et al., 1997). Academics and practitioners analyze public policy in terms of causal stories (Stone, 1998), cost-benefit analyses, linear programming, queues, and measurable goals and trade-offs (Stokey & Zeckhauser, 1978).

Public policy can also be traced through the various stages of the policy process (Anderson, 1997; Lindblom, 1968). Although public policy books differ widely on this topic, their working definition of public policy process is almost always the same: "a historical series of intentions, actions, and behaviors of many participants" (Palumbo, 1994, p .8). All agree: the policy process is not stagnant. The process is seen as "a moving target."

In addition to the above, public policy process includes the following elements: it is a purposive course of action(s) (such as environmental protection, a Medicare drug plan, or the war on poverty), taken by appropriate government agencies (like the president, the courts, congress or a local police department), and it is designed to achieve specific goals or results (such as housing the homeless, cleaning the air, or reducing illegal drug use) (Anderson, 1997).

It is the rare textbook or college course that consistently emphasizes the social justice implications of public policy. The poor, the homeless, the welfare recipient, and the impoverished are indeed a focal point in some of the public policy textbooks (Bonser et al., 1996, pp. 162–190; Cochran et al., 1990, pp. 211–260; Rushefsky, 1990, pp. 129–158). But even here, social justice implications may not be entertained, or if they are they are usually raised in a substantive way only in isolated sections of the text.

Thus, we see that traditional public policy textbooks and courses do not incorporate, in a sustained way, the larger social justice themes articulated by social advocates like Medea Benjamin or social visionaries like Bill Drayton, the founder and chief executive of Ashoka, the organization responsible for coining the term *social entrepreneur*. If Benjamin's or Dayton's ideas are a part of a college course's discussion or readings, in most classes, they are simply one among many perspectives. In truth, in most public policy classes, the greater focus is on the neutral analytic precision of a policy and the impartial details of the public policy process.

Social Justice as the Course Theme

It is possible to make social justice the dominant theme of the class even while teaching with traditional materials. One can teach policy analysis and the details of the policy process in a way that lends itself to social justice insights. For example, if the class subject is public policy and welfare, poverty, or the homeless, where so much of the data reflects deprivation, suffering, inadequate social programs, and unequal treatment, the social justice concerns may emerge effortlessly. Then it is the job of the instructor to give coherence to these concerns and lead students to understand their larger implications.

This can be accomplished by having students evaluate the creation and impact of public policy within the framework of primary values delineated by Prilleltensky (1997), values that promote social justice. These include caring and compassion, self-determination, human diversity, collaboration and democratic participation, and distributive justice. In examining institutions in which they serve or work, students should ask the following questions:

1. Are the institutions established or influenced by public policy that is caring and compassionate?
2. Do policies create roadblocks that prevent citizens from self-determination?
3. Is there a universal respect for human diversity that allows individual citizens opportunities to create their own personal maneuverability?
4. Are there veritable collaboration and democratic participation, such that those who receive services on the basis of public policies do not have their personal rights violated?
5. And finally, with regard to distributive justice, is there evidence that public policies ensure that there are plenty of resources available to enact the programs that they promote to enable citizens a greater degree of self determination?

The challenges are a little greater, but the same is true for other courses on public policy such as public policy courses on the environment, on aging, or on illegal drugs. Unequal distribution and unequal treatment can be developed as course themes in these and in other public policy classes. Faculty are always free to address moral implications while using classical texts. This is the case in the public policy class discussed below.

Teaching Public Policy and Social Justice

The class that we describe in this chapter is a University of San Francisco (USF) public policy class whose focus is on homelessness. The class is a regularly scheduled upper-division class with required readings, lectures, class discussions, and group projects. As a part of the class requirements, students are assigned to work in community organizations as interns for a minimum of two hours per week over a period of 12 weeks.

The syllabus, divided into distinct sections, is designed to turn the students into public policy specialists. Topics involving the policy process require that the class examine the sudden emergence of homelessness onto the public agenda, its historic context, the political debate over solutions, and the many public and private responses to the problem. Topics engaging the class in an analysis of the homeless problem enable the class to explore how homelessness has been defined, how the homeless have been counted, how the problem has been analyzed in terms of "causes," and how policies have been evaluated in terms of their success.

The assigned readings for this course were selected to familiarize the students with a wide variety of literature written by advocates, bureaucrats, journalists, historians, sociologists, political scientists, economists, and even architects. Within each topic, social justice implications arise and are discussed; this is illustrated in the following brief description of one seemingly straightforward topic, "counting the homeless."

Public policy analysis depends on data. For the section on "counting the homeless," students read two assignments: chapter 3 in Peter Rossi's *Down and Out in America* (1989), and chapter 2 in Christopher Jencks's *The Homeless* (1994). The readings explain social science "best practice" techniques for surveying large numbers of hard–to-reach people, but the readings also capture the political nature of the count.

In this section of the course, students see how most attempts to count the homeless population are doomed to undercount them. Many homeless are invisible because they are hidden, because they are in dangerous places where surveyors do not go, or because they do not *look* homeless. The homeless are also undercounted because the surveys are usually organized as a "one-night count" rather than a survey conducted over a period of time. A "one-night count" drastically underrepresents the large population of episodic homeless.

Students learn more than just survey techniques and sample designs. They soon see how counting the homeless is far from a neutral process. Because money and services are always at stake, the fight over numbers has significant consequences. When students study how the homeless have been counted and undercounted, they soon understand how the powerful have exerted influence on the process, and they are alerted to many social justice implications.

Faculty who teach a public policy class on the homeless have to be creative in order to make the problem real as opposed to a mere academic exercise. Along with tracing the policy process and analyzing the policy arguments, the students need to learn to scrutinize the policy players who are making the arguments. The students must learn to ask not only, "how will public policy solve the homeless problem?" but also, "how might past public policy have contributed to the problem in the first place?" The class needs to be able to assess public policy in terms of who benefits and who does not. This creates a healthy suspicion about policy players and can directly lead to social justice implications. The framework described below that can be used to envelop this kind of questioning is called *social constructions*.

We can guide students to more automatically address social justice issues if we include in our policy analysis a framework to understand the social construction of players. Anne Schneider and Helen Ingram's book, *Policy Design for Democracy* (1997) presents the social construction paradigm. "Social constructions" are perceptions we have of "target groups." The target groups of public policy are the groups affected by public policy that can benefit or be hurt. The target groups can have varying degrees of political power and also experience varying degrees of social inclusion. Their social inclusion can be displayed with four distinct categories: advantaged, contenders, dependents, and deviants.

The "advantaged" groups have political power and are seen as deserving. They are likely to be beneficiaries of public policy. The "contenders" have some political power but are viewed as less deserving. "Dependents" may deserve and be treated sympathetically, but they have less political power to make demands on the policy system. "Deviants" lack social inclusion and political power. In fact, they are likely to be hurt by public policy.

Schneider and Ingram use these four categories to demonstrate that the U.S. public policy process is currently being crafted in a way that widens the chasm between the advantaged and the other categories. By consistently and systematically looking at who is getting what from public policy, students can begin to generalize in a methodical way about the patterns of exclusion. Thus, all at once, we have temporally removed the morally neutral stance that is typically taken in a public policy class.

These categories can so easily be applied in a public policy class on the homeless. The homeless fit the category of deviant; the well-off are advantaged, and the well-off are much more likely to be beneficiaries of public policy. This is demonstrated in the many books and articles available that describe the recent history of housing policy. For example, Cushing N. Dolbeare's short chapter, "Housing Policy: A General Consideration," describes the decades of generous public policy toward the housing needs of the rich and middle class and the neglect of the poor and less well-off (in Baumohl, 1996, pp. 34–45). Another example is Jennifer Wolch and Michael Dear's introductory chapter in *Malign Neglect* (1993). The chapter outlines a list of economic and welfare-restructuring policies produced during the last decades that benefited the rich, ignored the needs of the poor, and contributed to the growing number of homeless. But, however insightful and value laden the academic exploration in the classroom is, it may all still seem quite theoretical. The students learn how some people are consistently excluded from receiving much-needed benefits. Now, the challenge is to get the students to care about the excluded groups.

With experiential learning, and with appropriate community groups, students can personally get to know the human targets of public policy espoused by Schneider and Ingram (1997). They will know if the community members were helped or hurt, heard or ignored. Students will come to know firsthand about the human impact of public policy through community internships and service learning.

Teaching About the Homeless

A public policy course on the homeless is a perfect vehicle for teaching about social justice. The topic allows students to understand how the homelessness problem can be seen as a direct result of decades of public policies that ignored the poor. Among these past policies were those in housing, welfare, taxes, minimum wages, mental illness, and illegal drugs, among others.

By using the social construction paradigm (who received what and why) as a tool for connecting to this range of past public policies, students are able to see an emerging pattern in policy outcomes that have led to a crisis in homelessness. The well-off, not the needy, are the major beneficiaries of economic policy. For example, policies have provided low-interest loans and mortgage tax deductions for the middle class and the rich in contrast to inadequately funding policies to create a social net for the poor, the ill, and the disabled. Homelessness in America can be seen as a by-product of these and many other past and current public policy decisions.

While the students are learning these academic lessons, they are also out in the field experiencing the social and economic impact of public policy. The homeless policy arena is rich with internship and service-learning opportunities. The learning objective for the internship experience is that students appreciate the human consequences of public policy. In fact, in the study of homeless public policy, the goal is for students to be so fully engaged with the homeless community that the homeless will have a conceptual presence in all their discussions. It would be impossible to participate in an abstract discussion of agenda setting and tactics, or to engage in a policy calculation based only on efficiency and cost-effectiveness when discussing public policy toward the homeless. Instead, what naturally emerges for the students are discussions of public policy that include and are directly linked to human consequences.

Class lessons, no matter how engaging, never seem to be as effective as student internship experiences for raising social justice issues. Based on the results of student surveys, all students in the USF homelessness class say they were personally affected by their internship experiences. But more important, based on open-ended answers to the class-administered surveys, they were affected in unexpected ways. According to their own testimony, what students got out of the internship experience is different from what they *thought* they would get out of it.

In the spring semester of 2005, 15 students enrolled in the homelessness class. They were surveyed in January during the first week of classes and surveyed in May during the last week of classes. During the first week, just after they selected and contacted their prospective agencies, they were asked to describe the accomplishments or impact they hoped to have from working in their agency assignments. The agencies varied.

Students chose their placements from a faculty-prepared list with contact names and numbers provided. They selected from among local public and nonprofit agencies. The list included Shelter Plus Care, a city agency that evaluates and places homeless people into transitional housing; the McKinney Grant Project, which monitors federally funded programs and directly assists homeless people; and nonprofit service providers like Tenderloin

Housing Clinic, which directly assists the homeless, and the Episcopal Community Services, offering a range of services including a homeless senior center and a skills center. Shelters for women and children where students could work included Hamilton Family Shelter, St. Anthony's, and the Marianne Women's Shelter. These shelters offered opportunities to prepare and serve food. Students could also choose to work with advocacy groups, such as the Coalition on Homelessness, where they could participate in organizing and in outreach or at Home Base, a public interest law and policy center, where they could be involved with surveys and research projects.

On the first class survey, administered during the first week, the goals the students listed most often for what they hoped to get out of the experience were particular skills and information they wanted and specific knowledge of the workings of their agency or organization that they hoped to learn.

At the end of the semester, the descriptions of what they got out of the internship were quite different. What they said they valued most was the personal connection with homeless people. They wrote about connecting with the homeless, "understanding the homeless," and "firsthand experience" because of "speaking with the homeless." They wrote about an empathy "for those who do not have food" and about "heartwarming relationships and friendships" with homeless children.

The students measured the importance of their work not by skills, knowledge, and reports they produced; the value of the internship for them was in the human connection with the homeless it afforded them. When the homeless had a face, a name, a story, it changed the way the students studied and understood public policy.

About the Public Policy Homeless Course

There are homeless people living on the streets of San Francisco and on the streets of almost all American cities. We can see them. They grew in numbers as the United States grew wealthier during the "dot-com boom" of the 1990s. Their numbers continue to grow. This begs two questions: (1) Why are so many people homeless? and (2) Why have government programs failed to adequately address the problem? In the process of answering these questions, we got to know the stories of homeless teens, Vietnam veterans, the mentally ill, homeless families, and many more people who were strangers to us.

Class Visits

The class, as a group, visited a neighborhood advocacy group, an adult homeless shelter, a family shelter, and two single-resident-occupancy hotels (SROs). All visits were conducted during class time.

Service Learning

As part of this class experience, students were required to work with an agency in the community for a total of 24 hours (an average of 2 hours per week for 12 weeks). Students chose their organization from a list provided that included a description of the organizations, contact names, and contact numbers. Students followed a journal guide provided to help them prepare their journal entries describing their community experiences.

Learning Outcomes for the Public Policy Homeless Class

The goals for the traditional classroom part of the course were achieved. The outcomes were measured by exams, student projects, a final paper, and the content of their classroom contributions. By the end of the semester, the students were able to compare for accuracy sampling techniques used to count the number of homeless; organize descriptive data (including statistical material and interviews) to understand the many subsets of the homeless population such as the mentally ill, substance abusers, members of minority groups, families with children, and so on; understand how factors such as race, poverty, gentrification, globalization, deindustrialization, deinstitutionalization, housing policy, and inadequate welfare policy have contributed to homelessness; and evaluate different government programs as to their ability to address the problem of homelessness.

The outcome for the service-learning component of the course was more than achieved. As already described, the human connection with homeless people informed the students' understanding in all of the classroom discussions and exercises.

Conclusion

As we have demonstrated, public policy classes can be used to raise important social justice issues in a focused and methodical way. In addition, public policy classes that include an internship and service-learning component allow for exposure to real people with real problems. Internships also expose students to the institutions that are designed to provide a better life for the citizenry. These out-of-the-classroom experiences enable students to decide for themselves whether public policies and the institutions that implement them are leading to a more promising set of life circumstances.

Students ought to leave their service-learning or internship experience with the belief that, through social justice advocacy, public policy can be improved and political and social institutions changed for the better.

References

Anderson, J. E. (1997). *Public policymaking, an introduction.* Boston: Houghton Mifflin.

Baumohl, J. (Ed.). (1996). *Homelessness in America.* Phoenix: The Oryx Press.

Bonser, C. F., McGregor, E. B., & Oster, C. V. (1996). Policy choices and public action. Upper Saddle River, NJ: Prentice Hall.

Bryner, G. C. (1995). *Blue skies, green politics.* Washington, DC: Congressional Quarterly.

Cochran, C. E., Mayer, L. C., Carr, T. R., & Cayer, N. J. (1990). *American public policy: An introduction.* New York: St. Martin's Press.

Cochran, C. L., & Malone, E. F. (1995). *Public policy perspectives and choices.* New York: McGraw-Hill.

Fritschler, A. L., & Hoefler, J. M. (1996). *Smoking and politics: Policy making and the federal bureaucracy.* Upper Saddle River, NJ: Prentice Hall.

Heineman, R. A., Bluhm, W. T., Peterson, S. A., & Kearny, E. N. (1997). *The world of the policy analyst.* Chatham, NJ: Chatham House [acquired by CQ Press in November 2003].

Hird, J. A. (1995). *Controversies in American public policy.* New York: St. Martin's Press.

Jencks, C. (1994). *The homeless.* Cambridge, MA: Harvard University Press.

Kikuchi, D. (2005, October 26). *What is social justice? A collection of definitions.* Retrieved from Read and Teach Web site, http://www.reachandteach.com

Lindblom, C.E. (1968). *The policy-making process.* Englewood Cliffs, NJ: Prentice Hall.

Melosi, M. V. (1981). *Garbage in the cities: Refuse, reform and the environment 1880–1980.* Chicago: The Dorsey Press.

Mills, C. (1992). *Values and public policy.* Fort Worth, TX: Harcourt Brace Jovanovich College Publishers.

Palumbo, D. J. (1994). *Public policy in America: Government in action.* Fort Worth, TX: Harcourt Brace.

Prilleltensky, I. (1997). Values, assumptions, and practices: Assessing the moral implications of psychological discourse and action. *American Psychologist, 52,* 517–535.

Rich, B. M, & Baum, M. (1986). *The aging: A guide to public policy.* Pittsburgh: University of Pittsburgh Press.

Rossi, P. H. (1989). *Down and out in America: The origins of homelessness.* Chicago: University of Chicago Press.

Rushefsky, M. E. (1990). *Public policy in the United States: Toward the twenty-first century.* Pacific Grove, CA: Brooks/Cole.

Schneider, A. L., & Ingram, H. M. (1997). *Policy design for democracy.* Lawrence: University Press of Kansas.

Sharp, E. B. (1994). *The dilemma of drug policy in the United States.* New York: Harper Collins College.

Smith, T. A. (1988). *Time and public policy.* Knoxville: The University of Tennessee Press.

Spitzer, R. J. (1995). *The politics of gun control.* Chatham, NJ: Chatham House [acquired by CQ Press in November 2003].

Stokey, E., & Zeckhauser, R. (1978). *A primer for policy analysis.* New York: W.W. Norton.

Stone, D. A. (1988). *Policy paradox and political reason.* Glenview, IL: Scott, Foresman.

Switzer, V. S. (1994). *Environmental politics: Domestic and global dimensions.* New York: St. Martin's Press.

Theodoulou, S. Z. (1996). *Aids: The politics and policy of disease.* Upper Saddle River, NJ: Prentice Hall.

Vig, N. J., & Kraft, M. E. (1997). *Environmental policy in the 1990s.* Washington, DC: Congressional Quarterly.

Wolch, J., & Dear, M. (1993). *Malign neglect: Homelessness in an American city.* San Francisco: Jossey-Bass.

8

SOCIAL RESPONSIBILITY BY DESIGN

Interior Design, Graphic Design, and Photography
Students' Close Encounter with Homelessness

Jill Pable

Some homeless people report that they find
themselves staring at people's keys, a poignant
reminder of the extent of their own loss, since
they no longer have the things that require keys:
a home, a car and an office.

—Sam Davis, *Designing for the Homeless:
Architecture That Works* (2004a, p. 18)

I n developing an effective design for any community, an intimate relationship must be established between the designer and the client. The
designer must understand the functional aspects of the environment
from the perspective of those who use it and must choose an aesthetic with
this in mind. This is how designers treat all other clients; why should the
homeless and disenfranchised be treated differently?

This chapter will describe a service-learning project that sought to
heighten students' awareness and empathy about homelessness while immer-
sing them in several different areas of design: the architectural renovation of
a homeless shelter, creation of the shelter's graphic communication system,
and recording the photo-based personal stories of the homeless clients that
reside there. Students of interior design, graphic design, and photography

each investigated the nature of homelessness from their distinct point of view. These individual efforts coalesced into a unified project for the purpose of proposing a tangible contribution to the project's client, the homeless shelter. As I am the faculty member representing the interior design contribution, the project will be described primarily from this point of view.

The design profession per se encompasses many fields, such as interior design, architecture, graphic design, and product design. Most people are aware of well-designed interior spaces such as elite restaurants and hotels, but the most recent decade has witnessed the rising ubiquity of "democratic" design and its potential to enhance the comfort, convenience, and aesthetics of persons of all means. Fueled by the lengthy and prosperous period of the nineties, this current serendipitous crossroad of technology, prosperity, and cultural awareness has led in part to the new "golden age" of design (Gibney & Luscombe, 2000). Thus, on the whimsical end of this idea, Michael Graves designer toilet brushes can be had at Target stores by all, and on the potential-filled side of things, there is opportunity to design psychologically healing environments for those less fortunate. Design students may be uniquely positioned to explore the application of democratic design because their learning experiences allow time for necessary research. The project described within this chapter sought to provide such a democratic learning experience for students. The students' efforts also proved to be of unanticipated and significant, tangible benefit to the shelter community partner. Through their ability to analyze existing problems and generate innovative drawings, models, and graphic design solutions, the students likely helped prompt renewed thinking on the part of the shelter's capital facilities committee. In a closing thank-you letter to faculty, the shelter's administrator reported that the students' efforts prompted renewed and invigorated interest in the committee to explore upgrades to the shelter's facilities. Coincidental with review of the students' work, the capital facilities committee chose to boost the building fund-raising target from 1 to 5 million dollars.

Such an outcome was not anticipated as project planning got under way. As a new assistant professor in the Department of Design assigned to facilitate the interior design students' final senior design project, I found myself looking for ways to bring meaning and relevancy to their experience. I questioned the often-used, mundane imaginary clients and a given set of instructions.[1] I was motivated to seek out a "real" client for them to interact with, to get their hands dirty with the squishiness of real life, and get them engaged with tangible challenges. Moreover, I wanted them to see the actual implications of their lines drawn on paper and realize that their decisions in interior-place making have consequences for real people. While it was naturally unlikely that the students' paper designs would actually be built, the effort nonetheless seemed worthwhile.

I was not alone in my interest in trying a new approach, and two faculty department colleagues, Gwen Amos in graphic design and Johanna Latty in photography, were coaxed into coming along as well. Our university's office of service learning fortuitously found a recipient of our efforts in the Salvation Army Transitional Shelter of Sacramento. Admittedly, it was not until this point that it fully dawned on me that the students' experience in this setting, in addition to its advantage of "realness," would be even further enhanced by their interaction with a community issue. Homelessness became the project's pervasive unifier, plus considerably more, as will be described below.

Social Justice and Homelessness

As I began looking into the homelessness issue in my project preparations, it became clear that, among issues of social justice, homelessness is likely among the most persistent and enduring of societal ills. In December of 2005, the United States Conference of Mayors representing 24 American cities released their yearly survey of the status of hunger and homelessness. They have done so since 1982. Among its findings and projections for 2006:

- There was a 12 percent average increase in food requests in 2005 over the previous year, and 18 percent of emergency food requests for families went unmet in 2005.
- 32 percent of requests for shelter by families were unmet in 2005.
- The average length of time people are homeless increased in 2005 to seven months.
- Lack of affordable housing is the leading cause of homelessness, not substance abuse or criminality.
- More than 85 percent of the 24 polled cities expect requests for emergency food and shelter to increase in 2006.

Such statistics bear out disturbing trends in the evaporation of government support for housing and a shift in the demographics of who in the United States are finding themselves homeless and why. Sacramento, California, is not exempt from the presence of a homeless population, and as the focus of our service-learning project, the Salvation Army's Transitional Shelter was geographically well placed to do what it could to confront this problem. Located on the industrial side of town, the shelter was housed in a converted office building. While the shelter's many programs have helped numerous people to a more positive, stable life, the facility in its current physical condition seemed at times to work against these positive activities. Though well maintained, the building presented an interior environment largely devoid of interest, with glare-filled lighting, check-in areas with dirt floors, storage rooms prone to flooding, and generally tired surfaces, fixtures, and equipment. The reception room, while serviceable, presented a sterile and psychologically forbidding introduction to the shelter. As the students' background research came to suggest, the current facility was far removed from its potential as "a means of establishing trust between the provider and the homeless" and "a way to create a sense of belonging for those with little or no social connection" (Davis, 2004b).

Among the challenges the shelter faced was an expanding population of homeless who were sometimes turned away due to lack of space. While newly funded programs successfully installed more beds at the facility, a recently established interim care program brought persons recently discharged from hospitals who had nowhere else to recover into the shelter. This somewhat shifted the shelter's focus of care and broadened its scope of services. It was into this situation that the service-learning project was initiated.

Project Development and Preplanning

As faculty planning progressed for the project, goals for student learning oftentimes meshed well with the needs of the project client. For example, a growing body of information exists within the architectural design sciences that identify aspects of interior environments that promote psychological and physiological healing.[2] It was decided that such research would be a cornerstone of the interior design students' work so that the resulting redesigns would benefit from these insights.

Similarly, communication graphics held great potential for making a contribution to the project. In particular, environmental graphics' ability to heighten social interchange is crucial in the case of a transient population that requires orientation to a new facility. Signage, way finding, and messaging become paramount to a traumatized person's comfort and orientation within a new environment. The graphic students' efforts were focused toward this end.

In a somewhat different fashion, photography proved to be a powerful and emotional tool through its ability to examine and communicate states of the human condition to others. Exemplar photo essay collections in the past have effectively brought social justice issues into strong relief.[3] Thus, the photography students would embark on an effort to chronicle the life stories of those they encountered at the shelter.

Faculty recognized that in order for the project to be successful for students, it would have to integrate effectively into their current understanding of their respective design fields. For example, the senior interior design students came to the project with a great deal of practical content already under their belts in such areas as building codes, space planning, finish, and furnishing selection. However, their deficiencies were threefold: they lacked

- an awareness of the theoretical underpinnings of this content;
- the skills to properly apply this fact base to an actual human population; and
- the understanding and empathy for persons unlike themselves that is a necessary framework for good design decision making.

By nature of the project, a personal and even phenomenological strategy emerged for the project. Through interview, observation, and other means, we decided the students would wrestle with an emergent set of design goals rather than being spoon-fed a predetermined set of rules. Thus, students would be exposed to how design really gets accomplished with all the dynamic untidiness inherent in real design. Pedagogically speaking, such a project strategy would make us as faculty confront how and when to call a halt to the various project phases and how to deal with issues such as conflicting information and the dilemma of the design "moving target" that presents itself when clients change their minds.

Student learning goals emerged during final preplanning preparation, as this example from the interior design project details:

1. Students will demonstrate empathetic thinking with regard to design decisions stemming from knowledge of homeless persons' perceptions about and use of interior space.
2. Students will demonstrate social responsibility within the context of their professional skills by applying their knowledge for the benefit of the community.
3. Through study of those lacking shelter, students will recognize, explain, and justify through the design solution and its verbal defense that interior space has causative ramifications for humans' well-being.[4]
4. Students will incorporate the ideas of graphic design and photography into their own expressions to realize design solutions enriched with multiple points of view.[5]

Project Procedure

In all three study areas, the students engaged in the project were of senior status and capable of intermediate to advanced class work. Many were working to put themselves through school. Ages ranged from the traditional 18 or 19 to early forties in the case of career-change students. I placed the interior design students in teams of three, as much of professional commercial design work is undertaken in a team environment, and group decision making is a crucial skill. Coming at the end of their four-year degree, the summative commercial project for the interior design students is always a daunting one, and represents a substantial part of their graduating portfolio. Fifteen weeks in length, the project is characteristically a large-scope undertaking of at least 10,000 square feet of interior architectural space over multiple levels. With this semester's addition of an actual client with a real building, the project scope blossomed to 42,000 feet of inside and outside square footage, over three levels in two connecting structures. Students were understandably nervous about this undertaking, but no less so at the prospect of multiple field trips to an actual homeless shelter and working with students in the other design professions. In-class discussions and a policies and procedures document providing details (an excerpt of which is shown in Appendix 8.A) helped to bring structure and dispel uneasiness.

The course syllabus provided students with information on expectations and tentative schedules of the many related field trips and events (see Appendix 8.B for the syllabus). Because many students knew little about the issue of homelessness, background research on the issue became the obvious first task. A video that interviewed previously homeless persons was shown in class, and a homelessness quiz developed by the Loaves and Fishes organization was used to dispel inaccuracies and present factual evidence. Students' answers to a reflection exercise directly afterward suggested some were surprised to hear that homelessness is not always the result of personal irresponsibility, and that homeless persons increasingly include families, single women, children, and the elderly in addition to single males. Some students were themselves all too familiar with the issue, and one student privately confided to me that she herself had previously been homeless for six months, sleeping in her car. Another revealed that her father was currently absent and presumed homeless. Through class discussion, I sensed the issue was beginning to make a personal connection to a number of the students.

The Project Phases

One of the key concepts design students must grasp and apply in their professional careers is a strategy for creating effective design solutions. Typically called the design process, this procedure employs "a sequence of unique actions leading to the realization of some aim or intention" (Koberg & Bagnall, 1991, p. 10). By following such a procedure, one can evolve thorough background research into alternative draft solutions, then filter and narrow down these possibilities through multiple revisions to reach an effective final design. This service-learning project applied four of this process's six phases to reinforce this crucial procedure with the interior design and graphic design students:

1. Research: Gathering information relevant to client needs, the site, budget, and time schedule
2. Programming: Initial processing of the research into an organized response
3. Concept Design: Development of multiple possible solutions in rough form
4. Design Development: Refinement and client presentation of the strongest solution

Research

The first phase involved the students in a series of immersive activities designed to help them understand the nature of the clients' needs, the building's opportunities and limitations, and the content of scholarly research regarding homeless shelter design. As appropriate, all three student groups were involved to build a sense of collaboration. A variety of activities engaged the students in these efforts:

- *In-depth research* on a topic, such as the Salvation Army organization, lighting, defensible space, furnishings durability, and color and psychology. Interior design students divided up these topics, verbally presented their findings, and contributed to a final collaborative research document.
- *Guest lecture* by UC Berkeley architect Sam Davis, author of *Designing for the Homeless: Architecture That Works* (2004a). The students organized a show in the department's gallery designed to inform attendees about the statistics of homelessness in the Sacramento region. Among the student presentations was a full-size mockup showing the square footage of personal space allotted to a homeless client in a shelter (typically a bunk bed and a locker) and an actual shopping cart and contents as might be used by a homeless person in an urban setting.[6]
- *A field trip to homeless shelters in San Francisco.* This was probably among the most impactful of the introductory activities, through both the good and the deplorably bad conditions that we witnessed. To middle- to upper-income students, images such as large bowls of free condoms and signs stating "No spitting on the walls" proved to be both a culture shock and necessary introduction to the issue at hand.[7]
- *Multiple trips to the Salvation Army Transitional Shelter* to engage in different fact-gathering tasks:
  a. On-site measurement and photography of rooms, ceiling heights, lighting placement, and other details.
  b. One-on-one interviews with staff and homeless clients. This proved to be a huge learning step for many of the students. The shelter staff arranged to have a number of homeless clients available on our day at the shelter. After much prompting on my part, I finally convinced each student to introduce him- or herself and sit down to have a one-on-one lunchroom conversation. Students were generally surprised to find the clients more

than willing to talk about their situation and feelings about being in the shelter. While this activity was probably of limited value in decision making for space planning, the encounters were profound in their effect of making the project real to the students.

c. Group interviews with homeless clients and the students. This tactic proved less successful than the one-on-one interviews, though not for the reason I anticipated. I was initially concerned that in a group setting it would be difficult to prompt a dialogue about potentially sensitive subjects such as "how does dormitory life make you feel?" I quickly learned that posing an open-ended question such as this prompted much discussion, but the interviewees were prone to quickly drift into minutiae, such as a prolonged debate over what time the lights were turned off the previous evening.[8]

These various fact-gathering activities culminated in the students' group collaboration on a background-research book they presented to the Salvation Army.

Programming

The considerable amount of gathered research data was then massaged into a multipage "criteria matrix" by the students (see Appendix 8.C). This information-organization tool began a process of migrating verbal, text, and image information into a workable document used to guide later design decision making.

Students broke up this task into equal sections, sharing sections of it via e-mail and assembling it into a single Excel spreadsheet. Again, this document was shared with the Salvation Army staff for feedback and correction. In retrospect, I believe it was at this point that the Salvation Army staff began to see the depth of critical thinking the students were capable of, and they began considering how the students' skills might further the organizations' goals beyond the bounds of this project.

Schematic Design

In reaction to the criteria matrix and the wealth of research information gathered in the first phases, the schematic design phase represented the "first pass" at a graphic-style design solution. This phase involved an intense back-and-forth dialogue among the interior design student teams and me and represented the "heavy lifting" of problem solving, including code-compliant exits, fire walls, and space psychology such as corridor widths and circulation. Given the large project scope, student team members typically broke up the work into one student per floor. While this managed the workload, this also resulted in a design often fractured along building levels and required much discussion and alteration to evolve the design solutions into a coherent whole.

The schematic design phase resulted in preliminary perspective drawings of key areas within the facility: "bubble diagrams," plan views, and building sections, among other elements. These early ideas were shared not only with me but also with the student teams' interior design mentor, a local commercial interior designer who volunteered time to offer advice and guidance to a specific student team. A significant part of the project grade stemmed from this phase so that students knew the status of their progress as the project progressed.

The graphic design students similarly wrestled with their design solutions for a messaging system within the shelter. "Growth" became the watchword signifying homeless persons' escape from the street and was explored by the graphic students in the organic lines and shapes of a tree leaf.

Photography students were deeply engaged in weekly interviews and photography sessions of willing homeless persons arranged by the shelter staff, plus photography of the shelter itself and the interior design students' activities in the project.

Design Development

The semesterlong project culminated in the final design development phase. For both interior design and graphic design students, this part of the project essentially involved selection and refinement of the strongest of the schematic design ideas into a client-presentable solution. For interior design, this meant three-dimensional models of the building, color-rendered perspective drawings and plan views, plus further "deliverables" such as construction drawings of custom seating units and other details (refer to Appendix 8.D).

Graphic design students enriched their strongest ideas of the leaf concept, and then developed them into full-wall panels that engaged the stories and photos of the homeless generated by the photography students. In turn, some of the interior design teams successfully integrated these panels into the interior renovations for the waiting room or corridors of the Transitional Shelter. Pedagogically speaking, this movement of designed works from one student group to the next proved to be among the most challenging of the project's aspects for faculty. This was due in part to scheduling, as it takes time for each student group to develop their strongest ideas. These ideas then may or may not be passed on to the next student group in time for them to appropriately incorporate them into the larger design. As a result, only a small number of the interior design student teams incorporated the graphic wall panels effectively.

The project grand finale was the students' verbal on-site presentations of their solutions to the Salvation Army staff, homeless persons, university administrators, and their interior design mentors. Due to the project's scope this was a fairly elaborate event, as each interior design student team produced at least 10 large presentation boards. The students' verbal presentations were videotaped for their later review.

Each student team also presented recommendations for spending $50,000 toward facilities improvements at the shelter, a figure that, while certainly not sufficient to see through their re-visioning plans, represents a typical grant the organization often obtains. This aspect of the project acquainted students with the cost realities of such items as bed mattresses, replacement lighting fixtures and computers for clients' business training, and other items the student team deemed most immediately crucial to the shelter.

The student commitment to the project was palpable during the verbal presentations, and was likely heightened by the presence of the shelter staff and homeless persons, whom the students had grown to know through their repeated visits. I noted this was a significant change from previous projects, in which the client had been imaginary and I as the instructor served as the "client." One student in particular grew emotional as she described a stylized tree and pond for the shelter's garden that symbolized the drawing of strength from a healing source. Graphic design student solutions were also on hand, and the photography students' images and text stories gathered from the homeless clients were uniquely displayed on laundry rope lines temporarily strung across the shelter's day lounge.

Project Assessment and Reflection Components

Given the various dimensions of the project, I concluded that a multimodal final assessment approach would acknowledge its complexity. Some aspects of the final assessment for the interior design component are as follows:

- The final phase assessment represented 50 percent of the project grade, with the other half of credit tied to the student's performance in the research, programming, and schematic design phases. This is because it was crucial both that students understood their work's strong and weak points as this long-term project moved along and that they consistently made progress on its many requirements.
- The verbal presentation represented a small but significant part of the final phase assessment. In the design fields it is crucial not only to devise an appropriately functional and aesthetic solution but also to express its character in a professional, effective manner. Doing so maximizes the chance that the project will be understood and embraced by the client.
- Five percent of the final grade was based on students' evaluations of each other's team commitment and sharing of responsibilities (see Appendix 8.E). This requirement was announced from the outset of the project. I was the final arbiter of the grade resulting from this component, and sometimes I was forced to make judgment calls based on the reported comments of the team members.[9]

It was important to gauge the students' reaction to the project, especially with regard to its service-learning character. An anonymous final-reflection written assignment provided a window into how the interior design students viewed various project aspects. On the nature of having real clients with real issues and an actual building:

> "It made the project mean something, not just a grade or portfolio piece."
> "It made me want to try harder to please and impress them . . ."
> "I was designing for someone else and that pushed me more."

On the opportunity to interview shelter staff and homeless persons:

"[The project provided the] chance to build personal relationships."
"It proved stereotypes false, which helped a lot!"
"Their excitement about all of our ideas made all the work involved seem worth it."

On the field trip to homeless shelters in San Francisco:

"An experience like that, what you take away is priceless. I have never seen the experiences of a homeless community up front and personal."
"[Shelters] aren't as scary as I thought they'd be."

On the project as a whole:

"I learned a lot about humanity."
"My research has been an incredibly humbling experience."

Perhaps most telling, some students' attitudes regarding the issue of homelessness appeared to evolve over the course of the project:

"Previous to this semester I accredited homelessness to carelessness and laziness."
"I learned there are homeless people who really work hard to get their natural life back."
"I used to think that homelessness was the fault of the person. Now I realize that that is not always the case."
"I now have a greater understanding of the struggles and hardship many go through."

Of course, not all students expressed new insight or an attitude change stemming from the project, and some asserted that their feelings about the causes of homelessness had been accurate from the start. However, it was interesting to note the students' growing ability to confront the issue with self-confidence. Early visits to the shelter were marked by students clinging to each other in tight-knit groups as they moved amongst the rooms to document and photograph the building. As the semester progressed and the students grew to know the shelter staff and some of the homeless clients, this tension visibly eased. By the project's end (and contrary to my direct instructions), some students returned to the shelter on their own to obtain a last measurement or photograph.

Spin-Offs

The conclusion of the semester project brought a sense of accomplishment to our relationship with the Salvation Army organization. During the next semester, I engaged the interior design senior students in the project again, and the photography students continued their development of the collected photographic images and stories of the homeless persons.

While we as faculty had been pleased with our students' individual efforts, their collective outcomes did not quite gel as we had hoped. One reason for this was the difficulty of class scheduling and the sheer number of students involved. Rich, true collaboration was going to require more intense faculty guidance than had been possible. It was at this time that a grant opportunity presented itself, and we applied for funds that would allow us to take a more concentrated approach to this collaboration.

This new project would combine the creative efforts of graphic design, interior design, and photography to convince homeless persons to stay and commit to recovery programs at the Transitional Shelter. This was an important objective, as shelter staff described to us that the homeless are often suspicious of institutional help. After discussion, faculty decided that it might be effective to demonstrate to these persons that others before them had successfully escaped from homelessness to better lives through their participation at the Transitional Shelter. This would allow us to use the projects' photographs, stories, and graphic wall panels to achieve a specific end and address a very practical need. The effort came to be known as the "Wall of Hope" project and was developed by two hand-picked students of graphic design and interior design (see Appendix 8.F). Through dialogue with the Salvation Army administration, a proposal and budget were developed to renovate the existing waiting room to achieve the following goals:

1. Place the Wall of Hope graphic display panels within the waiting room for prospective clients to view, hopefully convincing them to stay at the shelter.
2. Provide better seating that would also convert to beds—important, as this room served as an overflow area on cold nights for the homeless who had nowhere else to turn.

The project proposal is currently under review by the Salvation Army shelter administration. The Salvation Army hopes to raise sufficient funds to actually construct the project in the future.

A second by-product of the original service-learning project proved interesting in that it addressed the role of student idea generation within charity organizations. Salvation Army administration graciously extended the invitation for our students to display the results of their senior projects at their annual donor luncheon, an elaborate event attended by 1,500 local businesspersons who support the Salvation Army's activities. During the event, the organization's Social Services Committee chairman reviewed the students' work and later requested digital images of their ideas.

An often-heard criticism of student portfolio work is that it is creatively unrealistic, does not conform to real budgets, and, by extension, is essentially a flight of fancy that cannot be built. In the case of this project, students worked diligently to adhere to rigid standards of durability and maintenance in space planning, finish, and furnishing selection, while offering a research-justified solution intended to promote physical and mental healing.

While it was not this service-learning project's intention at the outset, the students' creativity may have been fortuitously timed to aid the Salvation Army in their goal of building a new shelter. In spring of 2005 I was informed that the Capital Facilities campaign for this objective had recently been boosted from 1 million to 5 million dollars. It is at least tempting to think that the student's efforts as "visioneers" helped the appropriate persons see a space that reaches beyond function to support human betterment and recuperation.[10]

As for graphic design, the Salvation Army remains excited at the prospect of continuing to work with these students, especially in the development of business identity including brochures and business cards, a messaging center for the shelter, and other inclusions.

The photography students completed their work with the development of the book *Shelter Lives,* a compendium of photo images and stories of staff and homeless persons at the Transitional Shelter. The Salvation Army organization is interested in publishing copies for sale as a fundraiser for its ongoing activities.

The possibilities for collaboration with the Salvation Army remain strong, and a good baseline rapport now exists for future opportunities. The Salvation Army staff are now regular contributors to new faculty service-learning orientation sessions at California State University–Sacramento, and other CSU programs of study are considering working with the organization.

Some Final Reflections

As this project represented one of my first forays into a community-collaborative student project, I learned a great deal through the experience. I am convinced that service learning, through its interaction with real needs, people, and situations, enables students to vividly see the implications of their choices as considerably more than lines on paper—and to begin to recognize their potential to create environments within which disenfranchised persons can not only exist but thrive, learning once again to socialize and trust.

Including the reality of service learning into a class project implies considerable work on the part of faculty. In part, this is due to the unpredictability of real life. What if a person the students are to interview is sick that day? What if there is insufficient parking, forcing students to park across the street next to the triple-X bookstore? A measure of tolerance and patience is necessary as well as the means to improvise.

Project workload is even more intense when collaborating with other faculty and student groups. While we encountered few problems in our faculty collaboration together, it became clear that project commitment and ability to put time into the project was enduringly important. Occasional differences of opinion, especially in design decision making, enhanced class discussion and added another component of reality to the process.

When working with a community partner in the context of three different student groups, it is vital to have a point person within the organization who is patient, positive, and willing to work with the inevitable stumbles of scheduling and events that occur. We were fortunate to have a facilities director who was unfailingly upbeat, supportive, and respectful of the students and open to new ideas.

On an individual and somewhat self-serving note, I have found service learning to be a personally fulfilling undertaking that has enhanced my own empathy toward others. As a new faculty member currently seeking tenure, my efforts in service-learning pursuits have stimulated my research agenda into areas I was previously unacquainted with, and I am looking forward to projects that will enable me to investigate the role of self-esteem within physical facilities for the homeless. This project has revealed content to me and provided contacts who can assist me in this endeavor. Service-learning projects have also gained me entrance into faculty advisory boards for service learning and helped me realize the satisfaction of receiving the "Best Faculty Presentation" award at a recent research and teaching conference.

While these occurrences are gratifying, they do not approach the satisfaction of knowing that it is possible that my teaching activities are making a difference in my students' understanding of their civic and professional responsibilities. In a closing reflective exercise, one student summed up the experience by describing how she will now engage a homeless person in conversation who has taken up residency in her workplace's doorway instead of merely walking by. In the larger scheme of life, this seems to be a positive outcome.

Appendix 8.A

Excerpt From Orientation Document: Rules of Conduct and Dress

Interacting with Salvation Army Staff and Homeless Guests

You will be asked to collect your programming material at the beginning of the project, much of it through site visits during class. You must be very efficient with our field trips, gathering as much information as possible during these times. If further questions arise, please refer them to me, and I will compile a question list from everybody. This way we will not duplicate our questions as I ask them of our clients.

Please keep the following in mind as we observe and speak with the clients and their homeless guests:

- Absorb as much as possible on your initial walk-through. Take a camera with you. This will allow you to avoid asking obvious questions later in time.
- Staff are always very busy. Do your homework in advance, and be efficient with the use of their time.
- You will find homeless persons staying at the shelter to be on the whole calm and in many ways like you. However, remember that they are going through tremendous trauma in their lives. *Approach these persons at all times with respect, patience, and understanding.* Be tactful in your questioning. They may seem standoffish, as they have often

learned not to trust strangers. We may find that they would very much like to share their story with you.

Salvation Army policy dictates that the homeless guests are largely not present in the facility during the day when we visit on our field trips. On our visits, staff will arrange to have several homeless guests available to interact with us.

Dress

Our project site and purpose is unique, as it serves as a refuge for many who are marginalized in our society. It is important that you are prepared to appear professional during our field trips. This is so you will prompt others to trust you and take you seriously. This does not mean a business suit—casual school dress is fine. However, do not wear clothing that is overly revealing, suggestive, or brief, such as spaghetti straps and midriff-bearing clothing. I would also avoid shorts.

Appendix 8.B

Excerpt From Syllabus Describing Service-Learning Project Expectations

Select Course Requirements In-Depth

Details of projects not listed here will be supplied when projects are assigned.

- Salvation Army Community Center Project
  This project will immerse you in the issues of an actual design project with its complexities of user analysis and existing site/building shell parameters. This endeavor offers tremendous potential in engaging in socially responsible and sensitive design. Additionally, you will be working with students in other majors—specifically graphics and photography. Consequently, the project can be a powerful participant in your student portfolio given its real-life nature and the substantial programming and design that you will be engaged in.

- Reflective Journal
  You are embarking on a project that likely deals with individuals you are not very familiar with. You will keep a journal that records your personal thoughts on this learning experience that will encourage you to reflect on what you have learned and how it has changed you.

- SWAT Design Team Activity
  The Salvation Army Project will at times require individual tasks to be done that benefit everyone. These include assisting with displays within our Gallery show, generating measurements or drawings for everyone's use, or assisting with the organization of a class event.

- Field Trip and Guest Speaker
  At least one field trip will contribute to class activities. Every effort will be made to respect your transportation needs and time constraints. I will distribute a letter that will explain the trip for your other instructors. Note that the **September 10th field trip is mandatory** and a vital part of research and programming for the project. Grant funds permit us to travel to San Francisco without substantial cost to you.

  You will also be required to attend a guest presentation organized expressly for our Salvation Army project. This will occur at **5:30–7:30 on Thursday, September 16th.**

  Due to the nature of research and other activities you will be engaged in, there are days when the class will not meet as a group. You are responsible for knowing when these days are and being present in class when it is required.

Appendix 8.C

Excerpt From Student-Created Criteria Matrix From the Research Information Gathered to Guide Their Design Creation

TABLE 8-C-1
Excerpt From Student-Created Criteria Matrix

DESIGN PROGRAM CRITERIA MATRIX			
Salvation Army Community Services Center 1200 N B Street			10/05/2004
Area/Department	Exterior		
Area/Department	Parking	Front door approach	Intake patio
Description of function	Vehicle approach from N B Street entrance	Client/visitor entrance from parking lot	Exterior waiting area for clients
Quantity	1 to 2	1	1
SF size or number of persons served	37 spaces		
Near to +/or far from		Access to intake area	Same
Desired prominence in the overall design	35 spaces—2 ADA	Main entrance is on the side, would like more of an entrance overhang with signage to invite clients into the facility	Private area away from main entrance walkway; sound wall surrounding, with plenty of shade in outdoor area. "Town Square" approach
Availability, Walk-ins, admitted clients, staff other guests	Walk-ins, admitted clients, staff and guests	Admitted clients, staff, and guests	Walk-ins, admitted clients, staff, and guests. Additional privacy will be needed for one-on-one interviews
Finishes	Reflective paint	Updated exterior materials and/or paint	Durable, easily maintained surfaces

Furnishings			Durable stackable seating and all-weather tables
Lighting	Low level horizontal illum 6 fc. 4 stalls: 1 fixture	Mid-level horizontal 4.5 fc (40tx)	Mid-high horizontal and vertical luminance 7.5 fc
Daylighting	Yes	Yes	Yes
Privacy level	Low	Low	High—good neighbor
Security risk level	Moderate	High	Moderate
Key priorities or comments	Expand to southern vacant lot.	Would entrance walkway be separated from intake patio area?	Wants to be inviting with landscaping/gardens. Wants it shielded from neighborhood (vice/versa)

Appendix 8.D

Revised Exterior Entrance Proposed by an Interior Design Student Team.

Appendix 8.E

Excerpt From a Self-Assessment Report That Students Used to Rate the Performance of Their Team Colleagues

INTD126B Advanced Commercial Studio

Your name: _____xxx_____

Salvation Army Service Learning Project

Team Self-Evaluation

Please complete the following regarding your opinion of the team's ability to share work on the assigned topic. Your answers will be held in my confidence and may influence up to 10% of an individual's project grade.

Rate your own performance on the project from 1 (poor) to 5 (outstanding) regarding your follow-through and attendance to high quality in your project responsibilities.

1 2 3 4 5

☐ ☐ ☐ ☒ ☐

Your Project Partners

Reflect on your partners' contributions to the project. Rate their performance from 1 (poor) to 5 (outstanding).

1 2 3 4 5

Partner 1 name: _____xxx_____   Rating: ☐ ☐ ☐ ☐ ☒

Explain/justify your rating here:

_____xxx_____ *was a much better group leader than I was. She is very organized, and took on a lot of responsibility for the completion of the project. We met often, and got a lot accomplished. I feel that* _____xxx_____ *did more than her fair share of the work. In retrospect, we should have divided up the work differently, but I think the outcome would have been the same, with* _____xxx_____ *and I taking on a majority of the work.*

Appendix 8.F

Perspective and Plan View of the Renovated Waiting Room as Proposed in the Wall of Hope Grant Project

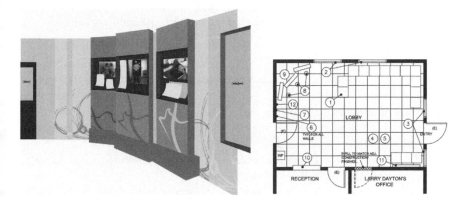

Notes

1. Imaginary clients and projects are often used in interior design education because actual construction, of course, costs thousands of dollars. It is the rare client indeed that is willing to commit to a student's vision of a solution.

2. For example, lighting that produces "disability glare" due to poor placement not only creates heightened irritability but also represents a security hazard as it conceals visitors' facial features and expressions (Leibrock, 2000). Creating designs that avoid problems of space planning, finish selection, security, and a host of other considerations is often no more expensive than not addressing them in the first place, and their application is simply a matter of preplanning.

3. Isay, Abramson, and Wang's *Flophouse: Life on the Bowery* (2001) and Goldberg's *Raised by Wolves* (1995) are efforts that examined homelessness and "throwaway" children respectively. The public relations potential of such photography projects remains powerful, much as Steinbeck's *Cannery Row* exposed the conditions of fishery workers half a century before.

4. Well-designed space holds huge potential for human psychological and physical healing. In a study of postsurgery patients, where half were provided a view of trees and the other half a view of a wall, those with the wall view stayed in the hospital longer, needed more medication, and had increased complications (Carpman, 1986).

5. Collaboration among design students is not untested. Richie and Spafford's groups of interior design, graphic design, and landscape design students led them to

confirm the value of multiple perspectives, especially in projects tightly integrated with social considerations (2002).

6. I was surprised to learn that the student sought out a homeless person in Sacramento and purchased some of the contents of his cart for the display, such as bags of recyclable cans. The homeless person additionally offered extensive advice on what makes up these near-ubiquitous mobile living devices.

7. Some images of the field trip that stayed with me (and undoubtedly the students as well):

- Sights and smells of the third-floor medical ward where flies prevailed and iron beds backed up to each other, recalling photographs of third-world countries.
- Use of only metal bed frames in dormitories. We would later find out this is due to the tendency of bedbugs (which are nearly impossible to eradicate), to nest within wooden beds.
- Painted out windows so that clients could not expose themselves to occupants of other high-rise buildings.
- Personal effects of clients in their dormitory rooms. Drawings by both children and adults and stuffed animals revealed a vulnerability that likely few of the homeless would show to others on the street.
- Separate shelter entries for adults and families with children to prevent exposure of children to potential sex offenders.
- The sensitivity and compassion of social workers and staff assisting those homeless persons afflicted with AIDS.
- My students' sharing of hand sanitizer on the bus after exiting the main downtown San Francisco shelter.

8. These group encounters also occasionally brought to light the diverse backgrounds of the homeless clients. One was a screenwriter from Hollywood down on his luck. Two others were a married couple forced to sleep separately in the male and female dormitories. Another client sitting next to me revealed through the content of the discussion that he had recently been released not only from jail but from three continuous months of solitary confinement for an offense he did not detail.

9. On occasion this project aspect caused minor grade reductions when I determined from multiple reports that a student was not fully supporting his or her team colleagues. While the impact on the final grade, at worst, was minimal (from B+ to B, for example), students were rarely pleased to learn of the ramifications of their actions. Despite the occasional difficulties this requirement creates, I maintain that it is important so that students grasp the nature of holding up one's end of the bargain in team dynamics.

10. A letter from the Salvation Army divisional secretary was heartening in its discussion of the students' work: "I have personally spoken to the members of our Social Services Committee and they are eager to see these designs and to talk about the future of our Transitional Shelter. None of this would have been possible if it

were not for the creative imaginations of your students. They truly captured the essence of what we are trying to achieve in our program. . . . We look forward to seeing what will happen in the future with this project as people are really getting excited about the potential" (May 15, 2004).

References

Carpman, J. R. (1986). *Design that cares*. American Hospital Publishing.

Davis, S. (2004a). *Designing for the homeless: Architecture that works*. Berkeley: University of California Press.

Davis, S. (2004b). *Sam Davis architecture*. http://sdavisarchitecture.com/homeless.html

Gibney, F., & Luscombe, B. (2000, March). The rebirth of design. *Time 155*(11). Retrieved December 27, 2005, from http://www.time.com/time/archive/preview/0,10987,996372,00.html

Goldberg, J. (1995). *Raised by wolves*. Zurich: Scalo.

Isay, D., Abramson, S., & Wang, H. (2001). *Flophouse: Life on the bowery*. New York: Random House Trade Paperbacks.

Koberg, G., & Bagnall, J. (1991). *The universal traveler: A soft-systems guide to creativity, problem-solving and the process of reaching goals*. Los Altos, CA: CNSP Publications.

Leibrock, C. (2000). *Design details for health*. New York: Wiley & Sons.

Richie, T., & Spafford, A. (2002). Bluebonnet Swamp Learning Community: The design of a collaborative studio. *Proceedings of the Interior Design Educator's Council International Conference*, 76–77.

United States Conference of Mayors. (2005, December). Hunger and homelessness survey: A status report on hunger and homelessness in America's cities. Retrieved December 5, 2005, from http://www.usmayors.org/uscm/hungersurvey/2005/HH2005FINAL.pdf

9

PROVIDING HUMAN SERVICES WITH A SOCIAL JUSTICE PERSPECTIVE

Robert C. Chope and Rebecca L. Toporek

Moral virtue comes about as a result of habit. We become just by doing just acts. . . ."
—Aristotle, *Nicomachean Ethics*, Book II, chapter 1 (in Aristotle, 2001, p. 952)

There has been a recent dramatic increase in the intertwining of social justice with vocational counseling psychology and career development brought about by leadership of Division 17 (Counseling Psychology) of the American Psychological Association and the Counselors for Social Justice, a division of the American Counseling Association (Toporek & Chope, 2006). The significance of these two organizational commitments has given professional support for a more thorough integration of social justice as a central role in counseling and human services provision. As faculty who teach in a California State University department devoted to training professionally competent, culturally sensitive practitioners, we have attempted to integrate these social justice principles into a service-learning package that includes both classroom instruction and clinical experience.

Our approach to integrating social justice in counseling training includes attention to students' personal feelings as well as professional skills and strategies. In this chapter we describe some of the activities and exercises that address each of these areas with service-learning students in developing a greater understanding of the concept of social justice and the systemic causes of injustice, and we learn how they as professionals can address these issues for individuals as well as institutions. While prime examples are seen in the vocational domain of human services, our specialization, we believe that the ideas and exercises described in this chapter are generalizable to a wide range of other graduate and undergraduate programs and disciplines. Some of these exercises are experiential in nature and designed to facilitate reflection and discussion in the class and are not used in an evaluative way. Other exercises provide an opportunity to assess the students' insight, awareness, knowledge, and skill in particular areas as well as their analytical and research process in investigating a problem or situation. These exercises may be more appropriate for evaluation and are graded to determine the extent to which the objectives of the assignment have been met and learning has occurred.

Personal Feelings About Social Justice

In the time that our students complete their 60 units of instruction for the degree program, they are required to spend a minimum of 840 hours in service learning, gaining direct, nonbookish experience with real-world clients as they develop their clinical skills. With each semester that the students are in a service-learning placement, they are also enrolled in a small seminar of 12 students that is used to support and evaluate their educational development in case analysis, case management, and of course counseling. The seminar involves academic learning with a healthy dose of self-disclosure and addressing personal feelings about becoming a counselor or human services provider.

In the first seminar that is connected to the service-learning experience, we have our students consider and discuss how they might incorporate social justice attitudes into their thinking and conceptualizations of service provision. The seminar begins with a thorough examination of a definition of social justice such as the one drawn from Janna Smith (2003). Smith posits that a socially just world is one where everyone has access to the following:

> Adequate food, sleep, wages, education, safety, opportunity, institutional support, health care, childcare, and loving relationships. "Adequate" means enough to allow [participation] in the world . . . without starving, or feeling economically trapped or uncompensated, continually exploited, terrorized, devalued, battered, chronically exhausted, or virtually enslaved (and for some, still, actually enslaved). (Smith, 2003, p. 167)

To help students in the service-learning seminar identify critical social justice experiences that may have helped shape their attitudes, education, career, and/or life path we utilize two exercises: visualization and one we call "pivotal points." We have found that these exercises are best used to stimulate thinking or discussion rather than for evaluative purposes in order to promote safety and honest self-reflection.

Exercise: Visualization

Since we also teach visualization as a clinical skill, we are comfortable using the power of visualization to help us introduce a social justice paradigm to our students. For educators who may wish to try this we suggest a passage taken from Franz Kafka's *The Metamorphosis* (1972) originally published in 1915. This short novel is timely and can be used in bringing forth a new context for understanding:

> As Gregor Samsa awoke one morning from a troubled dream, he found himself changed in his bed into some monstrous kind of vermin . . . his great brown belly, divided by bowed corrugations . . . and Gregor's legs, pitiably thin compared with their former size, fluttered before his eyes. (p. 1)

Kafka's perplexing beginning to his famous story seems at first to be taken from an impossible dream. But what would it be like to awaken one morning where nothing is familiar and your body has changed dramatically? You don't feel clean. Your room and its accoutrements are unfamiliar. Transformation occurred so rapidly that the fabric of support of your life along with all tangible comforts has disappeared.

Capitalizing on this example, we ask the students to close their eyes and listen to the following words for a Kafkaesque visualization:

> You awaken one morning and you're in a tiny hotel room in an impoverished part of an unfamiliar town. You don't feel well, no toiletries are available, your clothing has a distinctive odor that doesn't resemble yours, and you have a headache. You crawl out from under the dirty sheet and thin blanket and grab your pants only to realize that you have no money. The phone in your room is blocked, and your cell phone has been turned off because the bill hasn't been paid. You're hungry. You're not sure where you are or how you got this way.

This certainly is not a pleasant picture. But as a part of the exercise, we have the students discuss the following questions and then reflect on their personal responses:

What do you feel?
What would you do?
Who will you try to summon to help you?
What would you tell them about what happened to you?

To be sure, in large metropolitan areas, we all pass by homeless people every day; they are so familiar that we generally disregard them. Their clothing is usually tattered, and they often have distinctive street odors. The frequency with which they ask for money for a bus ride or a hamburger hardens us to their requests, as we automatically assume that any spare change will be invested in addictive substances.

Students characteristically remark that the experience elicited by the visualization could never happen to them. But as the many tragic events of the year 2005 unfolded several themes became apparent. The potential for disaster is always present: From late 2004 and through the beginning of 2006, the world was beset with the tsunami in Thailand, which extended to India, Africa, and Indonesia; hurricanes in the Gulf Coast of the United States and the east coast of Florida; an earthquake in Pakistan purported to have killed 200,000 people; drought in the Congo; landslides in the Philippines; and devastating military struggles in the Middle East. Disaster can occur frequently and rapidly, and the entire infrastructure of a person's life can be altered forever. The support system of family, workplace, and community can be lost with it. Moreover, our rehabilitation-counseling students remind us that we are all just a slip or a fall away from a permanent disability.

Exercise: Pivotal Points

The purpose of the pivotal points exercise is to prompt students to think about significant life events that may have influenced the way that they see social justice as well as to tap into emotional reactions that may reoccur as they engage in social change. We find that this approach helps to personalize the service-learning experience as the students learn to understand some of the origins of their own social conscience.

Instructors may choose to use this exercise as individual student reflection or as a part of a small group process. We have found that the benefits of the exercise are optimized when students complete the following questions independently, followed by sharing in pairs, and then come together in a larger discussion. The questions for the exercise include the following:

1. *Incident.* When did you first observe or become aware of an example of social injustice? Describe the situation in detail. Where were you? How old were you? Who was involved? What happened? Who was the receiver of the injustice? Who was the perpetrator?
2. *Your reaction.* What did you do? How did you know it was unjust? How did you feel, and what did you think?
3. *Lasting consequences.* How did this experience influence who you are today? Did it influence your choice of work or how you see your work?

In facilitating the discussion, there are several points that are valuable to consider highlighting. The first point of attention is the students' reactions to their experiences. When we think about these situations, almost all of us can recall an instance of new realization. However, the impact that these experiences have on us varies, as do our reactions. For some, these experiences form a core of understanding or commitment to make positive changes. For others, there is a search for an explanation or a rationale for the treatment received. For others, there may even be a minimization of the event so as to reduce the distress and confusion that might otherwise result. These are all reactions that are important to recognize and validate. Furthermore, we have found that discussion prior to the students' service-learning experience may be enhanced by integrating literature examining the relationship between prejudice and the constructs of cognitive dissonance (e.g., Eisenstadt, Leippe, Stambush, Rouch, & Rivers, 2005; Zimbardo & Leippe, 1991), attribution (e.g., Eagly, 2004; Toporek & Pope-Davis, 2005), stereotype disconfirmation (e.g., Wyer, 2004), and the "just world hypothesis" (e.g., Blader & Tyler, 2002; Lerner, 1980).

Professional Skills and Social Justice

In addition to developing a personal understanding of social justice, our students are being trained to be professional counselors and need the knowledge and skills of professionals to address injustice in the personal and institutional arenas. In the seminar we create a structure whereby we use four areas of *foundational knowledge* pertinent to a professional understanding of social justice (Toporek & Chope, 2006). These include interdisciplinary relationships, cultural competence, complex roles of providers, and social justice resources. These are particularly relevant in service-learning packages to help provide a cohesive approach. Again, while the lessons in our courses are intended for training human services professionals, these ideas are transferable to other disciplines.

We live in a world where the playing field of global competition is leveling or flattening (Friedman, 2005). But it is also a world with terrific mountains and valleys for individuals. Zakaria (2006) points out that people born into the right circumstances have the opportunities to attend schools that will educate them and connect them to others who will stimulate them and help them flourish. On the other hand, people can live in the United States but reside in communities where the schools are poor, the education is substandard, and where, most unfortunately, a pool of bright and creative children are not pushed or motivated to be the best that they can be. They are lost in the cracks; a life with encouragement and gusto is unavailable. For our students to be effective professionals, they will need a breadth of tools to employ.

Interdisciplinary Relationships

Many vocational and educational disciplines have a rich history of addressing social problems (e.g., social work, public health, public administration, community and social psychology, anthropology, sociology, education, law) and have informed the development of public policies concentrating on the most disenfranchised. Partnerships that combine the unique assets of many individually different disciplines have the potential to better serve client populations, while increasing the creativity necessary for demanding problem solving. Additionally, these partnerships have the potential to minimize redundancy of services, develop political alliances, and create greater prospects for public and private funding.

The first foundation, interdisciplinary relationships, begins when providers become familiar with the ongoing work of leaders and advocates in fields addressing social justice, including their own. They need to invest energy in becoming familiar with different communities needing specialized services. Developing as many relationships as possible with the community and with other professionals sharing similar interests is a good start toward assessing the work that is already being done and how a provider may contribute or further the efforts. A major contribution that can be made is simply facilitating communication among the community, existing providers, and policy makers.

We ask the students to create networks of knowledge regarding social justice principles and implementation. They are required to research their service-learning agency to understand its financial support and political connectedness. We ask them to understand the evolution of the agency from inception and to determine what might be needed for program or agency sustentation. We also ask that they become knowledgeable about the costs and benefits of the agency to the community. While this may take several forms, one example is to have students complete an agency *ecological network map* accompanied by supporting information. In the network map, students identify relevant individual, institutional (agency), community, and societal relationships. The map is constructed as a series of concentric circles with the student placed at the center. In the first ring, students identify the key individuals within the agency in terms of their relation to themselves. In the middle ring, they indicate the agencies and organizations that are affiliated with their agency. On the outer ring, they indicate the broader forces that influence their agency and clients. The students are then asked to address the following:.

1. Describe the links in the network map in terms of resources for you, your client, your agency including financial support and political connectedness.
2. Describe the evolution of the agency from inception and determine what might be needed for program or agency sustention.
3. Based on interviews with your supervisor and your observations of the community, describe the costs and benefits of the agency to the community.

The assignment is evaluated on the demonstrated level of insight, clarity and specificity of information, inclusiveness of political and financial connections, and articulation of the networks in the supplemental questions.

The exercise provides students with the opportunity to understand the existing political structure, alliances, and conflicts as well as untapped resources.

Developing interdisciplinary relationships requires knowledge and skill across the culture of various disciplines. Cultural competence in terms of sociopolitical privilege and dimensions of identity are also critical.

Cultural Competence

Cultural competence is the second foundation necessary for implementing social justice. Many human service and educational disciplines have developed some form of multicultural competence guidelines. As one example, Hargrove, Creagh, and Kelly (2003) proposed a guide for multicultural counseling competencies in career counseling based on Sue, Arredondo, and McDavis's (1992) tripartite model. This model asserts that multicultural competence requires awareness of one's own beliefs and attitudes, understanding of the client's worldview, and a repertoire of culturally relevant interventions. As with multicultural competence, we believe that social justice work in service learning requires that providers be aware of their own beliefs, values, and biases regarding work, money, and social responsibility. While the multicultural counseling competencies (Sue et al., 1992) emphasize race and ethnicity, social justice work must also attend to other dimensions of identity that represent marginalization and lack of institutional power, including being a women, of an ethnic minority, gay, lesbian, bisexual, or transgender, and an individual with a disability. It is important that the provider be familiar with literature that delineates competencies for working with the specific populations he or she is serving. Our seminar, along with another required course in multicultural counseling and integration of multicultural issues throughout all courses in the program, adds to the development of multicultural competence among the students.

Complex Roles of Providers

The third foundation is an understanding of the range of appropriate roles needed to address a range of social problems. In working with people experiencing systemic injustice, providers need to consider assuming a range of traditional and nontraditional roles given the problem, situation, and resources. For example, referring to the work of psychologists, Atkinson,

Thompson, and Grant (1993) asserted that the appropriate role should be determined by a client's level of acculturation, locus of problem etiology (internal or external), and the goal of the interventions (prevention or remediation). In addition to traditional roles such as counseling and psychotherapy, Atkinson et al. identified four roles (advocate, change agent, adviser, and consultant) that may be relevant when addressing problems that have an external etiology. According to the Atkinson et al. model, psychotherapy alone is not sufficient when social justice issues are created, or at least perpetuated by systems and institutions. This would reflect an external etiology; however, the problem itself may manifest as internal distress, behavioral dysfunction, or family and community conflict. Traditionally, psychotherapy and counseling has focused on working toward alleviating clients' feelings of distress or dysfunction without identifying or addressing external problem sources.

Other authors have described ways of integrating advocacy into human service work (e.g., Kiselica, 2004; Lewis, Lewis, Daniels, & D'Andrea, 1998; Toporek & Liu, 2001). Toporek and Liu described a range of counseling roles and goals on a continuum from empowerment (individual and small scale) to social action (systemic and large scale). Service-learning students who thought they would be providing only individual career counseling or psychotherapy are surprised at the potential complexity of their roles. We emphasize that where social justice issues are concerned flexibility in provider roles is needed to strike a balance among situational, contextual, cultural, and ethical needs.

Social Justice Resources

A fourth foundation that is necessary as a counselor and social change agent is knowledge of relevant resources or access to helpful information: for example, financial assistance, advocacy resources, affiliation resources, and others. This may also include knowledge of legislation pertaining to client situations such as employment (e.g., Equal Employment Opportunity Act [Title VII], Age Discrimination Act), education (e.g., Higher Education Act [Title IX]), and disability (e.g., Americans with Disabilities Act). In addition, addressing social justice issues is facilitated by familiarity with advocacy and enforcement organizations: for example, the U.S. Civil Rights Commission, Equal Employment Opportunity Commission, and local State Department of Civil Rights. In addition to being well informed, an approach that integrates legislation and policy conveys a proactive and supportive stance to clients and reinforces the validity of their worldview and experience. Attention to the societal and community levels of the network map can help the students maintain consciousness regarding ongoing policy developments and political influences that affect their agencies. And we want them to be sensitive to the basic interagency connections that exist.

To illustrate the integration of these four foundational areas, we provide the following fictional case study. In reading this case study, please pay attention to the complexity of levels involved as well as the sociopolitical and personal factors that might suggest areas for potential intervention.

Counseling Janna: An Individual Case Example

Janna, a self-identified Persian woman from Iran, 32-year-old mother of an 8-year-old son, has come to a community college counseling center seeking assistance in finding a job or career that pays more than her current office administration job and has more flexibility in her hours given problems that seem to be coming up for her son at school. Janna has worked as an administrative assistant for the past five years after completing a bachelor's degree in psychology. She did not pursue jobs in psychology because her son's father filed for a divorce, and she needed to get a job given that he has not followed through with child support payments. Her ex-husband, a U.S. citizen born in the United States, threatens that if she makes things difficult for him he will involve the INS and have her deported.

As a social justice–minded counselor, it is important to understand Janna's expectations and reasons for seeking assistance. In the vignette, it appears that Janna hopes to receive assistance in finding a job or career that pays more and is more flexible than her current position. Yet, if the provider focuses solely on this stated need without considering the complex systemic, environmental, and family issues impinging on Janna, the assistance would have minimal impact and could be potentially damaging.

It is important that the service-learning student understand the number of larger issues that Janna may be facing and consider the extent to which it may be important to receive assistance at multiple levels. By helping her only with finding a different job, some very significant circumstances may be ignored that will interfere with Janna's well-being.

An understanding of the levels of systems involved can help clarify the provider's role and the interventions that may be most helpful to Janna. In addition, a consideration of systems of power and oppression given culture, identity, and resources is helpful for all service-learning students to understand the full context. *Individually*, Janna is seeking a different job that is more fulfilling, pays more, and is more flexible. At the *family level*, she has a child and is undergoing a divorce. To what extent might her institutional power be influenced by her status as a woman or her identity as a Persian immigrant? The *community or school level* may be seen reflected in Janna's concerns about the problems her son is having at school. To what extent might his problems be related to cultural issues, the divorce, prejudice, and the greater political situation in Iraq as well as Iran? In terms of the community level, Janna's divorce and legal situation and concerns about immigration may be influenced by the resources in her community. At a *public or societal level*, what policies exist that may support or endanger Janna and her family, such as immigration law and child support?

In a social justice approach, Janna's provider would need to consider all of these levels. It would be important to honor Janna's original request for assistance while at the same time discussing the multitude of systemic barriers and concerns she seems to be facing. It is often the case that systemic issues faced by clients require expertise beyond a sole service provider. As a social change agent, it is within the provider's scope of duty to facilitate Janna's gaining some of the resources and skills to advocate for herself as well as her acquiring additional support and appropriate services. Sometimes this may require additional education or research. For example, a better understanding of immigration law and divorce law may be necessary. It would be essential that the provider is familiar with resources that can help Janna to gain access to those services.

The case of Janna clearly involves multiple levels, yet students often have difficulty shifting from identifying individual issues and interventions to addressing systemic ones. The following exercise, Observations of Social Injustice, is designed to help students identify situations of injustice in their service-learning environment (e.g., discrimination) and guide them in examining the multiple levels involved. This examination increases their sensitivity and awareness of the existence of these occurrences and sets the stage for action later.

Exercise: Observations of Social Injustice

The Observations of Social Injustice exercise is intended to facilitate students' identifying and examining daily observations of social injustice in their service-learning placements that can be used later as a springboard to developing a concrete plan for addressing a particular area of injustice. While the exercises we present are designed for students, we recommend that the instructor take some time to complete the exercises prior to using them with students to gain a sense of the experience.

As with the Pivotal Points exercise, we recommend that students initially complete this exercise independently, followed by dyad discussion and then large-group processing. The exercise contains a number of questions regarding an observation of injustice, the consequences and the students' reactions, and the different levels of systems that may be involved including individual, institutional, community, and public or societal. While this exercise is most often used to illustrate an analysis of injustice, it may also be used to evaluate a student's ability to conduct such an analysis. If used for evaluative purposes, we suggest articulating a grading criteria that includes completeness and clarity of response, depth of insight, and mechanics.

Levels of systems may be conceptualized in a framework similar to the bioecological systems model proposed by Bronfenbrenner (2005) in which the individual is influenced by increasingly larger and larger systems. Below are the stimulus items followed by an example providing an illustration of a student response.

Observations of Social Injustice Stimulus Points

1. Observation of social injustice:
2. Consequence for the client or individual facing the injustice:
3. Consequence for you as a provider (your feelings, reactions, and responses):
4. The influence of your identity, power, privilege, or oppression on your experience and reactions:
5. Level of issue:
   a. Individual:
   b. Institutional:
   c. Community:
   d. Public or societal:

To stimulate thinking about how students might respond, we present the following example. Upon reading the example, consider how this student's experience might be used to inspire social action.

Example: "Case Conference Bias"

1. *Observation of social injustice.*

"In case conferences at my placement, one counselor always gives more leeway to clients who are White women and describes them in more positive terms than she does clients from other ethnic backgrounds. No one seems to notice this except me, and because I'm an intern I am not sure if I should say anything."

2. *Consequence for the client or individual facing the injustice.*

"When other staff members recommend what should happen with a case, they provide more resources and support, like waiving session limits, for clients who are described positively by this counselor. Consequently, when this counselor describes her cases, the White female clients seem to get more services than the clients of other ethnicities, who seem to be terminated earlier."

3. *Consequence for you as a provider (your feelings, reactions, and responses).*

"I feel awkward and upset because it seems to be really unfair and racist, but I also feel really frustrated because I am afraid that if I say something I will have problems with the site. I feel caught and angry. I did not respond in the situation."

4. *The influence of your identity, power, privilege, or oppression on your experience and reactions.*

"As a White woman, I wondered if these kinds of beliefs influence me and whether I have been given special opportunities in the same way as these White clients. I wondered, if I was a person of color, would the counselor still be as oblivious to her bias? As an intern, I feel less power in the agency to speak up about things I disagree with."

5. *Level of issue.*
   a. *Individual.* "Individually, each client is affected, the counselor is affected, and I am affected. It seems individual because it is one counselor who seems to do it the most."

b. *Institutional.* "Everyone in the case conference and, by extension, the agency is perpetuating the injustice because no one seems to recognize it or say anything about this pattern."

c. *Community.* "If the profession of mental health service is considered the community, I know there is a history of unequal services and diagnoses based on race."

d. *Public or societal.* "In general, I know that people from different ethnic backgrounds have been discriminated against, and in the media people who are not White tend to be portrayed as more disturbed or just generally portrayed more negatively than White people"

This example provided a specific situation on a relatively small scale faced within the context of a service-learning experience. Processing this activity should work toward several objectives. First, this exercise is most useful when students are able to personalize the experience to the extent that they can identify a point of entry for intervention. Second, while the goal of this exercise is to identify a point of intervention, it is essential that students' feelings be recognized. These feelings and emotional reactions represent possible motivators or challenges for the student as a social change agent. Third, the follow-up discussion to this exercise can help students sort out their reactions and experiences, helping them determine the extent to which the situation results from systemic injustice or individual injustice or whether they may need to gather additional information before making that judgment. Fourth, it is helpful if instructors can facilitate students' identification of resources and knowledge that may be helpful in addressing the issue or situation they identify. In the case of service learning, it is important to attend to power differentials in the scenarios described by students as well as political situations they may be encountering. Helping students to think through the consequences of possible interventions can take place during the processing of this exercise. This brings us to the next focus area, developing strategies to address injustice.

Strategies for Social Action

As we noted at the beginning of the chapter, recognizing the need for social justice is a critical first step. However, without action, this recognition is meaningless. In this section, you are invited to apply the concepts described in this chapter into strategies to help service-learning students conceptualize a concrete plan for social action as a paper or a class project. To complete this exercise, it may be helpful for students to recall the data they generated in the previous exercise regarding their observations of injustice. It is often helpful for students to work in groups or dyads to provide opportunities for brainstorming and support. If this is used to assess a student's knowledge or analytical skills, for example as an assigned paper, we would recommend providing an opportunity in class for students to work in dyads or groups on their identified situations prior to writing it up independently. The grading criteria that we have found to be most relevant include depth of insight, clarity of expression, completeness of response, and mechanics.

The following is an outline designed to help students systematically identify a problem, set a goal, illuminate barriers, and strategize to overcome the barriers. In each section, we will provide additional points of inquiry that may be important to consider. For clarity, we will use the example presented earlier, "Case Conference Bias," for illustration, although these two exercises do not necessarily need to be conducted in conjunction with one another. We will follow the exercise with some suggestions for group processing and discussion prompts.

Exercise: Strategies for Social Action

1. What is the problem? Multilevel analysis and identification of recipient of injustice.
   a. What does the problem look like at each level of the system? (see student's response from "Case Conference Bias" example)
   b. Who is the recipient of injustice?
      Is this a client problem? Is this a problem you have experienced? "Clients of color in general are affected; there is not one specific client at this time. There might be other staff who are bothered by it also but haven't said anything."
   c. To what extent does this involve other people and imply collaboration? "Other people could be resources. At this time, no identified collaborators."
2. Goal: Choose a level of the problem and identify a specific goal.
   a. "Individual level, raise the specific counselor's awareness that it seems that ethnicity influences the way she talks about clients."

   b. "Institution level, raise the awareness of the case conference attendees regarding patterns of bias regarding clients."

3. What barriers might you perceive in reaching this goal?

   a. "Individually, I am afraid of the repercussions if the counselor gets
offended by what I say."

   b. "Institutionally, the staff might not want to acknowledge that
there is racism in the room."

4. Strategies for overcoming the barriers and establishing concrete goals:

   a. "Individually I can talk with my supervisor and other staff to find
out how the organization is politically with new staff to find out
possible repercussions. I might also try to find out more about the
extent of political power this person holds in the department.
Once I know this, I know what I am up against, and who could
be my allies in the worst-case scenario. I will also role-play ways of
stating my observations in order to get the point across most
clearly. Once I have some of this information, I will decide how
to approach them individually about my concerns."

   b. "Institutionally, I will advocate for multicultural training with an
emphasis on awareness of subtle biases. I can also recommend that
the case conference's discussions include countertransference issues related to cultural background in general."

The process described above is a simplified version of a very complex,
multidimensional process. The intent of this abbreviated version is to help
students begin to identify social justice issues in their service-learning work
and community and to identify at least one new way they will confront injustice as they see it. In facilitating a group discussion following the exercise,
there are several questions the instructor may want to raise. First, to what
extent have the students identified possible resources and allies? This is a
good opportunity for students to practice obtaining assistance and resources
from colleagues. It is also a good opportunity to practice consultation skills.
Second, to what extent have students identified manageable goals? One of
the valuable instructional lessons for students is the understanding that social
change is a very long-term process and that unrealistic goals can lead to burn-
out and ineffective service provision (Toporek et al., 2006). Conversely,

manageable goals are more likely to foster collaboration, stamina, and perspective on a situation. There are a number of additional discussion questions that may be relevant depending on the specific course and purpose of the exercise. The main point is to move students to action.

Conclusion

In this article, we have attempted to provide an overview of some general issues and concerns in integrating social justice into service-learning education. Interdisciplinary skills and knowledge help students learn to build bridges between various types of service providers and expertise including business, law, social work, public health, and others. The role of training in fostering students' ability to collaborate across disciplines is a critical task of educators. Further, training in ethics should facilitate students' examining their work and their role as change agents or bystanders in social justice concerns. The human service professions have a legacy of social change, it is our hope that our system of education for these professions serves to strengthen that legacy.

References

Aristotle. (2001). Ethica Nicomachea (Nicomachean ethics). In R. McKeon (Ed.), *The basic works of Aristotle*. New York: Modern Library.

Atkinson, D. R., Thompson, C. E., & Grant, S. K. (1993). A three-dimensional model for counseling racial/ethnic minorities. *The Counseling Psychologist, 21,* 257–277.

Blader, S. L., & Tyler, T. R. (2002). Justice and empathy: What motivates people to help others? In M. Ross & D. T. Miller (Eds.), *The justice motive in everyday life* (pp. 226–250). New York: Cambridge University Press.

Bronfenbrenner, U. (2005). *Making human beings human: Bioecological perspectives on human development*. Thousand Oaks, CA: Sage.

Eagly, A. H. (2004). Prejudice: Toward a more inclusive understanding. In A. H. Eagly, R. M. Baron, & V. L. Hamilton (Eds.), *The social psychology of group identity and social conflict: Theory, application, and practice* (pp. 45–64). Washington, DC: American Psychological Association.

Eisenstadt, D., Leippe, M. R., Stambush, M. A., Rouch, S. M., & Rivers, J. A. (2005). Dissonance and prejudice: Personal costs, choice, and change in attitudes and racial beliefs following counterattitudinal advocacy that benefits a minority. *Basic and Applied Social Psychology, 27*(2), 127–141.

Friedman, T. (2005). *The world is flat.* New York: Farrar, Straus, & Giroux.

Hargrove, B. K., Creagh, M. G., & Kelly, D. B. (2003). Multicultural competencies in career counseling. In D. B. Pope-Davis, H. L. K. Coleman, W. M. Liu, & R. L. Toporek (Eds.), *Handbook of multicultural competence for counseling and psychology* (pp. 392–405). Thousand Oaks, CA: Sage.

Kafka, F. (1972). *The metamorphosis.* New York: Bantam.

Kiselica, M. (2004). When duty calls: The implications of social justice work for policy, education, and practice in the mental health professions. *The Counseling Psychologist, 32*(6), 838–854.

Lerner, M. J. (1980). *The belief in a just world: A fundamental delusion.* New York: Plenum Press.

Lewis, J. A., Lewis, M. D., Daniels, J. A., & D'Andrea, M. J. (1998). *Community counseling: Empowerment strategies for a diverse society* (2nd ed.). Pacific Grove, CA: Brooks/Cole.

Smith, J. M. (2003). *A potent spell: Mother love and the power of fear.* Boston: Houghton Mifflin.

Sue, D. W., Arredondo, P., & McDavis, R. J. (1992). Multicultural counseling competencies and standards: A call to the profession. *Journal of Counseling and Development, 70,* 477–486.

Toporek, R. L., & Chope, R. C. (2006). Individual, programmatic, and entrepreneurial approaches to social justice: Counseling psychologists in vocational and career counseling. In R. L. Toporek, L. Gerstein, N. A. Fouad, G. S. Roysircar, & T. Israel (Eds.), *Handbook for social justice in counseling psychology: Leadership, vision, & action* (pp. 276–293). Thousand Oaks, CA: Sage.

Toporek, R. L., Gerstein, L., Fouad, N. A., Roysircar, G., & Israel, T. (Eds.). (2006). *Handbook for social justice in counseling psychology: Leadership, vision and action.* Thousand Oaks, CA: Sage.

Toporek, R. L., & Liu, W. M. (2001). Advocacy in counseling: Addressing race, class, and gender oppression. In D. B. Pope-Davis & H. L. K. Coleman (Eds.), *The intersection of race, class, and gender in multicultural counseling* (pp. 285–413). Thousand Oaks, CA: Sage.

Toporek, R. L., & Pope-Davis, D. B. (2005). Exploring the relationships between multicultural training, racial attitudes, and attributions of poverty among graduate counseling trainees. *Cultural Diversity and Ethnic Minority Psychology, 11*(3), 259–271.

Wyer, N. A. (2004). Not all stereotypic biases are created equal: Evidence for a stereotype-disconfirming bias. *Personality and Social Psychology Bulletin, 30*(6), 706–720.

Zakaria, F. (2006, January 9). We all have a lot to learn. *Newsweek,* 37.

Zimbardo, P. G., & Leippe, M. R. (1991). *The psychology of attitude change and social influence.* New York: McGraw-Hill.

Internet Resources

American Counseling Association Advocacy Competencies from http://www.counseling
.org/Content/NavigationMenu/RESOURCES/ADVOCACYCOMPETENCIES/
advocacy_competencies1.pdf

Counselors for Social Justice, a division of the American Counseling Association
from http://www.counselorsforsocialjustice.org/

Guidelines on Multicultural Education, Training, Research, Practice, and Organizational Change for Psychologists from http://www.apa.org/pi/multiculturalguide
lines/homepage.html

National Institute for Multicultural Competence Newsletter from http://www.geo
cities.com/nimc_newsletter/nimcnewsletter.htm

Operationalization of the Multicultural Counseling Competencies (AMCD Professional
Standards and Certification Committee) from http://www.counseling.org/Content/
NavigationMenu/RESOURCES/MULTICULTURALANDDIVERSITYISSUES/
MCC96.pdf

Psychologists for Social Responsibility from http://www.psysr.org/

The Radical Psychology Network (RadPsyNet) from http://www.radpsynet.org

SECTION FOUR

INTERNATIONAL PROJECTS

IO

SERVICE LEARNING IN THE WORLD COMMUNITY

Video Production in South America

Betsy J. Blosser

Injustice anywhere is a threat to justice everywhere. We are caught in an inescapable network
of mutuality, tied in a single garment of destiny.
Whatever affects one directly, affects all indirectly.

—Martin Luther King, Jr., "Letter from
Birmingham Jail," April 16, 1963

Students in the Broadcast and Electronic Communication Arts (or
BECA) Department at San Francisco State University (SFSU) often
assume they will leave school and enter a career in electronic media,
making programs for commercial television and earning a great deal of
money as they do so. With the highly commercial world of the media industries looming ahead of them, it is often difficult to get students to think
about how they might use the media for pro-social purposes rather than for
commercial gain. Often, they have become inured to the growing chasm between rich and poor in the United States, and have little conception of how
much greater that distance is in other countries. The mission statement of
the BECA department asserts that it trains students to use the media for
social good. Yet asking students to stop and think about the ends to which

The author thanks Dr. Gabriela Martínez of the University of Oregon for her valuable comments and
additions.

their work is devoted presents a challenge in the glitzy, commercial world of the media industries.

How might it be possible to encourage students to pause and reflect on the world outside the United States, and to consider how they might use the tools of their trade to work for social justice? One way to do so is to travel with students outside of the United States to countries where that social and economic distance between rich and poor is huge, and where students can put their media skills to work to be of service to people left at the bottom of the chasm. Working shoulder to shoulder with people whom the social structure has placed at the bottom, and living according to their country's norms, transforms previously abstract concepts—poverty, class, culture, social divide—into the faces of friends. Through this approach, the term *social justice* does not need to be defined or explicated; it is experienced. Students come to see their media skills as tools in the fight for social justice.

In three different years, BECA students have traveled to Latin America—twice to Peru and once to Brazil—to work with organizations aiding children and adults living in poverty and to make videos designed to assist the respective programs with their work. As rich description allows the reader of ethnography to enter the culture of its focus, this chapter is structured to provide the reader with access to the nature of this international experience. It also delineates the goals for the program and how they are met, and it explains how the program is evaluated. In addition, the chapter provides information on how the program is accomplished. Implicit in the experience, but inherent in every moment of it, is the teaching of social justice in this community service-learning program.

Peru, 2001

There they were—students carefully taking video cameras out of their cases, balancing them on their shoulders, and learning how to operate the controls. I had walked into a typical production class in the BECA department, except that this class was being held more than 5,000 miles from San Francisco, over 11,000 feet above sea level, and in the flowered patio of our temporary home in Cuzco, rather than in a windowless studio in the Creative Arts Building at SFSU. The students were considerably shorter than the average BECA student, they were all speaking in Spanish, and they were being taught, not by BECA professors but by BECA students, with occasional breaks to play "duck, duck, goose," to dance to music with an infectious beat, and to have a snack of juice and cookies rather than the customary java. I felt a surge of pride as I watched the BECA students in action, guiding, encouraging, and *having fun* with their younger charges. Pride swelled, too, as I watched their instructor, Gabriela Martínez, a former graduate student of the BECA department and now a faculty member at the University of Oregon, at ease in her role, and clearly in charge.

Gabriela had inspired me to propose "the Peru class," as we came to call it, to a mini-grant program created jointly by the SFSU Offices of International Programs and Community Service Learning. We proposed taking a group of 12 to 15 students to Cuzco to work with *Huchuy Runas*[1] during the summer of 2001 to produce public service announcements (PSAs) in English and Spanish to help promote the services of the organization. To prepare the BECA students for this experience, we would offer an orientation course the preceding spring. The proposal was funded, and much to our surprise, 33 students enrolled in the spring class!

Spring Preparation Course

As a precursor to the summer trip, the spring course established as its objectives that by the end of the semester each student would

Production Objectives
1. Work effectively as a member of a production team.
2. Display a specific production skill that contributes to the work of a production team.
3. Identify and define a target audience, and aim a production at that audience.
4. Effectively carry out content research for a production.

International Community Service-Learning Objectives
5. Demonstrate knowledge of the history and culture of [the Highlands of Peru] [Brazil], and of the current political situation in [Peru] [Brazil].
6. Explain the nature of a nonprofit organization in the United States, and of an NGO[2] internationally.

7. Discuss and employ principles of behavior that will enable the student to represent the BECA department, San Francisco State University, and the United States favorably while working and traveling in [Peru] [Brazil].

8. Complete preparation attitudinally, medically, and in terms of skills and paper work, for a 3 1/2-week trip to [Peru] [Brazil].

The first four of these, the Production Objectives, reflect aims common to any production course in the BECA department. Shaped by communication theory, department courses teach students to identify and become familiar with a target audience, and then to keep that audience in mind while developing a message that will reach that audience effectively. Similarly, students learn to do thorough research on the topic of their productions, to work well in a team setting, and to develop expertise in a specific production role.

In the spring, students develop these production-related objectives through their work with domestic organizations. In 2001, our efforts were much more modest than they became in later years (more on this below). Students rotated positions and teams to carry out production exercises that served the purpose of becoming familiar with the equipment they would use in Peru, but this work did not result in a production. Instead, each group—the membership of which had solidified by this time in the semester—had to develop a complete proposal for a PSA to support the work of a local community service organization of its choice.

The International, Community Service Learning Objectives are what distinguish this course from others in the department curriculum. Providing students with familiarity with the history, culture, and current political situation, as well as the media system, of the host country was a tall order. In the two classes in which we prepared for Peru, we used as texts *Peru: Society and Nationhood in the Andes* by Peter Klarén (2000) and *Andean Lives* by Ricardo Valderrama and Carmen Escalante (1996). The first is an extensive history of the country, which provides a broad background on Peru. The second is ethnography of a husband and wife who are Quechua, who live in the Peruvian Highlands, and whose stories are typical of the families of children at *Huchuy Runas*.

We accomplished the learning about nonprofits and NGOs (nongovernmental organizations) through our work with such organizations, both in the

United States and in Peru and later Brazil. While abroad, we spent a lot of time thinking and talking about the operation of the organizations where we lived and worked. While in Cuzco, we worked at *Huchuy Runas*, but lived at a second NGO—*Colegio Andino de Postgrado*—an arm of a larger NGO, *Centro Bartolomé de las Casas*, an international center devoted to Andean studies. This exposure broadened our perspective on the nature of an NGO.

To me, the most important objective was the seventh one—principles of behavior for traveling and working in another country. As a young person living in Spain, I had witnessed with embarrassment the U.S. airmen on leave from Torrejón Air Force Base, drunk and loud on the streets of Madrid. I had also come of age in the period when the book *The Ugly American* was popular (Lederer & Burdick, 1958). And countless times, I had witnessed the stereotypical U.S. tourist, pudgy under his Hawaiian shirt and Bermuda shorts, camera hung conspicuously over the neck, yelling, "Hey, Mabel! Will ya look at this??!!" loud enough to be heard on the next continent. In this context, I had a horror of being responsible for a group of college students, insensitive to the culture and customs of their hosts, making every possible *faux pas*, and talking *alto voce* in English wherever they went. To add to my worries, the policies of the Bush administration, with its war on Iraq, had intensified existing global hatred of the United States and everything it represented. The last thing I wanted to do was contribute to those feelings.

So I talked about these experiences that had shaped my perspective. The students were too young to remember the book, but they were familiar with the concept of the "ugly American." In most cases, the students recognized the need to "blend in" to the host culture, and understood their position as guests in, and learners about, the country and its customs. They were eager for hints on how to conduct themselves. Gabriela was extremely helpful here. She talked from the heart about her experiences with foreigners visiting Peru, and she emphasized that we were about to visit her *home*, where certain things were and were not appropriate.

We framed the seventh objective in terms of representing well the department, the university, and the country. In class discussions, we contrasted "typically American" comportment—loud, boorish, and insensitive to one's surroundings—with a more desirable effort to be inconspicuous, to blend in, and to be a learner in another culture. For the most part, this resulted in students adding to their political repertoire the need to be a "good guest" in a country not one's own.

Summer Course

The objectives established for the spring course applied, as well, to the summer trip. In addition, as a result of the international production experience, we expected that students would

1. Learn the stages of producing a public service announcement.
2. Learn conversational [Spanish] [Portuguese].
3. Acquire an overview of the communication system of [Peru] [Brazil].
4. Gain an introduction to the use of media in development.
5. Apply their technical knowledge to a third-world environment.
6. Transfer technology, by teaching Peruvian children to use video equipment.

The first objective makes concrete the expectation that students will produce a public service announcement, and acquire the skills to do so in the class. Although students have done some documentary-style production as well, each group has had to think about reaching an audience through a short PSA.

The second objective, language study, has been an essential ingredient of each trip. In advertising the class in the two years we traveled to Peru, we offered preference in enrollment to those with the ability to speak Spanish. This was unnecessary, however, because the potential of travel to a Spanish-speaking country in itself attracted students who spoke Spanish or had studied it. (It was a different story with the Brazil trip, perhaps because so few U.S. students study Portuguese.) Even so, it was a requirement of the course to take a language class while in the host country. In Peru, the schedule worked out so that students attended their respective language class in the morning, which left the longer afternoon to do production work. Because students with a wide variety of abilities in Spanish traveled to Peru, it was necessary to create three Spanish classes, beginning, intermediate, and advanced.

On each trip, the requirement to take a language class—and the necessity of going to class during the period when production was hot and heavy—was the thing students complained about the most. They felt it unnecessarily interrupted their day, and it forced them to shift gears into a different way of thinking from their production responsibilities; in short, it was an irritation. Unfortunately for them, I had little sympathy for their antipathy to language study, and I required them to continue with the classes. Part of living and working in another country is learning the language; making an effort to speak it is a way of learning to fit in and to understand the host culture. Students did make progress with their language skills during the short time in the respective country, and it paid off with positive responses to their efforts to communicate.

As students of mass communication, it was important to the third objective to learn about the media system of the country we visited. This was easier to do in Peru, as Gabriela, whose academic work lay in global communication with an emphasis on Peru, was able to explain in great detail the operation of the Peruvian media system. She arranged a visit to the set of the highest rated TV news station in the country, and we sat in on the taping of *24 Minutos*, a *Saturday Night Live*–like satire on the Peruvian news of the day, during our brief stay in Lima before going on to Cuzco. The biggest thrill, however, was visiting the brand-new cable station, *Canal N*, where all of the staff, including secretaries and receptionists, operate camcorders and ride *motos*. This station had recently "taken down" the Fujimori government by airing the tape of a congressman accepting a bribe from Peruvian intelligence chief Vladimiro Montesinos. In the politically repressive and corrupt environment of that administration, *Canal N* was the only station willing to take the risk of running the tape. Through the results of this channel's courage, students were able to see firsthand the power of the media to serve as a watchdog, or "fourth branch" of government.

The remaining objectives—to gain an introduction to the use of media in development and to apply technical knowledge to a third-world environment—were specific to the social justice goals of the course. We aimed to expose students to examples of how the media had been used in the respective countries, for better or worse, to move the country ahead economically. This involved discussing cases where media messages had been constructed intentionally to promote development, such as the inclusion of health and education messages in Latin American *telenovelas* in the mold of Mexico's Miguel Sabido (Singhal & Rogers, 1999), as well as considering the audience's increased desire for consumer goods, attributable to exposure to domestic and imported TV programming. But it also meant that students recognize the utility of video production skills, their own and those of members of the host culture, in development. That came from the experience of doing production and personally assessing the value of that production to the Latin American organization.

Linked to this, the concept of applying their technical skills to this environment had a dual meaning. In one sense, it meant being "of service" to the children or to the Peruvian or Brazilian organization through the use of students' video skills to assist them in meeting a goal. It was important that students realize the goal was defined *by* the organization. In the event that the organization was unclear about what its goal should be, this meant helping the organization to clarify its aims for *itself*, rather deciding for the organization what the students thought was "needed" and then imposing that goal. So self-determination by the host institution coupled with service to that organization were one part of the objective.

The other part involved students' learning to use their technical skills in a resource-limited environment. Students and faculty alike often complain about the not-quite-state-of-the-art equipment in the BECA department, and the musty studios with ancient lighting. In reality, the department has acquired a collection of just about any tool one would need for a given production problem, and the local Mac dealership is a few steps away at the campus bookstore. In both Peru and Brazil, such resources were inaccessible, and students had to improvise. And *that* was part of the learning!

The final objective, technology transfer, was a part of the two trips to Peru. At *Huchuy Runas*, teaching the children rudimentary video production skills and, by so doing, identifying children with natural talent for videography who could receive special training in video production allowed us to build rapport with the children. The screenings of the children's videos provided an opportunity for the children to see themselves on television, which was a new experience for most, and the screenings served as a social event to which the children responded enthusiastically.

Huchuy Runas

By June 6, the date we actually departed for Peru, the number of students had diminished from 33 to a more manageable 28, still double the number we had originally proposed. The students were prepared and eager to serve.

Gabriela had known about *Huchuy Runas,* an organization that educates, provides art training for, and in some cases houses street children, from her earlier work in Peru. Born in Yucay, a *pueblito* in the Sacred Valley of the

Incas outside of Cuzco, Gabriela had trained as a documentary filmmaker by apprenticing herself to ethnographic filmmakers working near her home. One of her early films portrayed some of the children of *Huchuy Runas*. *Vicuñitas: Girls of the Andes* (Martínez, 1989) is a documentary about girls living in the streets of Cuzco,who earn their livelihood by begging and by selling postcards and handicrafts to tourists.

Clara Silva, the director of *Huchuy Runas*, is simultaneously imposing and humble. Her warm, caring presence commands attention. On our first day at *Huchuy Runas*, after visiting the *talleres*, or workshops, where the children learn drawing and painting, jewelry making, carpentry, sewing and needlework, pottery, tinwork, and bread baking, we sat in the display room of the *Huchuy Runas* office amidst shelves and tables already bulging with toys, watercolors, and crafts made by the children in preparation for an exposition and sale to coincide with *Inti Raymi*, the famous Incan solstice festival later in the month. Clara explained that, with the amount of tourism in Cuzco, these artistic skills would enable the children to support themselves into adulthood. She talked enthusiastically—and definitively—of finding the artistic talent in *every* child, and of the academic education *Huchuy Runas* tailored to the needs of these children. Without *Huchuy Runas*, many of the children would not attend school even for a public primary school education, in part because their living situations do not facilitate regular school attendance. At *Huchuy Runas*, the children split their days between academics and artisanry. They complete the equivalent of a primary school education before leaving *Huchuy Runas*. Afterwards, not all of the children finish a traditional high school education. Of those who do, most do not continue into university. Instead, they work in manual labor as mechanics, cooks, or restaurant help.

At one point in the presentation, we asked Clara what she would do with the additional funding our PSAs were intended to attract. After observing, "There are so many needs!" she recounted cases of malnutrition among the children. Clara described a girl who had set her elbow down on a table, and the elbow broke from lack of calcium. Another child had a splinter in his foot, and due to poor nutrition the child's body didn't have the reserves to fight the infection. Ms. Silva indicated that the cost of regular milk was prohibitive, but that as often as finances would allow, her staff tried to purchase powdered milk for the children, sold there at three times its price in the United States. Milk is a luxury item that most poor people in Peru cannot afford. Cows require grass for grazing, which is in short supply in the

Andean Highlands. That means fresh milk must be transported, thus making the cost extremely high. Powdered milk is rarely produced in Peru; when it is, it comes from Lima. The scarcity of powdered milk, combined with its transportation cost, raises the price.

Clearly energized by their meeting with Clara, the BECA students went to work. They broke into four groups, each of which was assigned to a specific group of children. They spent the first week getting to know the children and teaching them some basic video skills. The children taped each other and their activities in the art workshops. A special screening was held so the children could see their tapes. Then the BECA students planned and shot their PSAs. Each group designed a PSA, which was dubbed in English and Spanish for airing in both the United States and Peru. All four of the PSAs captured the local, indigenous culture from which the children came. They all reported on the positive role *Huchuy Runas*, as an institution, plays in the lives of the children, who suffer from structurally based social injustice reflected in extreme economic hardship, racism, classism, and conditions such as alcoholism and domestic violence. The PSAs portrayed the children not as victims but as people empowered by the education they have received, and the skills they have developed, to "fight back" by becoming productive members of society.

More profound, perhaps, than the skills learned concerning video production were the lessons about poverty in the third world. In the first year, a young man—actually, a forty-ish, African American, returning student—signed up for the trip. He worked in a fish market in a town 60 miles north of San Francisco. His daily schedule involved rising at 4 a.m., driving a refrigerated truck to San Francisco to purchase fresh seafood, delivering it to the market by return trip, and spending most of the day selling fish before going back to San Francisco for class. Victor had never been out of the United States, and he commented any number of times during our preparations for the trip that my arranging this class was a huge service to "students like us who have never had this kind of experience before." The night before we left Cuzco for home, Victor pulled me aside to say, "I used to think I was poor, but now I know I'm not really poor at all. I'm rich."

Modifications to the Original Course Design

By spring 2003 we had modified the preparation course to require that students develop a short informational video for an actual client. That semester, they created a video to inform teachers and parents about a summer educational program held at a camp in Northern California. The program offers weeklong sessions for sixth-graders in elementary schools in California. The camp staff wanted to increase their clientele to more school systems and to help parents who, for cultural and other reasons, might not be inclined to send their children away from the family at that age to understand the value of the outdoor educational experience. One of the advantages of doing this project was that it meant students needed to travel together roughly three hours from San Francisco and stay in rustic cabins to get the job done. This also gave students practice in traveling with the equipment and using it in less-than-ideal conditions. (There is not much light under the redwood canopy, and electrical outlets are few and far between.) And of course, it was beneficial for students to practice working with children: to develop a rapport and to get them to behave naturally while ignoring the watchful eye of the camera.

For the 2005 class, students worked with a community organization called Inner City Youth (ICY), located in the Oceanside section of San Francisco, only a short distance from the SFSU campus. In this inner-city neighborhood, where churches compete with liquor stores and iron bars cover the windows of residences and businesses alike, gang violence has claimed the lives of far too many of its teenage boys. Out of a cramped storefront, ICY offers teens a place to "chill" and to get their lives together. There are writing and GED classes; there is a recording studio that attracts youth who aspire to become rappers; and most of all, there is support for efforts to make it through school, escape from gang culture, and find a job. Part of a citywide effort to stop the violence, ICY is a refuge where kids can hang out. Staff members hope to expand into a larger facility, preferably a vacant house across the street. Students directed their PSAs to helping ICY raise money for this move. Their production work prepared them for keeping a close watch on the equipment, and for a wide gap in life experience between themselves and the focus of their videography.

Brazil: *Salao do Encontro*

Two years after the last Peru trip, and much closer to sea level, a mixed group of SFSU students and new friends set out at dusk, ambling down the potholed streets of Betim, Brazil, led by a short woman of about 30 who walked with a decided limp.[3] It took quite a while to get there, but that gave us a chance to talk, spot establishment shots, and catch up on the day's events. Finally, Fatima proudly led us past a chain-link fence, over an obstacle course of discarded building materials, and into the tiny kitchen of her home. It was made entirely of cinder blocks, with no drywall covering the gray rectangles on the inside walls. Clothes hung on a line strung across the living room. Her son and husband watched TV on a couch in one of the rooms while we sat on the bed that covered the floor space in the master bedroom, and leafed through a photo album. She talked about the achievement the house represented after growing up in her mother's home with its mud floors. Before we left, she served us a snack of *doce de leite*[4] and cheese, and we took a group photo with the new puppy, in her husband's carpentry workshop in the basement.

Fatima had moved from her mother's mud-floored home to her own house as a consequence of her work for a unique "social service agency." Thirty-six years ago, Ms. Noemi Gontijo, then a young art teacher constrained by the rules of the public school system, set up shop in a *favela* in Betim, a small town 40 minutes from Belo Horizonte, Brazil's third-largest city, in the state of Minas Gerais. A *favela* is a housing development that springs up, usually on the side of a hill, one residence at a time. Future inhabitants—often people who have migrated to the city from an agricultural area—construct their individual shelters out of "found" materials: packing crates, cardboard boxes, and other items. Eventually, they become a community. The city of Rio de Janeiro is well known for the *favelas* that hang precariously from its hills.

Dona Noemi, as she came to be called, felt she could do more for children by providing their parents with jobs than she could through the schools. So she trained the adults in various crafts—weaving, furniture making, basketry, ceramics—and sold the products to secure the means to pay the artisans for their work. The project grew into an organization called *Salao do Encontro* (literally, "the meeting place") where adults earn minimum wage for their artisanry, their young children attend nursery school, the older ones receive homework help and learn crafts when they are not at school, and everyone eats the main meal of the day. There is an enormous showroom to display the crafts. Several blocks away, a set of duplexes—one-, two- and three-bedroom units—provide housing at a nominal fee for families who live there until they are able to save enough to purchase their own homes. When one family moves out, another obtains the opportunity to move in and do the same. Fatima and her husband had gradually built their house while employed at the *Salao*.

Once again, a graduate student in the BECA program had provided the contacts that led 11 students and me to Latin America. This time, it was Vanessa Pinhiero, the former host of a Brazilian television program, who suggested the trip. Hearing about the two trips to Peru in a conversation during her application to our master's program, Vanessa matter-of-factly observed, "You ought to come to Brazil." As she prepared to do her culminating experience, she showed me a book sent by her mother that described an organization working with poor children near her hometown. When the original plans for the 2005 class fell through in January of that year, I called Vanessa and asked her if she really had meant what she said about my taking students to Brazil. A quick call to *Mãe*, or Mom, launched the trip, and we prepared to visit the organization, which served both children *and* adults, portrayed in the book. That was *Salao do Encontro*.

In the first week, we all toured the *Salao*, asking questions, taking notes, and getting to know the organization in its entirety. We learned early on that each month the sale of artisanry covered 40 percent of the expenses for the operation. Partnerships with organizations and corporate entities met another 40 percent of the monthly cost. But 20 percent of the operating budget had to be met through other means, and each month it was a struggle. The *Salao* sought additional partnerships or, if necessary, donations to meet its operating expenses. After consultation with Dona Noemi and other staff members, we decided to target our production to the goal of raising that 20 percent. The production teams initially decided to target an international audience with one of their productions and a Brazilian audience with the other. (Later those plans changed, and both groups aimed their productions at very similar audiences.) The plan was to each shoot a mini-documentary detailing the work of the *Salao* and from that footage to also edit together a short PSA.

The second week was devoted to shooting, with the two production groups going in different directions until the end of the day, when we attended our Portuguese class and then gathered around the TV monitor to watch and critique the dailies. At the end of two weeks, when our access to the guesthouse ended, we moved into Belo Horizonte to concentrate on editing. The students spent that week holed up, transcribing tapes and editing around the clock.

Both videos offered a profile of the organization, showing each of the workshops where the artisanry is made, the artists at work, and the philosophy of the *Salao*. One of the videos used a family of a single mother and her four daughters as the centerpiece. The interviews of the mother and one of the daughters were selected to showcase the nature of the work, the educational programs for children, and the housing for families, as well as the life circumstances that take people to the *Salao*. The other focused on the family whose home we had visited, and featured the advances the organization had made possible for the couple and their young son. Since the media presentations were designed to encourage corporate partnerships, each video—over an audio track of Brazilian *samba*—emphasized the skills of the workers, the philosophy with which Dona Noemi had imbued the organization, and the opportunity for mutual enhancement a partnership with the *Salao* would entail.

Evaluation

The first means of evaluation is the production itself. Do students work as a team on its execution? Does each one pitch in with his or her respective talents and skills? Do they display enthusiasm, as well as professionalism, in the process? Do they handle the inevitable glitches with aplomb? Do they get the project finished? Do they incorporate lessons of social justice into the messages of the PSAs? This means not only working from dawn to dusk while in the country, but also scheduling themselves into the editing suite and spending hours of personal time on postproduction when they are back in San Francisco. For two of the three trips, students held a screening in October or November of the fall semester, which presented an opportunity to share their work with family and friends. Students served refreshments— Peruvian or Brazilian—and turned it into a memorable event. In each case, they took a few minutes to talk about the trip and what it meant to them, and these comments served as an evaluation. In each case, they used phrases like "life-changing experience," "trip of a lifetime," and "I'll always remember this."

Such screenings, in themselves, would be sufficient as a measure of what the students had learned. But there are other ways to assess course outcomes. One of those is through the journals that students are required to keep on each trip. The first year, I started out trying to read the journals from time to time, but I gave that up as it became obvious that students wanted to record both private and public information. Yet I continued to require the journals, because they served as a way for students to reflect and self-evaluate.

Another way to evaluate is through the constant contact with students while away. In Peru, the production instructor met with the producers each day, both to watch the dailies and to communicate in both directions with the students in each group. I frequently attended these meetings, and I often met separately with each of the groups, as did the production instructor. Occasionally, when there was a group decision to make, we gathered as a whole group to hash out a problem or make a plan. The fewer the students on the trip, the easier this process was to do. In Brazil, I sat in on the dailies every day. I established early on, even in the spring class, that whenever possible we would make group decisions. That didn't preclude my occasionally calling the shots when it was appropriate, but it did mean that students felt they had a say in decisions we made. That was how we hashed out sleeping arrangements, budgets, equipment failures, travel decisions, and other minutia of living and traveling together for nearly a month—and it worked.

But this constant contact meant that I had the pulse of each of the students during the time away. It was easy to see who was and wasn't pulling his or her weight, who needed sleep, who was having difficulty communicating, who worked particularly well with children, and so on. I heard and saw students' reactions to their experiences, and I kept a journal of my own to record these details. In my entry on the first day at *Salao*, I wrote, "I am so pleased with how the students are doing. They seem to take real joy in meeting the people and learning about the organization. I was so proud of them when they jumped in and started playing with the kids. Nothing like promoting international understanding!" In that same journal entry, I noted how one of the students, a skateboarder who'd taken his board to Brazil, had been out skating. A Brazilian child had admired his hat, so the student followed the Brazilian custom of making a gift of an item on which the other person has paid a compliment.

Finding the Social Justice

In this account of BECA's international community service-learning project, very little mention is made—at least explicitly—of the social justice content of these courses. So one might wonder, in this volume on social justice, where social justice enters into this project. I would argue that it is everywhere. The course objectives do not state such social justice aims as learning to be one among many, acquiring a sense of one's place in the world, and recognizing without arrogance the advantages of growing up in the United States, because they are not measurable. Instead, more concrete outcomes, like contributing to the work of a team and adapting gracefully to living and working in another culture, take precedence. Yet for many students, the trips are transformative. The students accomplish the concrete objectives and have a production to show for it. In addition, they contribute to the improvement of lives in a part of the world they barely knew existed six months before. They recognize, and contemplate, the enormous difference in the advantages their birth has given them, in contrast to those of the people with whom they work. And they see that the world does not end at the U.S. border, in part because they take a little bit of the place they have visited back with them.

Notes

1. In the Quechua language, a *runa* is a person, a highly evolved person, emotionally and spiritually, and *huchuy* means "small."

2. Literally, "nongovernmental organization" or an international nonprofit, usually aimed at development.

3. The ban on thalidomide as a remedy for morning sickness came late to Brazil, as did immunizations for polio. Limps such as Fatima's are common in Betim.

4. A sweet made of condensed milk, common in many parts of Latin America.

References

Klarén, P. F. (2000). *Peru: Society and nationhood in the Andes.* New York: Oxford University.

King, M. L., Jr. (2000). Letter from Birmingham jail. In M. L. King, Jr., *Why can't we wait.* New York: Signet Classics.

Lederer, W. J., & Burdick, E. (1958). *The ugly American.* New York: W.W. Norton.

Martínez, E. G. (1989). *Vicuñitas: Girls of the Andes* [Motion picture]. Berkeley, CA: Taruka Films (Cusco Association to Save the Children).

Singhal, A., & Rogers, E. M. (1999). *Entertainment-education: A communication strategy for social change.* Mahwah, NJ: Lawrence Erlbaum.

Valderrama, F. R., & Escalante, G. C. (1996). *Andean lives.* Austin: University of Texas.

SECTION FIVE

CULTURE AND EQUITY

II

CREATING SOCIAL JUSTICE IN THE CLASSROOM

Preparing Students for Diversity
Through Service Learning

Tasha Souza

"Historically American culture has valued assimilation and, as a result, the importance of diversity often is overlooked, diminished, and/or devalued. In addition, September 11th has caused public sentiment about diversity to rapidly become more negative" (Grant & Sleeter, 2004, p. 62). Yet, the United States is becoming increasingly more diverse (Carr-Ruffino, 1996) and so are our classrooms (Tetreault, 2004). The United States has experienced tremendous growth in racial and ethnic diversity, and as a result Whites are no longer the majority in many cities (Grant & Sleeter, 2004). If current trends continue, approximately 46 percent of school-age children will be of color by the year 2020 (Banks & Banks, 2004). "The nation's classrooms are experiencing the largest influx of immigrant students since the beginning of the 20th century" (Banks & Banks, 2004, p. 209). In addition to racial and ethnic diversity, social class is another important consideration. "Social-class inequality is greater in the United States than in any other industrial or postindustrial society in the world" (Persell, 2004, p. 87). A large percentage of today's students are poor and live in female-headed households (Banks & Banks, 2004). Further, the variations of students' abilities in the classroom have increased due to mainstreaming students with disabilities.

While our nation's students are becoming increasingly more diverse in race, ethnicity, religion, language, social class, and ability, most of the nation's teachers are not (Sleeter, 2001). In 2002, the typical teacher was White (87 percent), female (74 percent), and middle class (Banks & Banks, 2004). Nieto (1996) claims that most prospective teachers, regardless of social or cultural backgrounds, were raised and educated in pervasively monocultural, Eurocentric, English-speaking environments. The growing gap between our teachers and students brings one to question whether our educational system is making a concerted effort to be responsive to diversity in our schools. Are teachers prepared to teach in today's classrooms? Are students prepared to learn and build meaningful relationships with diverse peers? Are students prepared to function effectively in our increasingly diverse society? Do both teachers and students have a sense of social justice and caring for others who are different from them? Research suggests that we have a long way to go to reach a society where all groups experience equal opportunity and full social justice (Schuman, Steeh, Bobo, & Krysan, 1997).

Beginning teachers continue to feel inadequately prepared to teach diverse students and "seldom choose to teach in multicultural schools, especially those with high poverty rates" (Valli & Rennert-Aviev, 2000, p. 15). Often, they know little about and have biases against people marginalized in U.S. society such as people of color, GLBT (gay, lesbian, bisexual, and transgendered) students, people from low-income backgrounds, and the disabled (Sleeter, 1996). It is essential for teachers to understand how the dynamics of difference (e.g., race, class, gender, ability, ethnicity, language) influence classroom dynamics and educational opportunity in order to not create or reify inequities. According to Heward, Cavanough, and Ernsbarger (2004), "students who are different, whether because of race, culture, language, gender, or disability, have often been denied equal access to educational opportunities" (p. 323). There is a growing body of literature that suggests that schools reproduce structures of inequality and oppression (Banks & Banks, 2004; Grant & Sleeter, 1986; Nieto, 1996). If we wish to have schools reverse rather than reproduce racism, teachers must be prepared for the multicultural classroom.

Teacher education is central to helping prospective teachers enhance the academic achievement and future life opportunities for all youth (Vavrus, 2002). Although helping prospective teachers understand and effectively teach people different from themselves is acknowledged as being vital, multicultural education is given short shrift in teacher preparation programs (NCATE, 1996). Without appropriate preparation, novice teachers' instructional practices are driven by how they themselves were taught as students (Ball, 1990). Given the lack of focus on diversity in those earlier-life teaching models, many new teachers are left with little knowledge about and skill in educating students who are different from themselves. According to Gay (2004), student diversity demands variability in treatment in order for students to have the best chances to perform at maximum capabilities.

In addition to prospective teachers, education about diversity is important for students. Understanding, accepting, and valuing diverse cultures will help prepare youth to thrive in an ever-changing society. Students today are more likely than in the past to face challenges related to interacting with and working with people different from themselves. Negotiating daily contact with diverse peers has been theorized to require strategies to manage incongruities in values, beliefs, behaviors, and experiences that distinguish cultural groups (Hamm & Coleman, 2001; Phelan, Yu, & Davidson, 1994). In addition, research suggests that youth arrive in school with many negative stereotypes about and attitudes toward those who are different from themselves already in place (Aboud & Levy, 2000; Banks, 2001; Stephan, 1999).

The national focus on basic skills and standardized testing is diverting attention away from the education that students need to live and function effectively in a diverse nation and multicultural world (Banks, 2004). Although it is important for students to acquire literacy and numeric skills, "students need the knowledge, skills, and values that will enable them to live, interact, and make decisions with fellow citizens from different racial, ethnic, cultural, language, and religious groups" (Banks, 2004, p. 5). Horrendous atrocities committed upon others do not result from people not being able to read or multiply. "They result from people in the world—from different cultures, races, religions, and nations—being unable to get along and to work together to solve the world's problems," such as sexism, racism, and international conflict (Banks, 2004, p. 5). The United States suffers every year from hundreds of vicious hate crimes against people who are considered different and, therefore, less worthy (Oskamp, 2000). Greater social justice will result if students learn to respect one another regardless of categories of difference.

The increasing diversity in the classroom underscores the need for both teachers and students to be prepared to work effectively with and value those who are different. This chapter describes a service-learning course project that seeks to foster an appreciation for diversity for both students and future teachers. The following sections describe the course context, the theoretical underpinnings of the course, the community partners, the service-learning project, and reflection and assessment of the project.

Course Context

The course, Instructional Communication with Adolescents (Comm. 426), offered at Humbolt State University (HSU), is part of the Communicating Common Ground Partnership (CCG), which is a cooperative project between the National Communication Association (NCA), the Southern Poverty Law Center (SPLC), the American Association for Higher Education (which folded in the summer of 2005), and Campus Compact. The project integrates the interests of the sponsoring organizations in better educating youth to embrace the advantages of a diverse society, forwarding engagement of higher education with elementary/secondary education, and promoting service learning as an efficacious method for enhancing student learning and civic responsibility. The project creates partnerships across the nation between college communication programs and local P-12 schools or community groups.

Comm. 426 is a four-credit communication course designed to enhance student awareness, knowledge, and skill level of communication in instructional contexts in order to empower students to make more active, thoughtful, and effective choices in instructional communication with diverse adolescents. Students learn how to use effective instructional communication (e.g., discussion leading, active-learning strategies, question asking) in addition to learning about communication issues in teaching adolescents (e.g., diversity, adolescent development, student communication apprehension, adolescent relationships, adolescent risk behavior). The course is designed to bridge theory and practice by incorporating: (1) a theoretical framework designed to encourage students to reflect on power, privilege, and positionality, and (2) a service-learning project designed to help students progress from more theoretical understandings of communication, diversity, and adolescents to more practical experience as they engage in instructional communication in a service capacity.

The entire course is geared toward preparing for the service-learning project and is divided into three sections. The first third of the course focuses on instructional communication research, theory, and skills. For example, students learn about how one's theory of communication (e.g., social constructionist) impacts their instructional communication practices (e.g., use of lecture versus discussion). In addition, they learn the benefits and drawbacks of various active-learning strategies and how to implement them with diverse groups of adolescents. The second third of the course focuses on adolescent communication and development. For example, students learn that adolescents' greatest communication concern is that of identity management (see Manning, 1996). We discuss the ways in which their workshops (and future teaching experiences) will address this concern. The final third of the course is dedicated to the application of the material through internal and external workshops. At this point, students understand the importance of attending to diversity in instructional design, for it is woven into the curriculum and classroom activities throughout the semester.

The majority of students in the course are preservice teachers in their senior year of undergraduate work. A few communication majors interested in teaching or working with adolescents take the course as well. White students make up the majority of the class, with about one fourth of the students representing African American, Asian, Latino/a, and biracial backgrounds. About two thirds of the students are female, and the majority of students are considered middle class. Although the majority of the students come from fairly conventional backgrounds, they tend to be liberal minded and concerned with social justice. Humboldt State University attracts students who are interested in activism and environmental and social justice. The heart of HSU's curriculum and programs is a commitment to a healthy and just planet.

Theoretical Underpinnings of the Course Project

The idea of social justice is central to the theoretical underpinnings of the course. The course focuses on social justice in educational contexts and helps students to reflect on issues of identity and privilege in order to become more critically conscious. When people speak about diversity in the classroom, they often focus on finding strategies to work with student's differences rather than examining issues of identity and privilege. Educators look for things to "add" to the class in order to "include" all students. Rather than simply integrating tips for teaching diverse students into teaching practices, it is imperative that teachers examine and reflect on difference and how the positionality of the teacher can affect approaches to diversity in the classroom. *Positionality* assumes that important aspects of our identity (e.g., gender, race, class, age) are markers of relational positions rather than essential qualities (Harding, 1991). "Positionality helps us to see the multiple ways in which the complex dynamics of difference and inequality, which come from outside society, also operate powerfully inside the classroom itself" (Tetreault, 2004, p. 177).

Our educational and pedagogical experiences are shaped by our positionality. Carter and Goodwin (1994) contend that it is imperative for teachers to understand their own identity formations in order to better serve children of color because research suggests that a "normal" White person can develop negative racial stereotypes at as young an age as 3 or 4 and grow with these perceptions into young adulthood. According to Boyle-Baise and Kilbane (2000), "pre-service teachers need to question their own racism and biases, learn more about cultural diversity and pluralism, and grapple with realities from multiple perspectives" (p. 54).

In order to prepare prospective teachers to teach and learn about difference, I expect them to reflect on their own positionality. What informs their identity? In what ways are they privileged? In what ways are they marginalized or have they been oppressed? In what ways does their communication in the classroom reflect their positionality? What biases might they have as a result of their positionality? In what ways might their choice in curriculum or classroom practices privilege a particular person or group? Answering questions such as these encourages students to be reflective about what they bring to the dialogue on diversity and what they have yet to learn. Because the dominant Euro-American norms maintain power by remaining invisible, it is important to focus on diversity in a way that decentralizes the invisible center. Therefore, we discuss how the presumptions of Whiteness, heterosexuality, ability, and maleness act to constrict voice by universalizing the dominant positions.

In addition to reflecting on their own positionality, students examine, review, and critique theories and theorists related to the positionality of adolescents. We compare and contrast adolescent identity-development theories by such theorists as Piaget, Elkind, Erikson, Kohlberg, and Gilligan. We explore the positionality of the theorists and determine whom the theories best describe (e.g., White middle-class males) and who remains invisible. The students determine if the theories apply to their own adolescent experiences in addition to those of various diverse youth and reflect on how knowing multiple theories of adolescent identity development can inform and influence their teaching. I provide numerous examples of teaching multicultural youth (many from my own domestic and international teaching experiences) and ask students, based on what they know about adolescent identity development, to determine how the positionality of such diverse students would impact their own teaching in the future.

Consistent with the exercises and discussions about identity development and positionality, the class explores and promotes the concept of critical pedagogy. Critical pedagogy focuses on the construction of context-specific knowledge and alternative epistemology that allows students to articulate, engage, and transform the world in which they live (Freire, 1998; Shor, 1996). Many multicultural and diversity education programs that stress a liberal ideology of tolerance or color-blindness encourage people to accept individuals, cultures, and opinions that are different from their own, "but require little or no work from those in dominant groups to critique and confront systematically their own privileges and power" (Johnson, Rush, & Feagan, 2006, p. 426). bell hooks, a proponent of critical and engaged pedagogy, suggests that teachers should foster education as the practice of freedom rather than reinforce domination. She calls for a "recognition of cultural diversity, a rethinking of the ways of knowing, a deconstruction of old epistemologies, and the concomitant demand that there be a transformation in our classrooms, in how we teach, and what we teach" (1994, p. 30).

In order to empower students as future teachers, I encourage students to be reflective, to think critically, and to take action (Nieto, 2004). Students are expected to reflect on and examine the ways in which they "fit" into current power structures. The knowledge students learn can be used to explore the reasons for certain conditions in education and society and to seek strategies for changing them (Neito, 2004). I expect students to challenge old assumptions about education such as the banking system of education, in which students consume knowledge from the teacher and store it. Instead, I encourage students to examine the ways in which students and teachers coconstruct knowledge. The role of communication is foregrounded, and students are seen as active participants, rather than passive consumers, in the construction of knowledge. Penman (1992) states "meaning is a relational phenomena that is brought about *in* the interaction of participants" (p. 243). Because using critical pedagogy inspires students to question (Neito, 2004), to engage in dialogue, and to take action, I do my best to encourage and model this behavior and support students in doing the same with the adolescents during their workshops.

The workshops the students design are expected to be not only informative but also transformative. Our classroom focus is similar to Freire's emphasis on *praxis*—action and reflection upon the world in order to change it. I encourage them to assist the youth in thinking about and behaving differently, and more positively, toward difference. A workshop on sexual identity should not just describe the various sexual preferences, but rather a dialogue should occur that encourages the youth to be accepting of those whose preferences are different from their own. In designing a transformative workshop, the Comm. 426 students experience some transformation themselves. For example, students develop a deeper understanding of their diversity topic through the process of working as a team to grapple with complex content and instructional design issues. Previous notions of diversity topics, such as what it means to be disabled or what it means to have privilege, are modified as a result of learning to create, "own" the content, and adapt it to students' particular community partners.

Community Partners

The community partners for the course are eighth-grade students in social studies classes at a local middle school in the Arcata School District. The city of Arcata has a population of 16,381 and is located on California's redwood coast, approximately 275 miles north of San Francisco. As the only middle school in Arcata, Sunny Brae Middle School (SBMS) has an average enrollment of approximately 300 students. The typical ethnic makeup of the student body is 68 percent White, 12 percent Latino/a, 9 percent Native American, 4 percent African American, 2 percent Asian, and 5 percent multiracial and other. The school population draws from a wide range of socioeconomic groups, including children of white- and blue-collar workers, with approximately 50 percent of the families being on the free or reduced-cost lunch program.

The demographics of the particular middle school students (the community partners) who have participated in the workshops are similar to those enrolled in the school at large. Thus far, 53 total students have participated in the workshops during the semesters in which the Comm. 426 course was taught. The ethnic makeup of the students who have participated in the workshops was 61 percent White, 8 percent Latino/a, 9 percent Native American, 4 percent African American, 7 percent Asian, and 11 percent multiracial and other. Academically, the students were considered neither high nor low achieving but mixed, with a majority of the students considered (by the teacher) to be average. There were 23 females and 30 males who participated. Approximately 13 percent of the students were nonnative speakers with Spanish being the most common language spoken at home. Those considered special-needs students composed approximately 10 percent of the participants.

Issues related to student diversity are a concern at SBMS so the Comm. 426 students are meeting an expressed need by the middle school staff for communication and diversity education. The administration and staff at SBMS have been discouraged by the low level of tolerance for diversity among their students. Because SBMS has an increasingly diverse student body, the need for encouraging students to appreciate and celebrate diversity is imperative. In addition, SBMS teachers have suggested that there is a need for students to become more competent as communicators, which is a key ingredient to any social justice endeavor.

The Service-Learning Project

Service learning involves students learning about themselves and the relativity of their values, norms, culture, and background. They learn about the applicability of the course content, and they learn about the world around them. The interface between experience, community service, and subject matter prepares students to become concerned, considerate, and connected members of society (Dallimore & Souza, 2002). The utilization of service learning can be beneficial for preservice teachers in numerous ways. There is a growing body of literature that suggests that service learning (a) increases awareness and acceptance of cultural diversity (e.g., Hones, 1997; Sleeter, 1996), (b) has a positive effect on students' intellectual and social/psychological development (e.g., Conrad & Hedin, 1991), (c) challenges prejudicial, stereotypical beliefs (e.g., Fuller, 1998), (d) increases students' perceptions of learning (e.g., Souza, 1999), (e) develops more complex understandings of institutionalized racism (e.g., O'Grady & Chappell, 2000), (f) increases active involvement by students in the learning process (e.g., Krupar, 1994), and (g) heightens preservice teachers' commitment to teach diverse youth, particularly for European American teachers (e.g., Fuller, 1998).

As previously mentioned, the main goal of the course is for students to learn about both the content and process of instructional communication, adolescent development, and diversity education in order to be more effective teachers of diverse adolescents. The primary learning objective for the service-learning project is for students to design, facilitate, and evaluate a workshop as a team that will enhance the adolescents' appreciation of diversity and improve the adolescents' skill in and knowledge of communication. This objective is met through experiential activities and reflections. In order to complete the service-learning project, students must design a 40-minute diversity workshop using active-learning instructional strategies (e.g., small groups, discussion, exercises) for an adolescent audience, present an effective workshop (first to the class and then to the middle school students), and provide constructive feedback on one's own teaching and the teaching of others. In addition, students are expected to write a workshop proposal paper and a workshop evaluation paper.

The service-learning project begins with community building by the heterogeneous teams. After the team members have discussed individual strengths and weaknesses and what they can contribute to the team, the development of the workshops and proposal papers begins. They choose and research their particular workshop topic and are encouraged to be creative in their design choices for the workshops. I offer them a personal library of resources on diversity topics (e.g., books, toolkits, videos), encourage them to conduct research on their own, and provide grant money reimbursement for the purchasing of resources and supplies to assist them in developing their workshops and writing their proposal papers. In addition, they gather information from the teacher of the eighth-grade class at SMBS, Ms. Romo, in order to cater their workshops to the particular students with whom they will be working. Ms. Romo presents information and answers questions about her class and students during one class session and is available for questions during the entire semester.

Students write their proposal papers together in teams by integrating what they have learned about instructional communication, adolescents, and diversity to justify their workshop content and design. For example, students are expected to address how they are responding to student difference in their workshop content, design, and the instructional strategies chosen. They must address how issues of adolescent identity development have impacted their choices. They are expected to be sensitive to the adolescents' positionalities and communication concerns in addition to reflecting on how their own positionalities are impacting their pedagogical decisions.

After receiving copious feedback on the proposal paper, the students complete an in-class workshop. Some examples of workshop topics include social class awareness, intercultural communication, labels and stereotyping, gender and communication, sexual diversity, disability awareness, and power and privilege. The in-class workshop assignment assumes that designing and presenting an effective in-class workshop, as well as observing, evaluating, and providing constructive written and oral feedback for a variety of diversity activities, are useful in preparing for and designing the external diversity workshop for the middle school students.

I expect to see various skills and concepts in action during the workshops. First and foremost, effective instructional communication is a necessity. Many scholars have asserted that in order to have effective instruction a teacher's communication skills must be highly developed (Cooper, 1991; Fountain & Keenan, 1986; Hennings, 1975; Phillips, Butt, & Metzer, 1974; Wilkinson, 1982). Patel (1970) suggests that a teacher's communication process in the classroom is mainly responsible for appropriate educational growth of students. In addition, Hurt, Scott, and McCroskey (1978) state that a teacher's effective communication not only helps students "to develop specific concepts about classroom content, it also helps to shape their attitudes, beliefs and values about the 'real world' and the people in it" (p. 205). Effective instructional communication is central to the creation of a supportive communication climate. Prior to the workshops, we discuss the concept of communication climate and its impact on classroom communication, student voice, and learning. As a result, I expect the students to use immediate communication behaviors (e.g., eye contact) and engage in community building during their workshops in order to create a climate of inclusion and openness.

Consistent with the notion of praxis, the Comm. 426 students are expected to engage students actively in their learning and to create pedagogical situations that empower the students in the class. Students must use various active-learning strategies and be responsive to the different learning styles. It is imperative that they choose instructional strategies that will fulfill their specific instructional objectives (see Kibler, Cegala, Watson, Barker, & Miles, 1981). Each instructional objective is achieved best by strategically choosing a method of instruction that is devised to provide a productive learning experience. Therefore, the students must consider several factors in choosing instructional methods, such as the type and number of students, time available, type of content, instructor background, and, more important, what is most appropriate for the objectives they have chosen.

Peer evaluation teams and I provide feedback on these and other concepts, which the students use to redesign and improve their workshops for the middle school students. Oftentimes, a few teams of students realize that they spent too much time focusing on their particular diversity topic and not enough time focusing on meeting the needs of a diverse adolescent audience. This tendency to focus more on content than on process is consistent with research on preservice teachers (Staton-Spicer & Darling, 1986). Preservice teachers fear looking ignorant. Because both content and process are equally important, the lack of emphasis on process leads a few teams to a major restructuring of their workshops in favor of a more active-learning and varied approach in order to meet the needs of the SBMS students.

The workshop at SBMS is not graded. Students seem to have a sufficient amount of fear regarding teaching adolescents for the first time that they do not need the graded component as a motivator for achievement. I inform students that I can be present as a helper or observer during their external workshop if they would like; they can simply extend an invitation that in no way will impact their grade. Usually, one or two teams ask me to be present.

During the two-week period in which the workshops are being facilitated, Ms. Romo and I are in frequent contact about how the Comm. 426 students are doing and how the SBMS students are responding. In conducting their workshops, the Comm. 426 students use a variety of creative activities and thoughtful debriefing sessions that encourage the SBMS students to think differently about difference. For example, one team included the Bafa Bafa[1] simulation as part of their "Intercultural Communication" workshop. In this energetic simulation, students are divided into two fictitious cultures with differing characteristics and communication norms and artifacts that they must use in communicating with students from the other culture. Participants become personally aware of the issues around culture differences and feel the alienation and confusion that comes from being different. Thoughtful questioning initiated the transformative process encouraged in critical pedagogy. The "Power and Privilege" workshop is another example of engaging pedagogy related to issues of identity. One team of Comm. 426 students conducted an exercise that asked the SBMS students to stand in a straight line and move forward one step if a privilege statement was true for them (e.g., "step forward if you have never been discriminated against because of your religious preference"). Some students ended up at least 20 steps in front of other students. The debrief on this exercise was transformative; in fact, because the activity was done outside and the class time had officially ended, students from other classes actually joined the class discussion on what it means to have privilege—during the recess time!

After the external workshops have been completed, each team writes a workshop evaluation paper as a reflection tool. Students analyze and assess the diversity workshop, their team coordination, and their learning throughout the semester. This paper requires students to reflect upon and describe the process by which they defined needs, created a response to those needs, implemented a workshop, and evaluated its effectiveness. The experiential learning and continuous feedback have allowed students to achieve the primary objective of the service-learning project as well as other course objectives.

Reflection and Assessment

Reflection and assessment of the service-learning assignments and objectives continue throughout the semester. Students are expected to reflect on and write about their own performance as a teacher as well as the performance of their teammates and classmates. Students complete peer and self-evaluations to assess the in-class workshops' strengths and weaknesses. After the final (external) workshops have been facilitated, each team's final paper requires students to analyze and assess the workshop conducted at SBMS and their team coordination. In addition, each student evaluates each individual team member in written form, which ultimately impacts students' participation grades.

In addition to written reflections and assessments, students participate in several in-class reflection activities related to the service-learning project. For example, Ms. Romo conducts and leads a prereflection activity and discussion and a postreflection activity and discussion. Such activities and discussions help the students connect the content of the course with what is actually going on in an eighth-grade classroom and provide opportunities to debunk stereotypes about adolescents. Throughout the semester, I encourage students to reflect on their own adolescence, compare their personal experiences with the adolescents of today, and call into question both the media representations and the research about adolescents.

Students' abilities to master course objectives are measured using evaluation tools designed for instructional contexts, including evaluation on three of the four levels of evaluation for formal training programs (Kirkpatrick, 1994), which include reaction, learning, and behavioral change. *Reaction*, as the word implies, measures how students react to the course content. This level is often measured with classroom assessment techniques (see Angelo & Cross, 1993) such as critical incident reports and midsemester questionnaires. This level measures one thing: the learner's perception (reaction) of the service-learning project and course. Students learn better when they react positively to the learning environment. The next level, *learning*, is assessed through quizzes about the content, active-learning strategies (e.g., discussion) that require students to demonstrate their comprehension of certain concepts, and the written papers. The papers provide the best assessment of whether certain course objectives were met. In the papers, I expect students to interpret, apply, and evaluate various course concepts based on the stated objectives of the assignment and the course. For example, students are expected to discuss which theoretical perspectives of adolescent identity development influenced their choices in the content and design of their workshops. The level of *behavioral change* is defined as the extent to which a change in behavior has occurred as a result of what students have learned from the course. This level of evaluation involves the students actually performing learned skills during their workshops. I give students multiple opportunities in front of the room prior to the workshops, and, as a result, improvement in instructional communication is visible. Behavior data provides insight into the transfer of learning from the role as student to the role of teacher and the barriers encountered when attempting to implement the new techniques learned in the course. Using the various levels of evaluation introduces students to the importance of evaluating their own instructional communication and provides them with tools to do so.

In addition to assessing student reaction, learning, and behavior, the impact of service learning on our community partners, the SBMS students, has been assessed through a research project. The positive impact of service learning on community partners is often assumed and, as such, overlooked. I have sought to remedy this oversight through research that seeks to answer the question, *How do diversity workshops led by HSU Comm. 426 students for SBMS students influence SBMS students' perceptions of diversity and communication?* For two of these courses during different semesters, I assessed the impact on the SBMS students by conducting research using a pretest/posttest control group design. In addition, focus group interviews were conducted.

The survey research results suggest that the workshops have made a positive impact on the adolescents. They report that they are more accepting and appreciative of difference, more effective as communicators, and behave more kindly to those who are different. For example, in describing the most important lesson learned from the workshops, one student wrote, "That when you see someone, we label them. I didn't know that and I am trying to change that for myself." In response to the same question another student asserted, "I learned to communicate better with people who are different." The focus group interview results (conducted with small groups of students two weeks after workshops were completed) suggest that students enjoyed the workshops and are thinking and behaving differently as a result of the workshops. For example, when asked if and how the workshops have impacted them, one student stated that the workshop information "makes you realize . . . how you treat people. . . . someone might be really good at basketball but they are gay. You don't want them on your team, but then you like realize that it doesn't even matter." The research results have generated knowledge that may influence the ways in which diversity education and communication are taught to adolescents (and teachers of adolescents) in the future.

In addition to the research results, Ms. Romo and I gathered oral information from the middle school students on their reactions to the workshops as well. The students claim that they thoroughly enjoyed the workshops and believe that such workshops should be provided to all the students at the school each year. They also indicate that they feel as if they were fortunate and special to have been chosen as the class to participate in the workshops.

Although many Comm. 426 students claim that they believe they made a significant contribution during their service-learning experience, most students have focused on what they *received from* the experience during reflection and assessment exercises and assignments. One student wrote on an evaluation that "the service project was not only worthwhile but vital. There has been no other course that has showed me the joy and importance of teaching like this one. . . . We all learn theories and techniques but never get validation. This class gave me that." Another student wrote, "This course was crucial because it gave us practical, real experience being in the Sunny Brae Middle School classroom. Plus, the book-learning/lecture element of this class was of utmost importance to us in order to learn and understand proper pedagogy." On the one hand, the experience could be perceived as solely utilitarian and egocentric. On the other hand, however, the service experience could be considered positive because students learned how to make a difference in themselves and the world by making a difference in the middle school students' lives.

Conclusion

This chapter described a service-learning communication course that seeks to increase skill and knowledge in issues of communication and diversity for both college students and adolescent community partners. Information was provided on the course, the community partners, and the service-learning project. The majority of the students enrolled in Comm. 426 have the desire to teach adolescents at a middle school or high school as a professional career; this project helps them gain expertise in the teaching of communication and diversity issues. A short-term outcome for students is an increased awareness of diversity issues in education, the importance of diversity, and the complexity of communicating with diverse adolescents. Students learn about the content of diversity education (e.g., disability awareness, intercultural communication) as well as its processes (e.g., giving voice to minority students, teaching to different learning styles). A long-term outcome for students is to consider and address issues of diversity when teaching and to encourage their own students to appreciate and celebrate diversity.

The service-learning project has been positive for Comm. 426 students,

SBMS students, and myself, yet some important questions remain unanswered by the service-learning experience. Do students recognize the complexity of the dynamics of categories of difference (e.g., power, race, class, gender) as a result of the service-learning experience? What are the ethical considerations of such brief encounters with the SBMS students? What is the long-term effect of the service learning on the Comm. 426 and SBMS students? Are Comm. 426 students more likely to participate in the community or politically because of their service-learning experience? Will the service-learning experience cause the Comm. 426 students to work to create social justice in their future classrooms and schools? Although many students stated that they are more privy to issues of diversity and more confident in their instructional communication with adolescents, the difference in their future pedagogical practices remains to be seen.

Note

1. Bafa Bafa is a copyright of Simulation Training Systems, http:www.Simulation TrainingSystems.com

References

Aboud, F. E., & Levy, S. R. (2000). Interventions to reduce prejudice and discrimination in children and adolescents. In S. Oskamp (Ed.), *Reducing prejudice and discrimination* (pp. 269–293). Hillsdale, NJ: Lawrence Erlbaum.

Angelo, T., & Cross, P. (1993). *Classroom assessment techniques* (2nd ed.). San Francisco: Jossey-Bass.

Ball, D. (1990). *Unlearning to teach mathematics.* Report compiled by the National Center for Research on Teacher Education, East Lansing, MI.

Banks, J. A. (2001). Multicultural education: Its affects on students' racial and gender role attitudes. In J. A. Banks & C. M. Banks (Eds.), *Multicultural education: Issues and perspectives* (pp. 3–30). Danvers, MA: Wiley & Sons.

Banks, J. A. (2004). Multicultural education: Characteristics and goals. In J. A. Banks & C. M. Banks (Eds.), *Handbook of research on multicultural education* (pp. 617–627). San Francisco: Jossey-Bass.

Banks, J. A., & Banks, C. M. (Eds.). (2004). *Multicultural education: Issues and perspectives.* Danvers, MA: Wiley & Sons.

Boyle-Baise, M., & Kilbane, J. (2000, Fall). What really happens? A look inside service learning for multicultural teacher education. *Michigan Journal of Community Service Learning, 7,* 54–64.

Carr-Ruffino, N. (1996). *Managing diversity: People skills for a multicultural workplace.* Cincinnati: Thomson Executive Press.

Carter, R. T., & Goodwin, A. L. (1994). Racial identity and education. In L. Darling-Hammond (Ed.), *Review of Research in Education* (pp. 291–336). Washington, DC: American Educational Research Association.

Conrad, D., & Hedin, D. (1991). School-based community service: What we know from research and theory. *Phi Delta Kappan, 72*(10), 743–749.

Cooper, P. J. (1991). *Speech communication for the classroom teacher.* Scottsdale, AZ: Gorsuch Scarisbrick.

Dallimore, E., & Souza, T. J. (2002, December). Consulting course design: Theoretical frameworks and pedagogical strategies. *Business Communication Quarterly, 65*(4), 86–113.

Fountain, C. A., & Keenan, D. M. (1986). *Oral communication methods for the classroom teacher.* Dubuque, IA: Kendall/Hunt.

Freire, P. (1998). *Pedagogy of freedom.* Lanham, MD: Rowman & Littlefield.

Fuller, M. (1998, April). *Introducing multicultural preservice teachers to diversity through field experiences.* Paper presented at the annual meeting of the American Educational Research Association, San Diego, CA.

Gay, G. (2004). Educational equality for students of color. In J. A. Banks & C. M. Banks (Eds.), *Multicultural education: Issues and perspectives* (pp. 211–241). Danvers, MA: Wiley & Sons.

Grant, C. A., & Sleeter, C. E. (1986). *After the school bell rings.* London: Falmer.

Grant, C. A., & Sleeter, C. E. (2004). Race, class, gender, and disability in the classroom. In J. A. Banks & C. M. Banks (Eds.), *Multicultural education: Issues and perspectives* (pp. 61–83). Danvers, MA: Wiley & Sons.

Hamm, J. V., & Coleman, H. L. K. (2001). African-American and white adolescents' strategies for managing cultural diversity in predominantly white high schools. *Journal of Youth and Adolescence, 30*(3), 281–303.

Harding, S. (1991). *Whose science? Whose knowledge? Thinking from women's lives.* Ithaca, NY: Cornell University Press.

Hennings, D. G. (1975). *Mastering classroom communication: What interaction analysis tells the teacher.* Pacific Palisades, CA: Goodyear.

Heward, W. L., Cavanough, R. A., & Ernsbarger, S. C. (2004). Educational equality for students with disabilities. In J. A. Banks & C. M. Banks (Eds.), *Multicultural education: Issues and perspectives* (pp. 317–349). Danvers, MA: Wiley & Sons.

Hones, D. (1997, March). *Preparing teachers for diversity: A service-learning approach.* Paper presented at the annual meeting for the American Educational Research Association, Chicago, IL.

hooks, b. (1994). *Teaching to transgress: Education as the practice of freedom.* New York: Routledge.

Hurt, H. T., Scott, M. D., & McCroskey, J. C. (1978). *Communication in the classroom.* London: Addison-Wesley.

Johnson, J., Rush, S., & Feagan, J. (2006). Doing anti-racism: Toward an egalitarian American society. In E. Higginbotham & M. L. Anderson (Eds.), *Race and ethnicity in society* (pp. 426–430). Belmont, CA: Thomson Wadsworth.

Kibler, R. J., Cegala, D. J., Watson, K. W., Barker, L. L., & Miles, D. T. (1981). *Objectives for instruction and evaluation.* Boston: Allyn and Bacon.

Kirkpatrick, D. (1994). *Evaluating training programs.* San Francisco: Berrett-Koehler.

Krupar, K. (1994). Service learning in speech communication. In R. Kraft & M. Swadener (Eds.), *Building community: Service learning in the academic disciplines* (pp. 103–114). Denver: Colorado Campus Compact.

Manning, L. (1996). *Adolescents' communication concerns.* Paper presented at the annual meeting for the Speech Communication Association, San Diego, CA.

National Council for Accreditation of Teacher Education (NCATE). (1996). *Standards for preparing for the 21st century classroom.* Washington, DC: Author.

Nieto, S. (1996). *Affirming diversity: The sociopolitical context of multicultural education* (2nd ed.). White Plains, NY: Longman.

Nieto, S. (2004). School reform and student learning: A multicultural perspective. In J. A. Banks & C. M. Banks (Eds.), *Multicultural education: Issues and perspectives,* (pp. 401–420). Danvers, MA: Wiley & Sons.

O'Grady, C., & Chappell, B. (2000). With, not for: The politics of service learning in multicultural communities. In C. Ovando & P. McClaren (Eds.), *The politics of multiculturalism and bilingual education: Students and teachers caught in the crossfire* (pp. 208–224). Boston: McGraw-Hill.

Oskamp, S. (2000). *Reducing prejudice and discrimination.* Hillsdale, NJ: Lawrence Erlbaum.

Patel, I. J. (1970). *Communication in the classroom.* Baroda, India: Centre of Advanced Study in Education.

Penman, R. (1992). Good theory and good practice: An argument in progress. *Communication Theory, 2,* 234–250.

Persell, C. H. (2004). Social class and educational equality. In J. A. Banks & C. M. Banks (Eds.), *Multicultural education: Issues and perspectives* (pp. 87–109). Danvers, MA: Wiley & Sons.

Phelan, P., Yu, H. C., & Davidson, A. L. (1994, Summer). Navigating the psychosocial pressures of adolescents: The voices and experiences of high school youth. *American Educational Research Journal, 1*(2), 415–447.

Phillips, G. M., Butt, D. E., & Metzer, N. J. (1974). *Communication in education: A rhetoric of schooling and learning.* New York: Holt, Rinehart, and Winston.

Schuman, H., Steeh, C., Bobo, L., & Krysan, M. (1997). Cambridge, MA: Harvard University Press.

Shor, I. (1996). *When students have power: Negotiating authority in a critical pedagogy.* Chicago: University of Chicago.

Sleeter, C. E. (1996). *Multicultural education as social activism.* New York: SUNY Series.

Sleeter, C. E. (2001). Preparing teachers for culturally diverse schools: Research and the overwhelming presence of whiteness. *Journal of Teacher Education, 52*(2), 94–106.

Souza, T. (1999). Service-learning and interpersonal communication: Connecting students with the community. In D. Droge & B.O. Murphy (Eds.), *Voices of strong democracy: Concepts and models for service learning in communication studies* (pp. 77–86). Washington, DC: American Association for Higher Education.

Staton-Spicer, A. Q., & Darling, A. D. (1986). Communication in the socialization of preservice teachers. *Communication Education, 35*, 215.

Stephan, W. G. (1999). *Improving intergroup relations in the schools.* New York: Columbia Teachers College.

Tetreault, M. K. T. (2004). Classrooms for diversity: Rethinking curriculum and pedagogy. In J. A. Banks & C. M. Banks (Eds.), *Multicultural education: Issues and perspectives* (pp. 164–185). Danvers, MA: Wiley & Sons.

Valli, L., & Rennert-Aviev, P. L. (2000). Identifying consensus in teacher education reform documents: A proposed framework and action implications. *Journal of Teacher Education, 51*(1), 5–17.

Vavrus, M. (2002). *Connecting teacher identity formation to culturally responsive teaching.* Paper presented at the annual meeting for the National Association of Multicultural Education, Washington, DC.

Wilkinson, L. C. (1982). *Communicating in the classroom.* New York: Academic Press.

12

SOCIAL JUSTICE AND COMMUNITY SERVICE LEARNING IN CHICANO/ LATINO/RAZA STUDIES[1]

Velia Garcia

I know of no pedagogy more powerful for teaching and learning social justice than community service learning (CSL). Nothing offers a more profound learning experience than interviewing victims of police profiling for the ACLU or listening to Latino and African American youth locked up in juvenile hall talk about their lives, their families, and their experiences with teachers and police in the disenfranchised communities where they live, or discovering that in the home detention alternative to incarceration, all the homes are White homes, and those who are sentenced to the alternative are invariably White. In community service-learning internships, crime, poverty, and injustice take on human meaning, and the concept of social justice is infused with passion and commitment.

This chapter looks at approaches to community service learning that I have used in two interdisciplinary courses taught at San Francisco State University (SFSU) that illustrate the power of CSL to develop students' knowledge and motivation to work toward greater social justice. The courses, Race, Crime, and Justice and Criminalization of Latino Youth, are cross-listed between Raza studies and criminal justice studies. Discussion of the two courses follows a review of the central role that community service played in grounding and defining early Chicano/a studies with an emphasis on community-based activist research. This little known and largely unacknowledged early history of Chicano/Latino/Raza studies in community service learning was linked to the broader campus and community struggles for social justice that engaged a generation and ushered Chicano/a studies onto university campuses across the country.

History of Community Service Learning and Action Research in Chicano Studies

Today as social justice goals guide our teaching and scholarship and influence the academy it seems only socially just to credit the pioneering work of Chicano studies in community service learning 30 years ago. The history of Chicano studies itself provides an example of community activism and struggles for social justice. In part, Chicano studies emerged as a critical field of study because the research, education, and service needs of our communities were either ignored or ineffectively addressed by the academy. The early focus of Chicano studies on community self-determination forged organic links to community through fieldwork, service, and research viable today.

Efforts to integrate community service and action research into an academic curriculum were roundly discouraged by university committees on courses in the 1970s: Such courses were judged "not academic." Despite difficulties gaining legitimacy in the academy, action research, activist scholarship, and community service continued to anchor Chicano studies and influence early scholarship in the field. The community was perceived to be a learning environment and a means to praxis.[2] The Community Projects Office of the Associated Students of the University of California–Berkeley supported and funded many of these community service-learning projects. Several of the community-based organizations that exist in our communities today were literally built and staffed by student interns, including the Realistic Alternative Program still serving youth in San Francisco today; Clinica de la Raza in Oakland and Centros Legales in both cities were student- and faculty-initiated projects, as was La Familia in Union City and too many others to include here—a clear testimony to commitment and perseverance in community service learning, civic engagement, and social justice.

Some of my own most profound learning, clearest insights, sharpest critical thinking, and long-lived commitments have come from periods of research and activism in service of social justice goals of community empowerment. My teaching is shaped by these values. In 1972, when I first began my teaching career, I developed and taught a course titled La Chicana at UC Berkeley. When the UCB libraries yielded almost nothing pertaining to Mexican American women we turned to the local communities to collect data for class discussion and work assignments. No one among us was comfortable about getting without giving; the element of service became part of our work in the community. We served and we learned. We called it activist research in service to the community; we were 30 years ahead of our time.

Students organized into topical areas and collected data on labor, education, family life, gender relations, social activism, history of settlement, and Latin American revolutions from the perspectives and experiences of women. We pored over community newspapers and conducted interviews with community residents, friends and neighbors, community organization workers, youth, and social activists and seniors. In class we discussed issues that emerged from our research, analyzed the data, and had provocative, insightful discussions about what we learned. There was a focus on service to the community, the need for activism for social change, community self-determination, and social justice. We never questioned the importance of engaging the university in the community. Looking back, I recognize that the class contained all the critical elements of what today is called community service learning, civic engagement, and social justice.

Early community service-learning work was not just about linking the university classroom to the community through service, but also about framing the academic issues of the classroom and the research agenda in terms of community. Programmatic efforts to extend human and material resources from the university to groups and communities that had historically been denied access was not motivated by altruism in the strict sense; community partnerships were developed for mutual interest and benefit.[3] These views and efforts were shared and supported by key segments of the Chicano academic community,[4] and a powerful link between university and community that influenced the direction of research and scholarship in the field.

The introduction to one 1974 publication in which the editors describe the contents of the volume provides examples of this connection:

> Ernesto Galraza outlines the efforts of a collective Study Team in Alviso, California, to keep that . . . Chicano town from being swallowed up and

transformed by . . . San Jose. Guillermo Flores describes how a cooperative
effort between Chicano students and residents of Union City, California,
has attempted to reverse trends that are threatening to displace the barrios
in that Northern California town. . . ." (Barrera & Vialpando, 1974, p. 1)

In 1992, nearly 20 years later, the National Association for Chicano studies
took the scholarly theme of *Community Empowerment and Chicano Scholarship* (Candelaria & Romero, 1992) for the annual meetings. Today, after
more than 30 years, this pioneering work has been transformed and strength-
ened. Today it is wrapped in new clothes as an important academic program.
Today it is no longer discouraged; it is celebrated for its pedagogical values
and for its importance in teaching social justice and instilling values of civic
engagement. The very institutions that were once critical have now appro-
priated and renamed the endeavor *community service learning* (CSL).

The pedagogical model from which I initially adapted CSL to my classes
at SFSU came from the Vacaville Project at UC Berkeley, where I taught as
a lecturer in Chicano studies from 1970 to 1978. During those years I was the
initiating faculty sponsor of the Vacaville Project. The Associated Students'
Community Projects Office funded the cost of university vehicles, and I
traveled with groups of 10 to 30 students twice a week for the first two years
before prison authorities reduced access to once a week. Students taught
modules in ethnic studies for one hour, and in the second hour we participated in the convicts' meeting. Following the meeting there was a half hour
for informal conversation. Students traveling to the prison met for one hour
prior to leaving the campus to discuss what was to be taught and any special
concerns. We also met as a group for at least one hour after the return to
campus; we called this *debriefing and reflecting*. These shared reflections and
planning sessions were central to the learning, motivation, and general success of the Vacaville Prison Project. The Project lasted 20 years before it suc-
cumbed to the changing political climate and university priorities.

I'm not sure how fully I realized it at the time—these were my earliest
years of teaching, and I was still a graduate student myself—but it was in
the context of these shared experiences and direct confrontation with social
injustice that some of the clearest insights and some of the most engaged
learning took place for me as well as for my students and, I think, for many
of the convicts. What we learned inside the prison led to research and service
efforts outside the prison. Students organized to address problems of racial

discrimination, medical and psychiatric abuse, the indeterminate sentence, lack of rehabilitation, and pre-release programs. Students prepared and delivered testimony on prison conditions to Sacramento Committee Hearings held by the Senate Criminal Justice Committee; they organized community forums on prison conditions and alternatives to incarceration at Bay Area churches, universities, and community organizations; and they formed a "pre-release" group to facilitate convict reentry into the community. The project ran a campus radio program featuring convict poetry and call-in discussions about prison conditions and change. It was a time of intense learning and life-changing experiences. Community Service Learning in Raza Studies at San Francisco State University approximates the Vacaville Prison Project model.

Community Service Learning in Raza Studies: Two Approaches

All the classes I teach have a CSL component optional to students. I have chosen two courses that illustrate two different approaches to community service learning. The courses share similar content and pedagogy; both constitute critical analyses and bottom-up critiques of law enforcement, juvenile and criminal justice policies, and practices past and present. Racial and class biases and inequalities are viewed as systematic problems rooted in racialized U.S. histories of contact. Both courses analyze the impact of criminalization on individuals, families, and communities and examine successful impact-mitigating models and directions for change. The lived experiences of men, women, and children caught up and processed through the justice system are stressed; interviewed youth and adults speak for themselves. One course stresses the adult experience, and the other course emphasizes the experiences and perspectives of youth. The primary variation between the courses and the heart of the examples is in the ways the reflection component of CSL is integrated.

The first course example can only be done effectively in a small class of less than 25 students with some of the students situated in block internships that group 2 or more students in the same agency or organization. I require that students complete a minimum of 35 CSL internship hours in placements arranged by me or by the students themselves. Every third week of the course is devoted to group presentations and class discussions around key issues related to the internships.[5] In the second course example the placement of students in internships and their reflection work are handled separately in a three-unit online reflection course. The online reflection component as well as the discipline-based class assignments require students to link course learning and service learning through discussions and written assignments. Class lectures and discussions draw upon the experiences of students enrolled in the required online reflection course. Students choose course-writing assignments that link discussions and readings to the CSL internships.

In both cases course work includes choices of essays and research papers and class projects designed to help students understand the relationship between racial and social justice in a broader context. Students may choose to review an autobiographical or ethnographic study; observe, listen to, and report on cases brought to superior court or traffic court in a Bay Area city over the course of one or two days; go on a police ride-along in a local urban area and interview the police officer; or tour a prison or a jail and talk to inmates or staff. In these more public settings students see, hear, and are able to validate what they learn in the community and in the classroom. Students witness the relationships between race, crime, and justice as these relationships are played out and expressed in bureaucratically organized public arenas.

Exams focus on required course reading. Required reading is chosen to reflect course objectives. A minimum of 10 pages of writing is required. Written assignments are guided by course objectives and are designed to encourage critical understanding of the links between race, crime, and the justice system; foster analytical understanding of sources of inequality in U.S. history, society, and culture; examine effects of systematic and embedded biases of race, class, and other socially crucial invidious distinctions; provide specific information about the experiences of racial minorities, youth, women, and immigrants under the control of the criminal justice system; explore the effects of incarceration on individuals, families, communities, and democracy; and critically rethink and creatively redesign the criminal justice system in a more humane and socially just model.

Community Partners—CSL Internships

A mix of mainstream and activist community service and research-oriented internships satisfies diverse student interests, and the range of perspectives from law enforcement, juvenile and criminal justice, prison abolitionists, the incarcerated, social workers, youth, and community activists adds breadth to the classroom discussions. Contrasts of perspective and purpose between public and community-agency approaches add elements of controversy, offering opportunities to explore the concept of social justice in different organizational contexts. Our community partners have included mainstream institutions like San Quentin prison, San Francisco jails, and Bay Area juvenile halls. Some sites, such as jail home detention programs and SFSU's Project Rebound are established alternatives to incarceration. Activist research and action-oriented organizations such as the Prison Activist Resource Center in Berkeley, the Criminal Justice Program of the American Friends Service Committee in San Francisco, the Criminal Justice Consortium in Oakland, and the California Prison Focus newsletter are included in the mix, as is the mainstream jail-visiting organization, the Northern California Service League. A number of the placements are ethnic community-based organizations (CBOs) that provide direct services such as counseling and substance abuse treatment programs—Instituto Familiar de la Raza and Casa de las Madres—and legal services—Centros Legales de la Raza. These internships are best for the first course example focusing on adults.

The San Francisco Girls Justice Initiative programs, the Youth Guidance Center, after-school tutoring and mentorship programs, Youth Radio, the Real Alternatives Program, school and community-based mentoring programs like Mission Girls, arts and prevention programs like Precita Eyes, Youth Speaks, and Horizons are the kinds of community partners that work for both classes and are especially appropriate for the second course example stressing youth experiences and perspectives and organizations that work with locked-down youth, youth on probation, youth in gangs, substance abuse prevention, community involvement programs, recreational and cultural arts programs, and social activist organizations.

The First Course Example: Race, Crime, and Justice

CSL was fully embedded in this course; it was structured into the syllabus and required completion of a CSL internship of a minimum of 35 hours. Every third week classes were constituted as reflective seminar discussions centered on students' internship experiences. General reflection questions for each discussion week were posed to guide students to think about the questions in logical progression through the semester. Students were required to submit journals for review at the end of each third week. The four CSL discussion weeks spaced over the semester were briefly described to illustrate one way that CSL could be embedded and centered in an interdisciplinary course.

During the first discussion week students shared key facts about their internship placements, characteristics of the client population, professional and student roles and responsibilities, and issues entering the agency and community. About half of the students never had contact with community agencies or with ethnic communities. In the second group discussion students were asked to consider the social characteristics of their client population and to identify the broader social justice issues that their social locations raised. One student began:

> I don't think I really ever thought about it before but I will never read or hear the words "delinquent youth" again without thinking about the kids locked up in juvenile hall and the things that they told me about their lives and seeing how their lives will probably never change. The youth I worked with in juvenile hall do not fit their public image.

The third structured discussion linked the work with community partners to the issues raised in course readings, lectures, and class discussions. Readings and lectures addressed the racialization of the justice system and the criminalization of Chicanos, African Americans, and more recently Latinos. In the fourth and final class discussion students were asked to apply their community service learning to plans of action for social change in local communities. Students proposed more effective and humane ways of dealing with real problems of crime in our communities. Community-based prevention and rehabilitation strategies and alternatives to incarceration stressed student observations and insights from the internships.

The final paper assignment required students to design an alternative to incarceration for nonviolent offenders based on what they learned from course readings, lectures, and their lessons in the community as CSL interns. The same final paper assignment applied to the second course example discussed below.

A Second Course Example: Criminalization of Latino Youth

Criminalization of Latino Youth was first offered at SFSU in 2002 and cross-listed by Raza Studies and Criminal Justice Studies in 2003. The class draws enrollments too large to make it feasible to require CSL internships of all students. Students are encouraged but not required to choose CSL as an option. The big difference between the two course examples is that in this second case the crucial reflection component to community service learning is addressed in an online interactive Blackboard or Ilearn formatted CSL Reflections course specifically designed for reflective learning and supervised by a separate instructor. In this class, students choose the CSL option and focus their course assignments on the CSL internship, substantively linking required reading and class discussions to the reflective-learning experience gained from community service learning. The 12 to 20 CSL students that generally enroll in the adjunct course bring to class discussions examples drawn from their community-learning experiences. These examples are frequently studies in injustice, or they are examples of social justice triumphs; either way they serve to sharpen the critical point of view that characterizes these class discussions: "Everything I am reading in this class about youth in crisis, I am seeing and hearing from the kids I am working with in Juvenile Hall. It makes the reading more important. It's hard to believe what these youth go through but what the readings say, the kids say," and, "I'm convinced that you can't have Social Justice without social equality."

In terms of frameworks for analysis and learning objectives, the course is similar to the earlier example, but with a focus on youth and understanding youth as a special stage of human development with social and biological implications (see the Raza Studies 485 syllabus in Appendix 12.A). Like the first example, this course is taught as a counterthrust to mainstream academic theories, conventional approaches, and public attitudes about race, crime and justice, and youth. Stressing a critical bottom-up perspective is an effective device in helping students in ethnically mixed classes from various academic majors to see with different eyes from different vantage points. Popular culture images and mainstream parameters that contain the public discourse on crime and punishment are pervasive, profuse, and highly persuasive aspects of the culture. CSL is an effective pedagogical tool that can counter conventional wisdom in a way that the mere words of authors and professors cannot. Community service-learning internships put students more directly in touch with the human meaning of racial bias. Social justice stands in sharp relief to the social injustices students routinely encounter in the course of their work in poor, racialized ethnic communities, where urban neglect is matched by the repressive authority of schooling, human services, law enforcement, courts, and prisons.

Learning Outcomes

Nothing teaches social justice as effectively as community-based learning that engages students as whole human beings and illustrates academic concepts with real-life examples. Although different reflection modes are used in the two examples presented here, the end results in terms of learning outcomes are similar. The essential elements of group discussion are contained in both modes, and both address the community service-learning experience from a bottom-up perspective. The students' interface with youth and adults they engage teaches them what it means at a human level to be locked up, abused, homeless and abandoned, stereotyped and written off, and persecuted by the police; often unfairly judged, vulnerable, and without hope for change. They understand the sense of hopelessness they often see in those in less fortunate positions when unyielding authority frustrates their own intervention efforts and when they are faced with the rigidity of institutions of social control. The role of racial stereotyping, the demonization of vulnerable youth, how racial bias works in juvenile justice, and the pitiful lack of resources in the community to address these issues emphasizes for many the importance of activism in social justice work. One student from a southern California suburb said it this way:

> Nothing you say in class or that I read in the books you assign relates to anything I know, anything I experience, or anyone I know experiences or has ever seen. You talk about how the jails are filled with blacks and Latinos but I couldn't really believe it. When I walked into juvenile hall the first day of my (CSL) internship I believed it. I didn't see one white face.

And from an urban Latino in the same course collecting data on racial profiling for the ACLU:

> I always knew the cops harassed poor people and brown people. I've experienced it. I just never knew how widespread it is or that it's called racial profiling, that it's discrimination, it's just wrong and something can be done about it. What I like about CSL is that it teaches you that social justice is possible; you just have to do it.

Another student wrote in his journal, "Where is the social justice when kids are trapped by conditions they had nothing to do with and can't control; when they are victims!" He describes the circumstances of a youth he has been working with:

> It seems to me that this kid has no chance to go anywhere but jail. He came out of foster care; he spent years locked up when there were no foster homes even though at that point he had not done anything illegal and now he will be turned loose at 18. I don't see how he will be able to make it. He has no skills, barely reads and he has a history of petty crime and running from his foster homes. He made bad choices every time he was released to a different foster home because no one taught him how to make good choices. How is he supposed to learn how to make good choices? So, whose fault is this? This is a terrible social injustice and no one is held responsible.

Students are struck by the quickness with which impulsive youthful mistakes and bad choices turn into a lifetime of successive incarcerations.[6] Sometimes one or more students in the class will offer their own similar experiences, mishaps, and brushes with violence or the law and reflect on how differently their lives turned out despite youthful mistakes. Middle-class White students are struck by their own White privilege, and the contrasts of their own lives with those that others report get at what social justice is about: The political is personal. Students in CSL internships at schools, CBOs, and juvenile halls deal daily with youth casualties at the hands of schools and the juvenile justice system.

The youth crisis discussed by author Nanette Davis (1999) and her call for a social justice approach takes on real meaning for students from all ethnic backgrounds working in inner-city schools where teachers presume guilt and are quick to criminalize their students (Katz, 1997, p. 1) and to prepare them for jails and prisons (Duncan, 2000). Students compare the conditions of their own middle-class educations with the schooling of inner-city youth. The sometimes passionate student testimonies are real contributions to class discussions throughout the semester; they affirm Davis's analysis and put real faces and lives into the equation that challenge stereotypes and common assumptions. It can be moving and very powerful for the class as a whole to share in the insights of community service-learning students, albeit vicariously.

At her request, one student, a double major in psychology and Raza studies, was placed at the Youth Guidance Center in San Francisco as a mentor for girls. She learned a great deal about the life experiences of the young women and their circumstances. In class she effectively linked their plight to the harsh impacts of race, class and gender inequalities, and gendered role expectations in the society. She spoke to the enormous burden that inequalities and expectations posed and how they increased the vulnerability of young girls to exploitation. Poignantly she talked about what she called the "shiny potential" she saw in them and the limited opportunity they would have to achieve potential. She reported to the class the litany of statistical victimization of girls. The meaning of social justice stood in sharp relief against the injustice she witnessed.

Another student brought to the class discussion an example of what could only be seen as systematic racial bias in the home-detention-program alternative to incarceration where she was placed. The difference between those sentenced to jail and those sentenced to home detention for the same crimes was literally the difference between Black and White. Donna was able to identify the link between social justice and social equality as she worked in the intake unit and observed that cases of like crimes were accepted or rejected for alternative home detention most frequently on the basis of race. She said she knew that there was racial profiling but that it had "never occurred to me that race would have anything to do with who gets home detention and who gets jail." She thought such decisions were made on the basis of the seriousness of the crime.

These examples of commentaries by students placed in law enforcement, juvenile, or criminal justice agencies and programs are not atypical. The experiences students had as observers and participants in these mainstream internships increased their learning about social justice in large measure because they were exposed to alternative perspectives, interpretations, and points of view either directly experienced in the community or brought to class discussions by classmates. Students working at Project Rebound with young men at risk for gang activity and criminalization recounted the problems these men were having avoiding encounters with police who they maintained racially profiled and harassed them without cause despite their efforts to change and improve their lives.

The discussions, both structured and spontaneous in both classes, were wonderfully insightful, fully engaging, and not infrequently they sparked controversy as students confronted stereotypes and long-held assumptions. Clearly reflective discussions maximize the learning in community service learning. At times the learning in the classroom was almost palpable—a reminder that heightened learning states engage learners in holistic ways, and holistically engaged learners reach heightened learning states.[7] Social justice issues were highlighted by the inequalities and racial biases that students observed in the system. It was apparent in the discussions and in their written work that students identified the social inequalities they observed in communities as issues of social justice.

In at least one case that I am aware of, the CSL placement changed a student from a marginal performer to one of the most engaged students in the class. In the words of Jesse, who came from an impoverished background and was placed with the Oakland Criminal Justice Consortium, "It's humbling to realize that what I do or don't do affects someone else besides just me sometimes with serious consequences. It's an awesome responsibility but it makes me feel good about myself. What I am doing is about more than just my grade."

Conclusion

Community service learning is a pedagogical tool and a lesson in empowerment for students. To understand that you are actually making a difference in the well-being and life chances of others can be very empowering. One student wrote in her final paper, "This internship has made me look differently at myself and the choices I have to make in my life. I know now those choices have to include social justice work." The passion for social justice and the satisfaction of contributing to something larger than oneself often inspired by CSL experiences will lead to lifelong commitments to civic engagement in service of social justice goals. Community service-learning internships provide examples and experiences of how lives can be improved and systems changed through dedicated efforts.

As the history of community service learning is written it is important to recognize the early contributions of Chicano studies and to link them to the present-day "discovery." Today the Latino faculty embraces community service learning, social justice, and civic engagement, because for the most part this is very familiar territory. In the developing field of Chicano studies, the community was our learning laboratory, and service in the community for academic credit was a standard part of most of our programs, offered on many campuses across the country by the mid-1970s. Community was a main point of reference and a vast repository of knowledge; we gained access to the knowledge by doing and learning—hence praxis. Praxis and community empowerment are enduring values that continue to motivate and give greater purpose to our students. "The assumption linking civic engagement with service learning is that students will be more likely to become engaged citizens, insuring the heart of democracy in America, if they experience civic engagement first hand during their college years."[8] The Raza studies experience affirms this. Several of our former CSL interns are now working in community agencies where they are now supervisors of interns. It is lovely symmetry.

The place of community service learning in the academy is assured into the future; its institutionalization essentially complete. There is an Office of Community Service Learning on all California State University campuses; faculty are acknowledging the pedagogical advantages of CSL, a niche for scholarship; and an increase in research opportunities is forthcoming. A record of student hours spent in CSL internships is now included in official transcripts. Employers look for real-world experience from university graduates; students thrive and grow on CSL work; communities seek our students as interns; and community service learning has become a nationwide reality. Well done. The nation will one day reap enormous benefits from this truly progressive development in higher education. It is already producing a more socially conscious and empathetic educated class that takes civic engagement as a given, social justice as imperative, and race the most pressing issue of our time.

Appendix 12.A

Course Syllabus: Raza Studies 485

Jails Not Schools: The Criminalization of
Racialized Youth
Raza Studies 485
Fall 2005

Course Description

This course is a critical, bottom-up analysis of the juvenile justice system. The justice system is viewed as a historically rooted racial project. The contemporary problem of racial profiling and the disproportionate confinement of Chicano, Latino, and other racialized youth are foregrounded in this context. Juvenile justice decision-making processes are examined for differential outcomes by race. Myths, realities, and popular misconceptions about minority group youth and youth crime are identified. Structural sources of actual youth crime including schools, neighborhoods, and socioeconomic conditions are examined in this analysis. The social, political, and economic impact of juvenile justice on targeted individuals, families, and communities is addressed in terms of the costs, consequences, and casualties of criminalization. Youth voices speak out about schooling, police, gangs and drugs, "juvie," and social workers. Alternative approaches to juvenile "crime" and viable alternatives to juvenile incarceration are explored.

Course Objectives

- To familiarize students with the current research and researchers in the field of Raza studies and juvenile justice
- To introduce students to ethnic studies methods, perspectives, research strategies, and contemporary issues with respect to the criminalization of youth
- To foster critical analytical understanding of the relationship of U.S. social history to contemporary racial and ethnic overrepresentation in juvenile arrests and incarceration
- To enable students to develop a critical analytical understanding about

the juvenile justice system and its processes of criminalization and social control

- To encourage students to examine institutional sources and social contexts of the overcriminalization and disproportionate incarceration of racialized youth
- To examine of the impact of criminalization and overincarceration of racialized youth on individuals, families, and communities
- To facilitate an analytical consideration of the social costs and consequences of the overcriminalization and mass incarceration of youth for individuals, families, communities, and society
- To provide a bottom-up perspective on the experiences of Chicanos and Latinos in the juvenile justice system
- To review successful efforts to decrease disproportionality in the justice system and stimulate creative thought about more sensible alternatives to jailing youth

Required Reading

Course Reader Vol. I & Vol. II. (2005). Compiled for this course.
Davis, N. (1999). *Youth crisis: Growing up in the at-risk society.* New York: Praeger.
Mann, R. C., & Zatz, M. S. (Eds.). (2002). *Images of color, images of crime.* Los Angeles: Roxbury Press.

The Community Service-Learning Option

Students choosing the CSL option are responsible for completing all class assignments. Students may focus their papers on the CSL internship provided that required reading is substantively linked to the reflective-learning experience gained from community service.

Notes

1. A note on terminology: There is no generally agreed-upon identifier to describe the Mexican American, Chicano, Latino, Raza population. There is general agreement that the term Hispanic is not acceptable. Mexicano, Chicano/a, or Mexican American prevailed until the late 1980s, when large numbers of migrants came from Mexico and Central and South America. Chicanos defined these new arrivals as Latinos. Significantly, the term *Latino* is not used south of the U.S.–Mexican

border. Today the term *Latino* has become common usage as an umbrella term. If the Garcia and Morratta (2003) analysis of the 2000 census holds and the "other" category among Latinos grows numbers at present rates, the term *Latino* will likely become the dominant term. For the purposes of this paper I use the term *Chicano* or *Mexican American* historically when addressing premigration from Central and South America; otherwise I succumb to the umbrella term *Latino* that lumps together native born and immigrant populations.

2. Paolo Freire (1970), *Pedagogy of the Oppressed*. New York: Continuum. 1993 printing.

3. V. Garcia (1971), "Chicano Studies Proposal to Fund the Vacaville Prison Project With Associated Students Community Projects Funds. U.C.B." (p. 1).

4. *El Mirlo Canto,* Newsletter of the National Association for Chicano Studies (1972, Spring), "Founding Principles"; A. Valdez (1969), *El Plan de Santa Barbara*. It is interesting to note that MEChA has always required its members to contribute time and service to their communities and is often in the forefront of activism for social justice in our communities.

5. I strongly favor block placements for students. Two, ideally three or four, students at the same internship site provides for additional shared learning opportunities. Students learn so much from each other.

6. The California Prison Focus newsletter features the lockdown experiences, legal cases, views and reflection, and creative works of incarcerated men and women. Students work with correspondence and learn about justice and injustice from a bottom-up point of view.

7. I cannot stress enough the importance of reflection in community service learning. Before e-mail became standard for all students and before Blackboard and Ilearn, the journals and the structured discussions were the only reflection tools available. Other tools have since become available. I no longer require, though I still encourage, students to keep journals, and it is no longer necessary to structure reflective discussion into the course format. Blackboard and Ilearn discussion-format online programs are very effective; these programs add to the class but do not absorb as much classroom time.

8. Mary Beth Pudup, Andrea Steiner, & Abbey Asher, University of California, Santa Cruz, "What Difference Does Civic Engagement Make? The U.C.S.C. Experience," Progress Report to the California Campus Compact, Portland, OR, April 13, 2005.

References

Barrera, M., & Vialpando, G. (Eds.). (1974). *Action research in defense of the barrio*. Los Angeles: Aztlan.

Candelaria, C., & Romero, M. (Eds.). (1992). *Community empowerment and Chicano scholarship: Selected proceedings of the National Association for Chicano Studies*. Los Angeles: NACS.

Davis, N. (1999). *Youth crisis: Growing up in the high-risk society*. Westport, CT: Praeger.

Duncan, G. (2000). Urban pedagogies and the celling of adolescents. *Social Justice*, 27(3), 29–41.

Founding Principles of the National Association for Chicano Studies. (1972, Spring). *El Mirlo Canto, Newsletter of the National Association for Chicano Studies*.

Freire, P. (1970). *Pedagogy of the Oppressed*. New York: Continuum. (1993 printing)

Garcia, A. (Ed). (1997). La Chicana, Chicano movement and women's liberation. *Chicana feminist thought, the basic historical writings*. New York: Routledge Press. (Original work published 1971)

Garcia, J., & Morratta, S. (2003). Latinos in the United States 2000. *Hispanic Journal of Behavioral Sciences, 25*(1).

Garcia, V. (1971). *Chicano studies proposal to fund the Vacaville Prison Project*. Berkeley: University of California, Associated Students Community Projects Office.

Katz, S. R. (1997). Presumed guilty: How schools criminalize Latino youth. *Social Justice*, 24(4), 77–95.

Pudup, M. B., & Steiner, A. (2005). What difference does civic engagement make? The U.C.S.C. experience. Progress Report to the California Campus Compact given at the Eighth Annual Continuums of Service Conference, April 13, Portland, OR.

Valdez, A. (1969). *El Plan de Santa Barbara: A Chicano plan for higher education*. Oakland, CA: La Causa Publications.[1]

---

1. El Plan de Santa Barbara was actually the result of collective efforts by Chicano students and faculty from university campuses across the state of California gathered for a conference at the University of California at Santa Barbara to discuss Chicano Studies in Higher Education. El Plan de Santa Barbara established three key principles of practice for Chicano studies programs: (1) the necessity for self-determination, (2) the critical and inviolable link between Chicano studies and community, and (3) the key role of education in preparing students to serve community needs.

13

RECLAIMING A
FORGOTTEN PAST

The San Fernando Valley Japanese American Oral
History and Photograph Collection Project

Edith Wen-Chu Chen

Nancy Takayama is *Sansei*, or third-generation Japanese American from the San Fernando Valley. Her grandparents emigrated to the United States by 1914 and eventually settled in the Valley. By that time, there was an already growing Japanese American community in the Valley that had been coming to the United States since 1885 (Ichioka, 1988, p. 3). Her father, like most *Nisei*, second generation Japanese Americans, spent his childhood working with his family as tenant farmers in the Valley's primarily agricultural community. He attended North Hollywood High School during the weekdays and Japanese language school on the weekends. Nancy's mother, a *Kibei-Nisei*, was sent to Japan for her primary education and later returned to attend Glendale Hoover High School. Her plans for graduation were interrupted by the events surrounding World War II. Following the Japanese attack on Pearl Harbor, Franklin D. Roosevelt signed

I would like to thank the following people: California State University–Northridge (CSUN) students Cecile Asuncion, Teddy Avila, Tiffany Cheng, Jean-Paul deGuzman, Lindy Fujimoto, Yen Hoang, Amy Ikeda, Henderson Lee, Lori Monji, Joseph Kim, Scott Mitsunaga, Dinah Nghiem, Peter Ngotngamwong, Faith Ramirez, Michael Razon, Machiko Uyeno, and Tiffanie Young; CSUN alumnus Gary Mayeda; CSUN's Tony Hillbruner of Creative Media Services and Patricia Miller of Barbara Ann Ward Language Center; Robert Marshall and Mary Woodley of the Oviatt Library; and the Nisei interviewees who courageously shared their stories. Because of their efforts, the voices and experiences of Japanese Americans in the San Fernando Valley will be remembered.

Executive Order 9066 on February 19, 1942, which ordered the forcible relocation of 120,000 Japanese Americans, most of whom were U.S. citizens,
into internment camps (Chan, 1991, pp. 122–129; Takaki, 1989, p. 391). Nancy's mother and her family were sent to Manzanar, one of the 10 internment
camps set aside for Japanese Americans. It was during her internment at
Manzanar that she met Nancy's dad, fell in love, and got married.

Nancy's mother passed away in 1987, and her father in 1999. This was
later followed by the passing of her uncles and aunts. Rediscovering an old
box of family photos, Nancy began to realize that she did not know much
about her parents' history. Like so many Nisei (Hosokawa, 1969), "they just
weren't ones to talk," says Nancy. Their passing inspired her to search the
local libraries to learn more about Japanese American history in the San Fernando Valley. To her astonishment, she found nothing. What started out as
a personal inquiry grew into a two-year research expedition. When she was
not working at her regular job as an information systems operations specialist
in the computer field, she was hunting for information about the Valley's
Japanese Americans. The search started out locally, scouring multiple Los
Angeles Public Libraries, the Los Angeles County Records office, and the
Japanese American National Museum. The hunt then spread to the archives
in the libraries of the University of California–Los Angeles and California
State University–Northridge. Still finding little information that was specific
to the San Fernando Valley's Japanese American community, she used her
vacation time and personal finances to go to the different branches of the
National Archives, including the facilities in San Bruno, California; College
Park, Maryland; and Washington, D.C. She even went to the National Agricultural Library of the U.S. Department of Agriculture in Beltsville, Maryland. After much time, energy, and personal resources, she found very little
to help her understand her family's history. It was as if this community did
not exist. The lack of records betrayed this community's rich legacy.

Working with the San Fernando Valley Japanese American Community
Center (SFVJACC), she applied for a grant to help reclaim this lost history.
The community center needed wo-/man power as well as technical assistance
to help conduct and gather oral histories of the Nisei, who are now in their
70s, 80s, and beyond. She shared with me her vision for the project, which
included not only gathering the oral histories and photos but also a public
awareness campaign to bring attention to the contributions and experiences
of Japanese Americans in the Valley. A "Wall of Remembrance" would be
created, allowing viewers to walk through time as they learned about the

personal experiences and testimonies of Japanese American farming families leading up to World War II, the forced evacuation during the peak of harvest time, the detention in internment camps, and the period after the war when families returned to their farms, or maybe to no farm at all. This exhibit would be displayed at multiple venues and bring public awareness to this forgotten history.

I was moved by her commitment and passion for this project, and excited with the prospect of helping reclaim a past that has been left out of traditional history. Part of what drew me to the discipline of Asian American studies was to participate in social justice projects such as this one. One should be reminded that Asian American studies and ethnic studies were founded so that the material being taught in the classroom could help empower our communities (Hu-DeHart, 1993; Murase, 1976; Tsao, 2003). While service learning is currently considered in vogue by many universities, it was not an idea that has always been accepted by mainstream academics. In fact, Asian American, African American, Chicana/o, Native American, and progressive White students had to endure violence, academic probation, and police arrests to establish a discipline that was relevant to communities of color (Murase, 1976). While service learning may be a relatively new concept in some academic fields, the idea of "giving back" to the community has been the basis for the founding of Asian American studies. Personally, I find it much more interesting when the research question is initiated at the community level, rather than within the academy.

After a meeting with Gordon Nakagawa, who at the time was chair of the department, we decided to carry out the project through the AAS 390 class (Asian American Communities: Field Practicum). This is an upper-division course typically taken by juniors and seniors. As the name of the course suggests, this course emphasizes field study, observation, and participation in community institutions, which naturally lends it to service learning. By participating in this project, I also learned along with students the rich history of Japanese Americans in the San Fernando Valley.

Japanese Americans in the San Fernando Valley: A Hidden History

The San Fernando Valley is a suburb of metropolitan Los Angeles. Some of the cities in the Valley include Glendale, North Hollywood, Van Nuys, Burbank, Sun Valley, Lake View Terrace, Pacoima, Arleta, Chatsworth, and San

Fernando. It has been better known as the playground of Hollywood stars such as Lucille Ball, Bob Hope, and Clark Gable, and later as a growing Los Angeles suburb for young White middle-class families (Roderick, 2001). Few people are aware of the small Japanese American community in the Valley, whose origins can be traced back to the early twentieth century (Iwata, 1992, p. 409).

Prior to World War II, 3,200 Japanese Americans, primarily farming families, lived in the San Fernando Valley. There were many attempts to limit the Japanese population, including the Alien Land Act of 1913, which along with local laws hindered where Japanese American farmers could farm, therefore maintaining the Valley's majority White population. Despite this, Japanese American farmers were a major part of the California agricultural economy, growing fruits, vegetables, and flowers, and were largely responsible for turning California's "wasteland" into the agricultural mecca that it is today (Chan, 1991, p. 38; Osumi, 2006, p. 20). However, after the bombing of Pearl Harbor, Japanese Americans were forced to evacuate and experienced severe losses including land, vehicles, household goods, and personal property. After internment, many returned to their farms only to discover that they had been taken away or that their property had been destroyed.

Why is this important piece of Valley history not well known? The experiences of Japanese Americans, like those of other people of color, have been omitted from the traditional narrative of the American experience. History, as traditionally taught, is not an objective rendering of events, but rather stories from the point of view of the powerful, wealthy, and privileged (Zinn, 1999). Until recently, most of the American public did not care to know what Japanese Americans had to say, and Japanese Americans had little choice in how they were being portrayed during this hostile period.

In addition, personal documents of Japanese Americans prior to World War II are especially difficult to come by. Since Japanese Americans were suspected of being the enemy during World War II, FBI agents would routinely search the family belongings of Japanese American homes. Any material that linked them to Japan would be seen as further evidence that they were not to be trusted. Consequently, many Japanese Americans families destroyed or buried their photos, letters, and personal mementos. When ordered to evacuate from their homes, Japanese Americans could only bring what they could carry, often leaving behind or losing their family photos and other precious belongings.

As the Japanese American community tried to rebuild their lives, not talking about the past was a common coping mechanism for moving on. This included not sharing their experiences with their children, who are now middle-aged. The necessity of collecting these stories has become urgent, given that the Japanese Americans who lived through this time period are in their 70s, 80s, and beyond. Too many have passed away without their stories having been recorded. An important piece of California history is in danger of being lost forever.

Finally, the modesty of Japanese Americans of the Nisei generation is another reason why their stories have gone untold. Nancy Takayama had the challenging task of asking Nisei if they would agree to be interviewed. Some would respond, "I was just a poor farmer, why is my experience important?" Similarly, Mr. Noda, one of the Nisei, was initially reluctant to be interviewed, saying, "Why do you want to interview me? I'm nobody. You should find someone more interesting to interview." Another of the Nisei informants even apologized to one of my students stating, "Sorry you have to sit here and listen to boring old me talk instead of being out and about."

Description of Field Practicum Course

This project was conducted through the AAS 390 Field Practicum, which was modified to incorporate service learning, in partnership with the San Fernando Valley Japanese American Community Center (SFVJACC). The field practicum course naturally lends itself to service learning. The course introduces students to field methods such as interviewing techniques, participation/observation, and other forms of documentation of the Asian American experience. The aim of this project was to document the Japanese American history in the San Fernando Valley from the 1910s to the 1960s. During 15 intensive weeks, the students busily participated in oral history workshops, video training workshops, a field trip to Manzanar, and field trips to the Japanese American National Museum and Little Tokyo; attended community center senior luncheons; conducted and transcribed the interviews; collected photos; and performed library research, archival research, and film editing. The students' long, hard work culminated with several exhibitions including a multimedia presentation at the SFVJACC, CSUN, Mission College, the Pasadena Cherry Blossom Festival, and the San Fernando Museum of Art and History.

Most of the students who took the class were juniors and seniors majoring in Asian American studies. Although all the students taking the class were Asian Americans, they came from diverse backgrounds: Japanese, Hong Kong Chinese, Taiwanese, Filipino, and Korean American. The class size was small: the first-semester class had 10 students, and the second-semester class had 5.

The class was designed to meet the project goals of the SFVJACC. Students were expected to spend 3 hours in class time to work on this project (for a total of 45 hours of class time for the semester) and 6 to 9 hours outside of class working on this project (for a total of 90 to 135 hours outside of class time for the semester).

Oral history is a common methodology in Asian American studies, ethnic studies, and women's studies. As stated previously, the voices of people of color and women have not been given as much attention in mainstream U.S. history and media. Part of the mission of Asian American studies since its founding is to emphasize the voices that have previously been excluded. As Lam, Lam, Matsuda, and Tran (2006) aptly note, oral history can be seen as a form of cultural and sociopolitical resistance that ". . . gives us access to the voices, experiences, and perspectives of people who have been oppressed or ignored" (p. 204). Since most of the *Issei*, or first generation Japanese Americans have passed away, the remaining who have firsthand knowledge of pre- and postwar Valley life are the elderly Nisei. These are second generation Japanese Americans, most of whom were children during this time period. As there is not a great deal of readily accessible documents that testify to their historical presence, oral history is the best and perhaps the only way to recover this part of Valley history.

In preparing for their interviews with the Nisei, students read general readings on the Japanese American experience, as well as about local Valley history (see syllabus in Appendix 13.A). In addition to these readings I assigned two books, *Through Harsh Winters: The Life of a Japanese Immigrant Woman* (1981) and *Promises Kept: The Life of an Issei Man* (1991), both written by anthropologist Akemi Kikumura. Not only do Kikumura's engaging works provide insights into the lives of some first generation Japanese Americans, but they were based upon oral histories of the author's family members. Both of these works also sensitize students to gender roles within the Japanese American experience.

Several class sessions were dedicated to preparing for the interview. This included questionnaire design, interviewing techniques, and video-recording techniques. Common problems for novice interviewers include lack of preparation, reading straight off the interview guide, and failing to ask appropriate follow-up questions. Assigning students to conduct mock interviews with each other, as well as role-play activities, can minimize these problems. Members of the SFVJACC were invited to the classroom so that students could practice with them as well as obtain feedback. The second time I taught the course, students had the benefit of watching the previous class's videotaped interviews, which allowed them to evaluate which techniques were the more effective. Students were also asked to come up with possible interview questions (see journal assignments 3 and 4 at the end of the syllabus in Appendix 13.A). We went over in class what kinds of questions elicited good storytelling, how to make the informant feel comfortable, and how to guide the informant through the interview process. Instructors should prepare students for a variety of informant response styles, ranging from those who give short responses to very talkative informants who may go off on tangents. Some informants will need more prompting than others. One prompt that can easily be used is, "Can you say a little more about that?"

If I were to conduct the class again, I would require the students to have a pre-interview session with their interviewees, such as a casual conversation over coffee or lunch. As with any group of interviewees, one will encounter a range of personalities, and some are more talkative than others. While some of the Nisei had no hesitation in telling their story, Nancy was particularly concerned about interviews with the "Quiet Nisei." According to Nancy, "the Quiet Nisei don't like to talk about the past, especially when it was so unhappy. They think, 'Why burden our children which such bad memories. It's just better to move on.'" Other Nisei may be reluctant to speak, fearful of saying the "wrong" thing or looking bad in the eyes of the community, noted Scott Mitsunaga, an Asian American studies major.

Then there is also the trust issue. Japanese Americans were the only group suspected of being the enemy during World War II, despite government reports that found no evidence of espionage (Munson, 1976). Yet they were still singled out for internment. You could say they have good reason to be cautious in sharing their stories with strangers. Interviewers who plan to conduct oral history with members that have a history of oppression may need to schedule at least one preinterview session. This works to reduce the anxieties not only of the interviewees but also of the students.

Students were divided into interview pairs. Based upon their interests and skills, one student was assigned to conduct the interview while the other was responsible for video recording the interview, and both took turns in each role. This encouraged cooperation, peer mentoring, and also reduced students' anxieties.

Although ethnic history is often marginalized from traditional history, within ethnic history the experiences of women are further marginalized. We found this to be somewhat the case in the interviews and photographs we collected. Most of the people who agreed to be interviewed were men, and they also tended to be more outspoken than the women. However, the men did speak of the important roles that women played, most of whom had the responsibility of cooking, cleaning, healing, and caring for the children in addition to working in the fields. Often women cooked meals and hand-washed laundry not only of their immediate family but also for other workers that their husbands employed. The photos we were able to gather were predominantly ones of men. Perhaps the mundane domestic duties of women were not seen as events worthy of a photograph. In addition, we knew from our informants that most of their mothers and sisters worked in the fields, but still we found few photos documenting this. Perhaps it was the women who took the pictures, since mothers often play the role of family historian. Or as Amy Ikeda, an Asian American studies/journalism major suggested, perhaps the women were ashamed that they had to engage in farmwork, as most did not work outside the home before their arrival to the United States. Proper Japanese women limited their roles to the home as "dutiful wives and intelligent mothers," not to a life of unending intense labor, as often was the fate of Issei women (Ichioka, 1988, p. 168). To balance out the lack of women's voices and photographs in our displays, we highlighted the roles of females as told by the male Nisei, as well illustrated in the interview excerpt below:

> You know the saying they have about women . . . the work is never done. That was absolutely true. Using my mother as an example, she woke up early, made breakfast for everybody. If there was hired help . . . she had to make them breakfast and send them off to work, and as soon as she finished that, out to the fields she went. Then come home half an hour early so she could prepare for lunch . . . So the women worked really hard. I

have to give them a lot of credit for that. (Interview with Ritsuo Takeuchi, San Fernando Valley Nisei, conducted by Jean-Paul deGuzman, AAS 390 student, November 15, 2004)

Student Learning Outcomes

Through this class, the students were able to learn about the history of Japanese Americans in the San Fernando Valley by interviewing the Nisei, or second generation Japanese Americans in their 70s, 80s, and beyond. While several of the students had grown up in the San Fernando Valley, few had known about the existence of the Japanese American community, much less their rich stories. On a larger level, as the role of Asian American studies and ethnic studies becomes more apparent, students question why they had not learned about this history in their middle school or high school history classes.

Cecile Asuncion, a political science and Asian American studies double major, wondered why most mainstream history books fail to include the pre- and postinternment experiences of Japanese Americans. She writes, "It is almost as if their lives are defined solely by internment." Through this project, students broaden their knowledge about Japanese American experiences, and deepen their understanding of how racism shaped their day-to-day lives beyond internment experiences. Jean-Paul deGuzman, an Asian American studies major and history minor, felt that it was important to dispel the notion that the Valley has been racially homogenous. Helping write the introductory panel of the exhibit, he summarizes aspects of the Valley's multiracial past: "Japanese Americans often hired Mexican Americans or Filipino Americans as laborers on their farms. Additionally, the wholesale marketplace was a focal point for interracial/interethnic interactions, as Japanese American farmers, Mexican American laborers, African American haul men and Chinese American buyers all mingled in one place." Students learn to question accepted truths, history, and, in particular, what has not been told.

Having students conduct oral histories can be a powerful teaching tool. For this particular project, in addition to hearing the stories firsthand, students also had to transcribe the interviews, requiring them to revisit the interviews in detail. Teddy Avila was one such student, who comments in his final reflection journal:

My understanding about Japanese Americans in general has grown dramatically. Experiences such as listening to firsthand accounts of struggles on the farm, multiple cases of racism and discrimination, events following Pearl Harbor, internment, and finally returning to SFVF were overwhelming.

Firsthand accounts also allow students to walk back in time and witness the emotional impact oppression had on the Nisei lives. Roy Muranaka, an interviewee, shared his parents' experiences as they quickly prepared for involuntary relocation during World War II.

They had a virtually new refrigerator, and the day before they were supposed to leave, a gentleman came to see if they wanted to sell anything. So my dad says, "I've got the refrigerator," and the gentleman says, "I'll give you a dollar for it." So my dad said no. The gentleman responds, "Well, it'll be free tomorrow 'cause you'll be gone and you can't take it with you." So my dad put it on the street and drove over it with a truck. (Interview conducted by Machiko Uyeno and Tiffany Cheng, AAS 390 students, March 21, 2004).

Amy Ikeda, one of the AAS 390 students, was also able to feel the past through her interview with Frank Emi, one of the Nisei who grew up in the San Fernando Valley prior to World War II. On an outing with his Caucasian peers, he was told he was not allowed to swim in the same pool with them. "Even though the incident happened over 70 years ago," she notes, "I could see the pain on his face as if it happened yesterday."

Finally, students saw their hard work pay off, as we debuted our exhibit at the San Fernando Valley Japanese American Community Center. This included 11 panels, each highlighting a theme of Japanese American Valley life, including Racism and Discrimination, Daily Routines, Getting Sick, School Life, Leisure and Holidays, World War II and Internment Camps, and Life After World War II. So impressed with our exhibit, some of the members of the SFVJACC asked us if we were from the "museum," referring to the prestigious Japanese American National Museum in Little Tokyo, next to downtown Los Angeles. This exhibit also included a 15-minute documentary. It was really moving to witness members of the Japanese American community sighing and laughing as they watched their friends recount earlier days.

Perhaps one of the greatest student outcomes is learning to work together as a team. During one of the first weeks of class, I asked students what were some skills they brought to the classroom and also what were some skills they wanted to develop. I tried to foster a model of Shared Leadership (Omatsu, 2006, pp. 183–194) inspired by grassroots movements in which leadership qualities are embedded in all individuals. Students brought different strengths to the project. Those that had strong academic abilities were good at synthesizing information and drawing out themes from the interviews. Others were dedicated and persistent and could always be relied on to help out with whatever challenge arose. Some who were adept with carpentry skills helped build the impressive frames and easels for the exhibit. Another student who was studying graphic design spent countless hours restoring images of the old photographs. In the second semester, we had one student who was a journalism major who wrote the press releases to advertise the events. Without a doubt, this project could not have been completed without the collective energy and talents of students.

Lessons Learned

When Nancy first asked me to help her out with this project, I thought, Sure! What a worthwhile project and what a great opportunity for students! Twenty interviews seems doable! This project has been one of the most memorable and rewarding teaching experiences.

This is not to say that working on the project was a smooth or an easy process. Students, Nancy, and I worked many long hours into the evenings and weekends. Some students could not keep their commitments, frustrating other students who were counting on them. It cannot be overstated that with a class such as this there can be many unforeseen challenges. When designing the course, faculty need to be realistic about the resources available to them, and plan accordingly. I naively thought that the required time for this course would be like any other course. As I now know better, students at CSUN often have very complicated lives. Most students work, many with full-time jobs, in addition to personal and family responsibilities. Time needs to be built into the schedule to deal with unanticipated human variables.

I probably overcommitted myself to what the students and I could do within one semester. The requirements for this class included transcribing oral histories of 20 Nisei, video-recording the interviews, digitizing photographs, constructing the exhibit, and a final presentation to the SFVJACC.

Keeping students on task, training students, dealing with unanticipated variables, meeting with community representatives weekly, and coordinating with faculty and staff across campus proved to be a daunting feat. Nancy and I spent many unanticipated days and nights at the Community Center to deal with unforeseen problems, especially when key tasks were not being carried out. Some students, although frustrated, took on the work of other students that could not deliver. In the end, most students were gratified with their collective work and the impact it had on the community. Machiko Uyeno summarizes the sentiments of many students:

> As I look back on the semester and on the project, I feel as though the road to the project was a very bumpy one. The class project has to have been the most interesting and informative project that I have ever taken; yet it also has been the most challenging one as well.

I would also strongly recommend discussing with community partners the nature of service learning. Although community groups may be initially enthusiastic about receiving assistance with their projects, it should be emphasized that students are also learning from this process. This means that mistakes and mishaps will occur, and community members should be asked to help students foster their leadership potential. Pedagogically, I believe that service learning provides an opportunity for developing leadership skills and tremendous personal growth, for all students.

Institutions can do a number of things to support service learning, thereby minimizing the frustration of students, faculty, and community people. Some faculty may be dissuaded from teaching service learning because of the time commitment, resources, and the complexities of community politics. At some institutions, extra units or credits are given to faculty for teaching service-learning courses. Extra staff support, or teaching assistance, can also provide invaluable assistance. I am glad that institutions are increasingly seeing the value of service learning in teaching and building community relationships. Hopefully, universities will take more steps to build an infrastructure that fosters faculty and student involvement with communities.

Although the AAS 390 course was conducted for two semesters, it has had long-lasting impact since the course has ended. The popular appeal of the subject matter has led to 10 exhibitions including at college campuses, community centers, a festival, and a local museum. The project was even honored by California State Senator Richard Alarcón. I am honored to have been part of this project and feel that my responsibilities as an educator/academic have expanded to that also of public scholar. Recently, I received a fellowship from the John Randolph Haynes and Dora Haynes Foundation to continue working on this project. The next step is to develop an educational documentary so that high school and college teachers can show it in their classroom. so that the voices and experiences of the San Fernando Valley Japanese American community will be known and remembered.

Appendix 13.A

Course Syllabus: Asian American Communities: Field Practicum

Asian American Communities: Field Practicum

Special Focus: Japanese Americans in the San Fernando Valley

Course Description

In this class, you will learn about the history and experiences of Japanese Americans in the San Fernando Valley through the combination of assigned reading, class discussion, research, and fieldwork. The history of the Japanese in the San Fernando Valley is not well documented, despite its significance. Prior to their internment, approximately 1,000 Japanese American families lived in Sylmar alone. Japanese American farmers once farmed even land that CSUN currently sits on. After World War II, many of the San Fernando Valley's Japanese farming families had lost their land due to tragic events while others struggled with what remained on their farms. Those who remain living are the aging *Nisei*, second generation Japanese Americans in their 70s, 80s, or beyond. Their knowledge and experiences is akin to a library that is slowly burning down. Hence, recording their experiences is timely.

This course introduces you to field methods such as interviewing techniques, video recording/editing, archival research, and other forms of documentation of the Asian American experience. This is a service-learning course in which our community partner is the San Fernando Valley Japanese

American Community Center. Another goal of this course is to develop leadership skills, improve awareness of your own individual strengths, and to develop autonomy and independence from faculty.

Course Objectives

- To learn about the history of Japanese Americans in the San Fernando Valley as well as the greater United States prior to World War II and after their internment
- To provide a community service to the SFVJACC
- To obtain interview skills (including questionnaire construction, interviewing, transcription, and analysis)
- To develop video recording and editing experience
- To learn about archival research
- To build leadership, cooperation, and interpersonal skills

Outcomes

We will assist the San Fernando Valley Japanese American Community Center in creating "The Wall of Remembrance: Japanese Americans in the San Fernando Valley from the 1910s to the 1960s," which would document this buried history. This exhibit will allow the viewers to "walk through time" as they learn about the personal experiences and testimonies of the Japanese and Japanese American farming families leading up to World War II, the forced evacuation during the peak of harvest time, the detention in internment camps, and the period after the war when families returned to their farms, or maybe to no farm at all. A large wall map of the San Fernando Valley will identify the location of the farms. There will be glossy photographs (e.g., of the farmhouses, fields, people, etc.) mounted on foam board along with large text.

Readings

- *Through Harsh Winters: The Life of a Japanese*, by Akemi Kikumura (1981)
- *Promises Kept: The Life of an Issei Man*, by Akemi Kikumura-Yano (1991)
- Reader

Journals

You will be turning in weekly journal entries, responding to the questions assigned for that week. Journals will be graded on completeness, demonstrated mastery of the reading materials, insightfulness, and clarity.

Journal Entry 1

In 500–600 words, discuss what you knew about the history of Japanese Americans in the San Fernando Valley prior to World War II. Were the experiences of Japanese Americans in the San Fernando Valley discussed in your high school or college history classes? What do you hope to learn in this class? What are you most looking forward to in this class? What are you most afraid of?

Journal Entry 2

In 650–750 words, discuss two things from the readings that you found to be the most interesting, disturbing, or surprising. In what way does this help you understand the Japanese American experience in the San Fernando Valley? Why is it important to learn about this history? How do the readings help prepare you to interact with the Nisei you will be interviewing? What do you think the Nisei will be like? What else would you like to know that the readings do not discuss?

Journal Entry 3

In 650–750 words, discuss two things from the readings that you found to be the most interesting, disturbing, or surprising. In what way does this help you understand the Japanese American experience in general, and the Issei and Nisei in particular? Why is it important to learn about their history? What is the significance of oral history in learning about Asian American history and experiences? Why is oral history important to this project? Why do you think *Through Harsh Winters* was assigned? How do the readings help prepare you to interact with the Nisei you will be interviewing? What else would you like to know that the readings do not discuss? Your readings should help you prepare a topic outline of questions you will be asking the Nisei. Prepare 10 interview questions.

Journal Entry 4

In 650–750 words, discuss two things from the readings that you found to be the most interesting, disturbing, or surprising. In what way does this help you understand the Japanese American experience in general, and the Issei and Nisei in particular? Whose point of view does *Promises Kept* try to give, and how does this differ from *Through Harsh Winters*? How do the readings help prepare you to interact with the Nisei you will be interviewing? What else would you like to know that the readings do not discuss?

Your readings should help you prepare a topic outline of questions you will be asking the Nisei. Prepare 10 interview questions and attach to your journal entry.

Final Reflection Paper

In 650–750 words, describe and analyze your experiences with this project. How has this project enhanced your understanding about Japanese Americans generally, and Japanese Americans in the San Fernando Valley specifically? What information did you gather that was previously not well understood or documented? What do you want others to know about the Japanese Americans in the San Fernando Valley? Is there a topic not covered in the displays or video that should also be included? Your paper should include specific, engaging, relevant examples.

In addition to the above, you should also comment on the leadership qualities you have gained from working on this project. What skills have you developed from working on this project? What skills have you learned from working with other classmates? Again, provide specific, engaging, relevant examples.

References

Chan, S. (1991). *Asian Americans: An interpretive history*. Boston: Twayne.

Hosokawa, B. (1969). *Nisei: The quiet Americans*. New York: William Morrow.

Hu-DeHart, E. (1993, September). The history, development, and future of ethnic studies. *Phi Delta Kappan, 75*(1), 50–54.

Ichioka, Y. (1988). *The Issei: The world of the first generation Japanese immigrants, 1885–1924*. New York: The Free Press.

Iwata, M. (1992). *Planted in good soil: A history of the Issei in the United States agriculture*. New York: Peter Lang.

Kikumura, A. (1981). *Through harsh winters: The life of a Japanese immigrant woman*. Novato, CA: Chandler and Sharp.

Kikumura, A. (1991). *Promises kept: The life of an Issei man.* Novato, CA: Chandler and Sharp.

Lam, M. B., Lam, J., Matsuda, M., & Tran, D. (2006). Oral history and multiculturalism. In E. Wen-Chu Chen & G. Omatsu (Eds.), *Teaching about Asian Pacific Americans: Effective activities, strategies, and assignments for classrooms and communities.* Boulder, CO: Rowman & Littlefield.

Munson, C. B. (1976). Japanese on the West Coast. In M. Weglyn, *Years of infamy: The story of America's concentration camps* (pp. 33–53). New York: Morrow Quill Paperbacks.

Murase, M. (1976). Ethnic studies and higher education. In E. Gee (Ed.), *Counterpoint: Contemporary perspectives in Asian American studies* (pp. 205–223). Los Angeles: Regents of the University of California and the UCLA Asian American Studies Center.

Omatsu, G. (2006). Making student leadership development an integral part of our classrooms. In E. Wen-Chu Chen & G. Omatsu (Eds.), *Teaching about Asian Pacific Americans: Effective activities, strategies, and assignments for classrooms and communities.* Boulder, CO: Rowman & Littlefield.

Osumi, T. (2006). Feast of resistance: Asian American history through food. In E. Wen-Chu Chen & G. Omatsu (Eds.), *Teaching about Asian Pacific Americans: Effective activities, strategies, and assignments for classrooms and communities.* Boulder, CO: Rowman & Littlefield.

Roderick, K. (2001). *The San Fernando Valley: America's suburb.* Los Angeles: Los Angeles Times.

Takaki, R. (1989). *Strangers from a different shore: A history of Asian Americans.* New York: Penguin Books.

Tsao, C. (2003, December 29). Recommitting Asian American studies to communities outside the academy: A critical task. In *Azine: Progressive, radical and revolutionary Asian American perspective.* Retrieved from http://aamovement.net/viewpoints/AAS&Community.html

Zinn, H. (1999). *A people's history of the United States: 1492–present.* New York: Harper Collins.

14

CULTURAL ISSUES IN
AMERICAN INDIAN
EDUCATION

Karren Baird-Olson

I approached a political science professor of
mine to ask if there was anyone in the department that I could talk to who could help me
make some connections between what I was
learning in class and what I know about tribal
government. His response was that no one he
knew was interested in that area of study. What
I don't understand is how you can study United
States government and not know the dynamics
of tribal government.

—Charmel McClure, Confederate Salish/
Kootenai (2006, p .11)

cClure's observation reflects the experiences of the majority of
American Indian postsecondary students who have remained
connected or want to regain ties with their traditional cultures.
Her insights also demonstrate the need for utilizing an engaging pedagogy
such as service-learning courses with First People organizations. Thus, the
interconnected purposes of this paper are to summarize the most striking
findings documenting the need for culturally relevant education for both
American Indians and non-Indians and to provide a sampling of pedagogical
approaches used successfully in an American Indian studies community-
partnership course taught at an urban California university.

Although more American Indians/Alaska Natives (AIAN) are enrolling in higher education across all institutions than they ever have before, AIAN still rank fourth among the four minority group categories (African American, Hispanic, Asian/Pacific Islander, and AIAN between the ages of 18 and 24), accounting for just 1 percent of enrollment (National Center for Education Statistics, 2005).

Furthermore, "Blacks, Hispanics, and American Indians remain less likely to graduate from college than other Americans. This national failure undermines the foundations of a free society, interferes with efforts to build a competitive work force, and raises doubts about our educational system's capacity to respond to oncoming demographic changes" (Richardson & de los Santos, 1988, p. 1).

Social Forces Contributing to the Push-Out Crisis

Today enlightened policy makers and educators no longer would argue that the goal of education for American Indian should be assimilation,

> a process [that was] believed would eventually lead to the extinction of indigenous communities residing within the boundaries of the United States as Native children were acculturated in Euro-American society. The goal was to convert young Native Americans into "white men," with future generations naturally following their lead since Western European–based society was "inherently superior" to tribal society. If extinction did not occur, adherents believed, at the very least Indian identity would be suppressed. One of the most outspoken proponents of these views was Colonel Richard Henry Pratt, a leader in the late-1800s movement to educate Native Americans based on a Western European model and founder of the Carlisle Indian School in Pennsylvania. The goal of educating "Indians," in Colonel Pratt's view, was to "[k]ill the Indian, save the Man." (U.S. Commission on Civil Rights, 2003, p. 84)

Given the magnitude of the educational crisis facing American Indian students, the retention problem is a social issue rather than an individual problem. Racism, cultural discontinuity, poverty, health issues, lack of educational role models, and school policies all contribute to the unmet needs of American Indian/Alaska Native students. Reyhner has noted: "Academically capable Native students often drop out of school because their needs are not being met while others are pushed out because they protest in a variety of ways how they are treated in school" (Reyhner, 1992, p. 1). Three consistent themes in the research literature on how to improve the retention of American Indian students and to increase sensitivity among non-Indian teachers, administrators, and students are (1) the need to reduce cultural discontinuity, (2) the need to honor American Indian personal and cultural identity, and (3) the need to create culturally relevant courses (Gordon, 2004; Reyhner, 1992; Richardson & de los Santos, 1988; St. Germain, 1995; U.S. Commission on Civil Rights, 2003).

Research that has been done to support American Indian student retention in public schools also has relevance for postsecondary retention. Jon Reyhner's (1992) following observations reflect the commonly held positions of traditional tribal leaders, who point out that indigenous students are sent to Eurocentric schools not to become non-Indian but to learn how to survive in the dominant culture[1]:

> Teachers need to build on the cultural values that Native parents give their children if teachers want to produce a strong positive sense of identity in their students. Attempts to replace students' Native identity with a dominant cultural identity confuse and repel Native students and force them to make a choice to either reject their families' values or their teachers' values. Neither choice is desirable or necessary. Students can be academically successful and learn about the larger non-Native world while at the same time retaining and developing their Native identity. (p. 19)

For the unique and heterogeneous nature of urban American Indian populations, most of whom are separated by vast geographical distances from their homelands, universities situated in areas with large numbers of First Peoples can play a vital role in assisting instructors and students by offering community partnership courses, thereby increasing student retention.

Creating Learning Communities Where Students Can Thrive

> Students are more likely to thrive in environments that support their cultural identities while introducing different ideas. The importance of such environments cannot be overstated. Such programs motivate students, support improved academic performance, promote a positive sense of identify

and self, stimulate favorable attitudes about school and others, and earn the support and positive perception of the community toward the school. (U.S. Commission on Human Rights, 2003, p. 87)

Because students who stay on their reservations and attend their tribal colleges are eight times less likely to drop out of school (American Indian College Fund, 2007), educators need to look at what tribal colleges and American Indian studies in nontribal colleges and universities are doing to reduce student alienation. This section will review the work begun by an urban American Indian studies program in a major urban teaching university. The first initiative of the program is to respect traditional identities and to increase retention of American Indian students.[2] The second initiative is to increase sensitivity of non-Indian students, teachers, staff, and administrators. One of the most successful pedagogical strategies has been the creation of a service-learning course that embodies the program's mission and learning outcomes.

Before describing the American Indian studies (AIS) service-learning course in more detail, I will briefly describe the AIS minor at California State University–Northridge (CSUN). AIS programs are unique in that they are multidisciplinary and take an indigenous rather than a Eurocentric perspective (Lobo & Talbot, 2001, p. 3). Why? As seen previously, cultural identity matters. Our AIS program's mission statement and five learning outcomes reflect this reality:

> Through its commitment to traditional indigenous approaches, American Indian Studies (AIS) education is learning-centered. AIS aims to provide access to the unique cultures and experiences of sovereign Indian nations and to educate a critical mass of students with knowledge of the voices, values, and traditions of First Peoples. Through AIS courses, student organizations, research, and community partnerships, [the university] provides an invaluable resource to the larger indigenous community. (AIS Program Mission)

AIS Program Learning Goals

1. Demonstrate the ability to further refine critical thinking, written and oral skills, and other creative endeavors.

2. Develop a critical and reflective perspective on Western interpretations of the experiences of First Peoples, in particular an understanding of internal colonialism.
3. Demonstrate an appreciation of the commonalities as well as the uniqueness of indigenous cultures and nations.
4. Demonstrate a commitment through effective community service to work cooperatively with indigenous peoples.
5. Demonstrate an enhanced professional ability to serve indigenous communities.

Since I came to CSUN six years ago, I have added four AIS courses to the interdisciplinary minor: AIS 101, Introduction to American Indian Studies; AIS 304, American Indian Law and Policy; AIS 401, Contemporary American Indian Social Issues; and AIS 499, Independent Studies. AIS 401 is a survey course that uses service learning to examine contemporary social issues of American Indians. Recognizing and accepting the unique sovereign status of American Indian nations, the students examine current social issues such as economic development, education, sports mascots and other negative symbols, mass media and American Indians, freedom of religion, Indian Child Welfare Act, health, Indian gaming and tourism, urban Indians, American Indians and the concept of place, the American Indian Movement, American Indian identity, affirmative action and human rights, multicultural education, public and private schools, American Indian colleges, criminal and civil justice and American Indians, peacemaking and restorative justice, environmental racism, economic development, and federal–state–tribal relationships. After the first two months of the semester, the majority of the course time is spent with the students' indigenous community partners.

The community partners have included the Fernandeno Tataviam band of Mission Indians, on whose land the university sits, as well as nonlocal First Nations; a citywide American Indian education organization; an urban American Indian center; an American Indian cultural center and park; a traditional American Indian woman who is employed as a county health educator for AIDS/HIV prevention; a traditional American Indian healer who works for an area youth correctional facility; and an American Indian law center. Since American Indian organizations and agencies are typically understaffed and have limited financial resources, oftentimes more than one student will partner with the same organization. The students work with their community partners to determine how best they may help them. To illustrate only a few of the partnership projects, students have helped tribes with their tribal enrollment data or with their youth programs; a First Nations student from out of state helped her tribe develop its initial plans for a tribal college; another student who not only helped with the upkeep of the physical grounds of a local cultural center but also went on to become a highly successful tour guide is now a student at an American Indian law school; and a non-Indian woman, who was a public school teacher, with the assistance of local American Indians developed a culturally sensitive and accurate American Indian teaching unit for third graders.

Drawing upon the American Indian studies program's five learning outcomes, AIS 401 focuses on outcomes 1, 2, 4, and 5 (see list at the beginning of this section). The students' mastery of these outcomes is assessed through the use of four evaluation techniques: participation, one exam, a journal, and a final report. Participation is based on active class partnership as well as the findings from my consultations with the community partners. The comprehensive objective-and-essay exam, given about two thirds of the way through the semester, is based on class readings, discussion, and specific community partnership experiences.[3] Each student keeps a journal of his or her community partnership experience, which I review at least twice during the semester. This requirement gives me the opportunity to give each student personal feedback as well as to see what topics or issues I may need to address. The journals also provide participant observation documentation and reflections that the students will need to write their final reports.

In preparation for the partnerships, I share my pedagogical philosophy, which includes the recognition that undergraduate and graduate degrees are tools of power. Historically, Euro-American schools have provided two formal educational services: professional preparation and personal life enhancement skills. In addition, a number of educational institutions have offered resources for learning how to be responsible as well as thoughtful community members and leaders. Learning, in the two latter cases, is seen as an ongoing process rather than a terminal product. My teaching ideals are not only to share my academic knowledge and experiential wisdom but also to motivate and assist students to learn how to become lifelong learners.

In order to most effectively achieve these goals, I teach my classes in an interactive style emphasizing cooperation and respect for individual and cultural differences. And the format is framed primarily in the traditional educational style of Native Americans, a pedagogy that has been largely experiential. Thus, community partnership courses are particularly relevant, as students are given opportunities to learn by listening, observing, and doing.

Based on student enthusiasm and appreciation reflected in the student reflective journals, their partnership reports, e-mail messages, personal discussions, and course/teacher evaluations, the educational strategies that I most commonly utilize to increase awareness, cooperation, and cross-cultural sensitivity are summarized in the following discussion. The pedagogical exercises, briefly described in the chronological order in which they are offered, are (1) course goals consensus exercise, (2) five core values for a successful learning community discussion, (3) Frequently Asked Questions and other myths discussions, (4) traditional communication styles and values discussion, (5) Frybread IQ exam (1991), and (6) the Talking Circle.

In order to provide another opportunity for students to get acquainted with each other, to provide practice in doing group work, and to allow each student to take ownership in the course, I do not begin the semester by handing out finalized syllabi. The first part of the first class period is spent getting acquainted with each other and orally identifying the overall goals of the course. The students learn that each can identify at least one goal and that, while some of the goals that they have discussed were the same, others differed, and all have merit. The next step in the goals exercise, given the necessity to facilitate communication in a course that involves both cognitive and affective learning, is to reach a harmonious class decision on the priority of the goals. I then give the students a handout listing the following seven goal statements, commonly used objectives for studying contemporary American Indian social issues:

1. To increase awareness about the experiences of all American Indian groups
2. To develop cross-cultural skills and values that will ensure successful social interaction with American Indians
3. To identify solutions for American Indian social issues that respect traditional cultures and the nations' sovereign status
4. To promote intercultural communication through an understanding of differing verbal and nonverbal communication styles
5. To advance American Indian identity by respecting cultural histories

6. To abolish myths about the modern American Indian experience

7. To identify and change negative conceptions about American Indians

After the students individually rank-order the goals, I randomly divide them into groups of no more than five students each. The group task is to reach consensus on the ordering as well as to provide three reasons for their first choice and two reasons for their last choice. Each group orally reports its rankings and reasons.

The students begin to see patterns of agreement as well as differences and that there are no right or wrong answers, only different ways of addressing shared concerns. The group rankings are later collapsed and included in the syllabus and also play a role in shaping the focus priorities in class discussions for that particular semester.

During the second or third meeting of the course I share five core educational values for a successful learning community identified and described by Ronald David Glass and Kendra R. Wallace (1996, pp. 355–356) and then compare them with parallel traditional indigenous values: creating learning communities; respecting every voice; seeking truth in all of life; compassionately understanding; and calling for nonviolent justice. I then ask the students if they are willing to live by these values. The response is typically unanimous in the affirmative. Later, if a student socialized into a Jerry Springer style of communication lapses into nonactive listening mode in the classroom, for instance, he or she is gently reminded of the core values. This framework for communication also helps prepare students for respecting cultural differences in the partnership sites.

Given the inordinate number of myths about American Indian historical and contemporary experiences and the critical need to address them immediately in order to prevent muddying the water of future discussions within the partnership sites as well as within the classroom, in addition to the required textbooks I provide a preliminary reading list of reliable materials and Web sites, and one class session is spent at the library learning how to do responsible research on American Indians. In addition, the students read and discuss in class a handout by the Bureau of Indian Affairs titled "Answers to Frequently Asked Questions" (n.d.). In order to help students begin to learn how to separate myths such as that First Peoples receive free money from the U.S. government and realities such as that American Indians do not receive free college education from the government, I also provide and discuss written guidelines on how to critique information. Students learn that even official documents can gloss over, minimize, and/or omit critical information about American Indians.

Another step in the preparation for going into the field is a discussion of cultural differences in verbal and nonverbal communication styles and values, particularly among more traditional peoples. To provide only two examples: The wisdom of the elderly is highly valued, and direct eye contact can be a sign of disrespect.

One of the most dramatic and successful exercises illustrating differences in cultural paradigms and increasing empathy is the use of role playing while taking the Frybread IQ exam (Baird-Olson, 2006). Several weeks into the semester after rapport and trust have been built, I come into the classroom dressed in stereotypical public school teacher clothing (think large cotton dress, droopy sweater, and clunky shoes), wearing heavy-rimmed glasses sliding down my nose (not a difficult position to maintain since my glasses typically end up there), and carrying a large wooden ruler. Before going into the Frybread IQ exam scenario, I ask the students to use their sociological imaginations to pretend that they are back in the sixth grade or junior high. I then leave the classroom and return in a few seconds as the "teacher from hell" to give them the exam "to prove how smart they are," pointing out who will do better than others, making other inappropriate remarks, and taking cruel actions such as threatening scapegoated students with the ruler. After the students take the "exam," they return to the present-day world and share their emotions and feelings of incompetence. In the debriefing, students share their utter sense of futility when they find that the vocabulary words are Lakota and the items are culturally relevant for First Peoples. They learn that exams can be culturally biased. For instance, the vast majority of non-Indians learn that in Indian Country and in urban indigenous communities *arbor* and *roach* have meanings they never knew. By demonstrating that knowledge is socially constructed, the exam exercise also facilitates communication with community partners.

By the end of the semester, the students have learned that by participating in an American Indian service-learning partnership each has been given a great honor. With that honor comes responsibility that goes beyond fulfilling the partnership agreements and also includes living out the traditional value of generosity. Each student decides what type of gift he or she will give to his or her partner. After working with their partners, they are able to determine with their partners' assistance what form of generosity would be useful and/or appreciated. Some forms that the gifts have taken are creating educational displays, brochures, and newsletters; giving talks; writing letters to the editor of relevant news sources; and writing reports on data that were collected for partners.

Finally, because of the type and intensity of cognitive and affective lessons learned in this community partnership course, the concluding activity is participation in a Talking Circle.[4] This experience provides another opportunity to appreciate the value of sharing and to hear that changes are being made to reduce the personal and ethnic stress experienced by First Nation peoples.

The students and I move our chairs into a circle one row deep. We attempt to avoid having an amoeba shape rather than a circle. Following my introductory and explanatory remarks, which I make while holding my talking stick made by a traditional Assiniboine healer and moving in clockwise direction, each student has a turn using the traditional talking stick to share, without being interrupted and without consequent critique, two or three of the most important partnership lessons he or she recorded in his or her journal and/or final report and one action he or she is doing or plans to do to respect the First Peoples of Turtle Island. At the conclusion of the Talking Circle, both Indian and non-Indian students are often tearful from their newfound respect for each other. Relationships that at the beginning of the semester were antagonistic are well on the road to being healed as they leave the classroom once again deeply engrossed in discussions.

Conclusion

This chapter has illustrated how American Indian studies community-partnership courses can work toward increasing retention of First Nation students and cultural sensitivity of non-Indian students. In addition, teaching activities to prepare students for their service-learning experiences with American Indians are identified and described. Student partnership responsibilities have ranged from working at the office of the First Peoples on whose land the university sits to assist in updating a tribal membership list in preparation for regaining federal recognition to serving as a tour guide at an indigenous museum, to assisting an American Indian filmmaker and producer in putting on the First Annual Southern California American Indian Film Festival, to working with American Indian youth at a city agency for First Peoples, to assisting a traditional healer with his highly successful program for incarcerated youth, to preparing a historical written and pictorial record of the university's powwow, helping a student's out-of-state, rural tribe's educational director with the needs assessment for their own tribal college, and designing an authentic educational American Indian unit for a local, urban third-grade teacher.

All Indian and non-Indian students as well as their First People partners have been highly satisfied with the results of the partnerships. Essentially, the non-Indian students' reactions have been "I never knew!" "Why haven't we been taught this before?" "How could I have been so insensitive [or ignorant] in the past?" and "I will never forget what I learned." All of the non-Indian students have been impressed by the values of traditional First Peoples and their ability to forgive and seek healing for all while still seeking respect for their traditional cultures and sovereign status. The majority of former students have continued to assist or support their partners or other American Indian groups and to refute myths about First Peoples. Their behavior and their community partnerships' responses have demonstrated that they have indeed learned the traditional First Peoples' values of generosity, respect, perseverance, courage, and the reality that we are all related. American Indian students appreciate the opportunities to have their traditional values validated and to be able to learn even more about their traditional lifestyles and how to incorporate their cultural ways into a global world.

Notes

1. Tribal leaders also call for more service-learning partnerships with tribal communities.

2. The university, which is located in an area that has one of the two largest American Indian urban populations in the United States, has over 33,000 students, yet at this point in time less than 200 are First Nations people.

3. Since exams are only one means of measuring achievement and ensure neither long-term retention of information nor respect for all learning styles, I give only one exam.

4. Talking Circles, also called Peacemaking Circles or Healing Circles, are based in the renewal of traditional means of solving conflict by talking and listening to each other. See, for instance, Barry Stuart and Kay Pranis (2006, pp. 121–133), James

W. Zion and Robert Yazzie (2006, pp. 151–160), and Institute for Higher Education Policy (2006, p. 3).

References

American Indian College Fund, http://www.collegefund.org/news/ad_TV.html (downloads/Ad-Kimberlly Benally.pdf). Retrieved March 26, 2007.

Baird-Olson, K. (2006). Summary report: Facing the educational challenge of tribal communities. Proceedings of the Chancellor's Conference on Higher Education and American Indians, sponsored by CSU, March 21, 2006.

Bureau of Indian Affairs. (n.d.). Answers to frequently asked questions. Retrieved March 11, 2000, from http://www.doi.gov/bia/aitoday/q_and_a.html

Frybread IQ Exam. (1991). (1991 adaptation of 1972 "test" obtained from the Montana Office of Public Instruction, Helena, MT [Georgia Rice, superintendent]).

Glass, R. D., & Wallace, K. R. (1996). A framework for educators. In M. P. P. Root (Ed.), *The Multiracial Experience: Racial Borders as the New Frontier.* Thousand Oaks, CA: Sage.

Gordon, R., Della Piana, L., & Keleher, T. (2000). Facing the consequences: An examination of racial discrimination in U.S. public schools. Oakland, CA: ERASE Initiative, Applied Research Center. Retrieved October 14, 2004, from http://www.arc.org/

Institute for Higher Education Policy. (2006, April). *Championing success: A report on the progress of tribal college and university alumni.* Denver: American Indian College Fund.

Lobo, S., & Talbot, S. (2001). *Native American voices: A reader.* Upper Saddle River, New Jersey: Prentice Hall.

McClure, C. (2006, May 17). *Internship paper: Tribal law and policy.* Northridge: California State University, Institute for AIS 499 Independent Studies.

National Center for Education Statistics. (2005). *Status and trends in the education of American Indians and Alaska natives.* Washington, DC: Author.

Reyhner, J. (1992). American Indians out of school: A review of school-based causes and solutions. *Journal of American Indian Education, 31*(2).

Richardson, R. C., Jr., & de los Santos, A. G., Jr. (1988). Helping minority students graduate from college—A comprehensive approach. *ERIC Digest.* Washington, DC: ERIC Clearinghouse on Higher Education. (ERIC Identifier ED308795)

St. Germaine, R. (1995). Drop-out rates among American Indian and Alaska Native students: Beyond cultural discontinuity. *ERIC Digest.* Charleston, WV: Eric Clearinghouse on Rural Education and Small Schools. (ERIC Identifier ED388492)

Stuart, B., & Pranis, K. (2006). Peacemaking circles: Reflections on principal features and primary outcomes. In D. Sulivan & L. Tifft (Eds.), *Handbook of restorative justice* (pp. 121–133). London: Routledge.

U.S. Commission on Civil Rights. (2003, July). *A quiet crisis: Federal funding and unmet needs in Indian country.* Washington, DC: U.S. Commission on Civil Rights.

Wilson, R. (2002). Evolution and revolution. In American Council on Education, Center for Advancement of Racial and Ethnic Equity, *Reflections on 20 Years of Minorities in Higher Education and the ACE Annual Status Report.* Washington, DC: ACE.

Zion, J. W., & Yazzie, R. (2006). Navajo peacemaking: Original dispute resolution and a life way. In D. Sulivan & L. Tifft (Eds.), *Handbook of restorative justice* (pp. 151–160). London: Routledge.